AF446829

CHAUCER: A CRITICAL APPRECIATION

CHAUCER
A CRITICAL APPRECIATION

Paull F. Baum

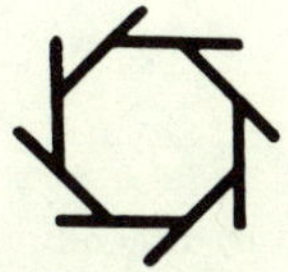

OCTAGON BOOKS

A DIVISION OF FARRAR, STRAUS AND GIROUX

New York   1982

Reprinted 1982

by special arrangement with Duke University Press, Durham, N.C.

OCTAGON BOOKS
A DIVISION OF FARRAR, STRAUS & GIROUX, INC.
19 Union Square West
New York, N.Y. 10003

Library of Congress Cataloging in Publication Data

Baum, Paull Franklin, 1886–
   Chaucer, a critical appreciation.

   Reprint. Originally published: Durham, N.C.: Duke
University Press, 1958.
   Includes bibliographical references and index.
   1. Chaucer, Geoffrey, d. 1400—Criticism and inter-
pretation.   I. Title.
PR1924.B3   1982   821'.1   82-2081
ISBN 0-374-90465-0   AACR2

Manufactured by Braun-Brumfield, Inc.
Ann Arbor, Michigan
Printed in the United States of America

THIS BOOK IS PUBLISHED WITH THE ASSISTANCE OF A GRANT FROM THE RESEARCH COUNCIL OF DUKE UNIVERSITY AND A GRANT TO THE DUKE UNIVERSITY PRESS BY THE FORD FOUNDATION

PREFACE

IF THE whole history of Chaucer studies is ever written, it will
show—along with a record of trial and error as the facts of his
biography and the essentials of background have been recovered
(so far as they are now recoverable)—a surprising phenomenon:
that seldom has there been anything but praise. Other poets
abide our question; not Chaucer. It has come now to seem dis-
loyal to hint a fault in "our incomparable poet": for if anything
in his poetry appeared irregular or unsatisfactory we have studi-
ously overlooked it or hurried to his defense with ingenious
contrivances of interpretation; if there was anything lacking we
have generously added it, imputing to him qualities to which he
made no claim and of which he never dreamed. Bagehot laid it
down a century ago "that the business of a critic is criticism;
that it is *not* his business to be thankful; that he must attempt
an estimate rather than a eulogy." But the critical premise of our
professional Chaucerians seems to have been that Chaucer was
a great poet and should therefore be adorned with all the high
qualities of other great poets. Whatever he did was always right
and nothing will do short of proving him so.

Thus our criticism has taken two wrong turns. One is that
of gratuitous supplementation—which I have illustrated specially
in the elaborate variations on the Pardoner theme (Chapter ii)
and in the Note on the Clerk (Chapter iii). No doubt by leaving
some things uncertain Chaucer has given the critics an opportunity, and they have taken every advantage of it. The other
turn is that of elevation: the discovery of profound latent philosophical or ethical meanings. This critical procedure is of course

not restricted to Chaucer. It is characteristic of much recent literary criticism, traceable partly to the nineteenth-century divagations on Shakespeare's plays and supported by the wide sweep of modern 'criticism' as it has enriched itself from the language of psychology and from a return to mediæval philosophy. This has led to a fashion of surrounding a work of art with a large phosphorescent nimbus, something outside though seeming to come from within, and producing an illusion of grandeur which would certainly astonish the author. A comprehensive review of the possibilities may be seen in Professor Fry's *Anatomy of Criticism*. Some of the encroachments of this fashion on Chaucer will be noted in the following pages. They have culminated (up to now) in a whole volume, by Dr. Jack A. W. Bennett, devoted to the 'Parlement of Foules.' Its model might have been Macrobius upon Cicero—that work over which the poet fell asleep.

The 'Parlement' is a brilliant little comedy on the theme of love-mating. It contains some of Chaucer's loveliest poetry and liveliest humor. But the scholars have labored over it as an 'occasional' poem, trying to identify the noble suitors and hoping to establish a date, and sometimes finding in the uproar of the lesser birds an echo of the Peasants' Revolt. They have consulted astronomers about the planet Venus in an unusual position and have added fanciful non-astronomical explanations. Dr. Bennett, however, will have none of "this misdirection of energy." Yet there seems to be something not quite right in a poem so plainly about love, a St. Valentine's Day poem of just under seven hundred lines which takes nearly three hundred lines to get started and comes to its *poynt* only at line 372; something not quite right in a poem which uses the august Scipio Africanus to introduce the dreamer into the Garden of Love and the Temple of Venus and which ends wistfully with the hope that some day he will have a better dream than this one produced by reading Cicero and Macrobius. Hence the need of interpretation, to discover some unifying principle. Ten years ago Professor Lumiansky (not mentioned by Dr. Bennett) found one in "Chaucer's unsuccessful search for a way of reconciling true and false felicity" or the service of love and orthodox Christianity. Miss Dorothy Everett has taken much the same view. Now Dr. Bennett, with an embarrassing wealth of annotation and far-flung allusion, in which a great deal of the poem is lost sight of, has translated this into the language of Professor Lovejoy: "the poem reflects the great debate of the age between the philosophy of plenitude and the philosophy of other-worldliness"; or, in simpler terms: "for all the values that inhere in love, the world of lovers is not the whole world; love is but a 'function' of Nature." African had pointed to the heavenly rewards of devotion to *commune profit* and the punishment of *brekers of the law* and *likerous folk:* thus the noble birds were without fruition and the commoners, the *smale foules,* enjoy the delights of plenitude. This indulgence in the intentional fallacy is in amusing contrast to what Chaucer knew of his aristocratic audience. One would like to have his opinion on it.

In social intercourse humor is a powerful weapon of defense; but on the printed page facing a body of professors after five centuries and more Chaucer's humor has proved treacherous. His interpreters, whatever they may be at other times, are eminently serious when they sit down to write an article. They forget or seem to forget that he was above all a humorist. Perhaps they recall his supposed deathbed retractions (a shambling list, as Manly said) of those *enditynges of worldly vanitees,* the poems which, with a few exceptions, we all read with the greatest pleasure, and would rescue them from Chaucer's condemnation (if it was his) and move them over into the list of *moralitee, and devocioun.*

The grounds for a proper criticism of Chaucer are, it seems to me, fairly simple: recognition of his position as court poet, with the limitations which that position implies; appreciation of his technique as prosodist (still neglected) and as narrative poet, with its ups and downs; and, negatively, avoidance of zealous effort to find in him æsthetic virtues which his kind of writing does not require or warrant. Such an approach is neither modern nor mediæval but rests upon criteria by which all poets are judged. It admits the conventions of mediæval rhetoric and of Courtly

Love as he adapted it to his special purposes; it omits deliberately the mediæval Four Levels of Meaning as inconsonant with his subjects and his ways of treating them. It sees him as a comic poet, whether by temperament or by the necessities of his milieu, and probably by both, endowed with very great gifts, and since poetry was his avocation, taking those gifts with a comfortable ease, untroubled by the severities which plague the dedicated artist; in two words, as *an amateur of genius:* a busy man of the world and very human who composed when it pleased him to do so poems which he thought would give pleasure to others. Yet even genius, the other side of the paradox, can be as fickle as Fortune, and we must accept its lapses. "A healthy sagacious man of the world," as Bagehot calls him, "has gone through the world; he loves it and knows it; he dwells on it with a fond appreciation." This is what delights us and earns our praise. Be glad, he would say,

Be glad, thow redere, and thy sorwe ofcaste.

Chaucer's art is pre-eminent in giving pleasure. He is companionable, our fellowman, sharing our whims and weaknesses, with no austere hatreds, no intense passions. It is his merit to be plain and earthy with our all-too-human earthiness, and we enjoy him for it; we even like to tolerate him when he is dull. Yet this is not to write him down as a mere entertainer. Comedy is never without its serious undertones, and if we sometimes deplore Chaucer's habit of seeming to laugh out of season, that is only to recognize a technical failure. *Seriousness,* in spite of Arnold, is not a word to conjure with; it is not a matter of subject but of treatment, of careful attention to getting the thing said in the best possible way. Has not Mr. T. S. Eliot told us that Villon's *Testament* is more serious than *In Memoriam?* In the same sense the Miller's Tale is more serious than the Knight's Tale, the Canon's Yeoman's than the Franklin's.

At the same time, we cannot safely overlook his historical position, which gave him little incentive to exceed his grasp, or to forget the first audience for which he wrote, an audience which, enveloped as he was in social and political confusions and wishing mainly to be entertained, was easily satisfied with what it could easily understand and would not greatly care for political, religious, or philosophical increments. He pleased them first with escape poetry from France and then, as his experience grew, with the comedy of low life, which also was remote from their personal concerns. His chosen models were Ovid and Boccaccio, and when he read the greater poets, Vergil and Dante, he used them for more stories and for fine phrases. All this is not to forget a few friends who would relish the philosophical increments; but even they encouraged him to no aspiration towards the highest levels of æsthetic experience which yield a sense of reality beyond the reality of appearance, which not only illuminate but enlarge the spirit. For Chaucer the word is *illuminates*. He had, as Mr. Coghill says, "an acute and questioning intelligence." His observations of the world are clear and comprehensive, especially its common frailties, rarely its tragic flaws. His reporting of it is both brilliant and tolerant; but not hortative. *Swich is this world* is his theme, and there he rested.

I know I have been accus'd as an enemy of his writings but without any other reason than that I do not admire him blindly, and without looking into his imperfections. For why should he only be exempted from those frailties, from which *Homer* and *Virgil* are not free? . . . I admire and applaud him where I ought; those who do more do but value themselves in their admiration of him.

Thus Dryden on Ben Jonson. But it is not dispraise to seem to take away from Chaucer certain qualities which he never had. The aura of uncritical praise—sincere and often disguised as ingenious subtlety—can be rightly diminished without occultation or derogation from his genuine gifts as poet, story-teller, and humorist. Some of the views here expressed may be open to the charge of heresy; they may irritate and offend the upholders of orthodoxy; but they may also (I hope) be *servysable* as well as *lowely*.

P.F.B.

CONTENTS

CHAUCER: A CRITICAL APPRECIATION

CHAPTER I. OBSERVATIONS ON THE LIFE OF CHAUCER

THE following observations attempt to collect the glimpses which our fragmentary and equivocal evidence yields into the personality of Geoffrey Chaucer. Fragmentation is necessarily the rule. There is first the record of his life as civil servant, which gives the illusion of fulness yet leaves out the important fact that he wrote poems. This section (i) on Chaucer's 'public' life is followed by a section (ii) giving particular attention to his last years, with a backward look at the chronology of the poems and the reasons why he left the *Canterbury Tales* unfinished. This leads to a section (iii) on Chaucer's position as a man close to the Court and the government and familiar, it would seem, with many of the leading figures, yet strikingly silent about the social and political events amid which he lived: in a word, his aloofness, as seen in his poetry, both from the political and the moral questions of his time. Discussion of this requires consideration of the poetical work, but only as evidence of character. In still other ways (section iv) Chaucer's poetry shows a kind of detachment from the world about him; for it omits a great deal of his immediate surroundings and experiences which might well have left their mark in his writing. Lastly, before the summing up, there is a section (v) on Chaucer and women, especially relevant because we know so little about his married life, because of the Cecilia Chaumpaigne affair, and because of his constant pose as an outsider in love. (See the Note on her at the end of the chapter.) Altogether, though we possess so many 'facts,' the picture will not come clear. The external facts and the internal evidence of his verse refuse to clarify, and we are left with hypotheses and generalizations which satisfy no one.

The outline of Chaucer's life, however, is simple.

I

He was born in 1345 or 1346,[1] of John Chaucer, a prosperous vintner, and his wife Agnes (a widow; her maiden name is unknown), probably in London. At the age of eleven or twelve he became a page to Elizabeth Countess of Ulster and wife of Edward III's second son Lionel—doubtless a sign both of the boy's promise and the father's influence.[2] Two years after this he was with the English army in France and captured near Reims; for (or towards) his ransom the king paid £16.[3] By 1366 he had married Philippa Roet, a damoiselle of Edward's Queen Philippa and sister of Katherine Swynford,[4] who was successively the governess of John of Gaunt's children, John's mistress and mother of the later legitimated Beauforts, and John's third wife. In 1367, when he was twenty-one or twenty-two, he appears as groom in the King's household *(valectus)* and two years later as esquire. His education meanwhile, including a knowledge of Latin and French, was such as a young man would get in the King's household. When the Duchess of Lancaster died in September 1369 he composed a considerable poem in the French manner celebrating her and also her surviving husband. (That he wrote this poem at the Duke's request or command is at best "a fanciful surmise.") In 1370 "he entered upon a diplomatic career," says Manly in rather grandiose terms. He had already crossed the Channel with a traveling account of £10; and for the next eight years he went abroad on various missions for the King, some of them secret or otherwise unknown as to purpose, sometimes alone and sometimes with more distinguished men, and on some occasions for several month's duration. Certainly he was in Italy in 1372—in Genoa for a trade treaty and in Florence. Then in 1374 he settled down, for twelve years, as controller of the Customs on wool, hides, etc., at an annual salary of £10, and later as controller also of the Petty Customs on wines. Now his duties brought him into contact with the commercial world, while his connections with the Court also continued and included further missions abroad. In the same year he took, rent free, the "whole mansion" of Aldgate, with the apartments over it and the cellar underneath, provided he keep them in repair—a short distance from the Customs House. These are apparently the only years he and his wife kept house together. During this period fall the appeal against him for *raptus* in 1380, and in 1381 the great Peasant Uprising, his appointment as J.P. for Kent, and his election to Parliament in 1386. After this he seems to have retired to Kent (though he held some minor offices) during or because of the rise of Gloucester and the decline of the Lancastrian party. His wife died probably in 1387. But when Richard came of age and assumed royal power, in 1389-1391, Chaucer was made Clerk of the Works at Windsor and other royal palaces. He was the victim of robbery three times in 1390. In 1390 also he was appointed deputy or subforester of North Petherton. Already in 1396 there are signs of favor from the Earl of Derby, soon to become Henry IV. On Christmas eve 1399 he took a long lease on a house in the garden of St. Mary's Chapel, Westminster. In June 1400 he drew his last recorded payment, and—according to his tomb in the Abbey (erected in 1556)—died 25 October. He was then fifty-four or fifty-five years of age.

The enigmas remain; for while we seem to know so much it turns out that we really know so little. Even the documented facts of his life as lay civil servant leave out the biographical essentials and because they are all we have they are often overworked. That he was in early life—till the age of say thirty—a valued esquire of the King's household is certain, as is testified by the number, though hardly the importance, of his missions abroad. That he stood well in the favor of both kings is also certain, since for a large part of his life he performed valuable services for the crown—"noster dilectus valectus," "quamplura ardua et vrgentia negocia nostra." But this too can be exaggerated, for the language of the documents is formalized. Very many Englishmen, greater and lesser, traveled on the Continent, and when Chaucer's journeys are lifted from the larger background they tend to look more significant than they actually were. For twelve years, from the age say of thirty to forty-two, he was employed as controller of the important Customs on wool etc. and at the same time was in business contact with the city magnates. He must have had also many personal friends in and around Court; for like his alter ego at the Tabard Inn he no doubt made friends easily. One imagines him to have been 'good company.' During these years the rewards in money for his various services were not munificent compared with those of other civil servants. Even the perquisites of clothing, an occasional wardship, his daily pitcher of wine, the payment (whether he sat or not) for sixty-one days in the Parliament of 1386, and a few other special gratuities, do not add up to an impressive amount; they mark him as a faithful and competent but not extraordinarily prominent civil servant. If he had not been also a poet he would have been lost to posterity along with the hundreds of others whose names repose in the public records.

Thus the facts are more teasing than satisfying. We should like to know—and the conflicting inferences of the specialists are proof that we do not know—just what were his personal relations with and his attitudes towards Edward III and Edward's notorious mistress; and with John of Gaunt and his political "gang"; whether their patronage had anything to do with his poetry; to whose influence the free lease of Aldgate was due; why Lancaster showed so many favors to his wife Philippa and only once (so far as the records go) rewarded Chaucer; why he lost or resigned the controllership and the clerkship; what he thought and where he stood through the last years of Edward's reign and throughout the misrule of Richard, amid the conflicts of political factions and Court intrigues; why he was made J.P. for Kent and whether he actually voted in the Parliament; and so on and so forth; what, in sum, his private life was like. Thesis and hypothesis, conjecture and fanciful surmise, we have in plenty; of certainty very little. To be sure, one may exaggerate downwards as well as upwards, but the tendency towards confident assertion is always a cautionary warning. The clearer things look, the more secure one feels, the more one should be suspicious of error.

II

So far as our records go, the last years are particularly obscure. In May 1389 Richard, then in his twenty-third year, assumed full royal power and in July Chaucer received his appointment as Clerk of the Works at the King's castles and palaces. From then until June 1391, when he resigned the office, he was certainly a busy man; and during that time he was thrice robbed of considerable sums (and at least once beaten up) and involved with the trials of the robbers. Moreover, the settling of his accounts—which were apparently in some confusion and at one point he was told to cease meddling—took a year. There could thus be two good reasons for resigning. But the confusion was as likely as not due to an inherited system of bookkeeping.

This was Chaucer's last office as civil servant. In the same year, however, he was appointed by Roger Mortimer VI (who as grandson of Prince Lionel would have been next in succession after Richard) as deputy forester of the royal forest of North Petherton. Roger died in 1398 and the appointment was renewed by his Countess. But just what his duties were and how much of the time he spent in Somerset is not known.

In 1394 Costanza, Queen Anne, and the Countess of Derby died; Chaucer's muse gave no sign. But he received a new annuity of £20 from Richard and in the following year a gift of £10 from the Earl of Derby, who four years later seized the throne. In 1396 he seems to have been living at Greenwich. In 1398 he seems (as Manly puts it) "to have been in a very peculiar position": he was sued by two persons for more than £25, and was granted royal protection for two years on account of "quamplura ardua et vrgencia negocia nostra . . . in diuersis partibus infra regum nostrum." On 13 October he petitioned successfully to the King for a butt of wine annually. Less than a year later Richard was no longer on the throne and exactly a year later, on the day of his coronation, the new King granted Chaucer an annuity of 40 marks in addition to the £20 from Richard in 1394. Meanwhile he had "casualiter" lost the patents for Richard's £20 and the butt of wine; Henry renewed them. On Christmas eve he took out the lease for a house in the garden of St. Mary's, Westminster.

What these few facts signify is hard to determine. A little more can be gleaned from his verse. The triple balade 'De Visage sanz Peinture' petitions the "Princes" to *releve him of his peyne* and the King to bring him *to som beter estat*. This is supposed to refer to the robberies of 1390; and in fact he was discharged 6 January 1391 of repayment of £20 taken from him "felonousement pres de le fowle Ok." The punning 'Complaint to his Purse'—

Beth hevy ageyn, or elles moote I dye—

would fit almost any of these last years when, though he may not have been in straits, he was obliged to borrow money frequently. The Envoy however, is a salutation to the new King (whom history regards as usurper):

O conquerour of Brutes Albyon....

But Chaucer adds duly and truly

Which that by lyne and free eleccion
Been verray kyng, this song to yow I sende,

perhaps meaning 'I refurbish my old Complaint with this new Envoy,'[5]

And ye, that mowen alle oure harmes amende,

i.e., all the tragedy of Richard's last years as well as Chaucer's,

Have mynde upon my supplicacioun,

which, since Henry was so prompt in granting his annuity and in confirming Richard's, may refer only and quite pleasantly to his 'casual' loss of those patents.

In two of the so-called minor poems we are permitted as nowhere else to see Geoffrey Chaucer plain and hear his voice. In 1396, one of the blank years otherwise, he rallied his friend Bukton—and whether it was Peter or Robert is no matter—on his approaching remarriage. The sentiments are conventional and are jocularly set forth with considerable solemnity. He began with the question put to Jesus 'What is truth?' and inferred from our Lord's silence that *No man is al trewe.* 'And therefore,' he continues, with remarkable logic, 'though I promise to tell you about the *wo that is in mariage* (the very words of the Wife of Bath's text) I must not speak ill of it for fear I should myself *falle eft in swich dotage.* If Satan were once freed of his chains *he* would never be bound again! Of course, it *is* better to marry than to burn, but you will be her slave. I warn you, I beg you to read *The Wife of Bath.* I pray God you will remain free.' So, marriage is a bondage, a trap, a dotage; beware. Bukton was probably no older than Chaucer, who was fifty and whose wife had been dead nine years, but probably he had his eye on a young girl. For besides the specific reference to the Wife par excellence, there seems to be an echo in

Ne no man him bewayle, though he wepe

of the Merchant's bitter cry,

Wepyng and waylyng, care and oother sorwe,

as he settled into the shocking story of January and May. Was Master Bukton persuaded?

This was simple chaff. The poem to Scogan is more lively and more revealing, and has more comic weeping and wailing. The date is set by *this diluge of pestilence,* which may refer to the heavy rains in the autumn of 1393 or to the wet summer of 1391. The heavenly statutes have been broken, all seven planetary gods, Venus especially, are flooding us with their tears, and I am frightened. And it is all your fault, for did you not say blasphemously that because your lady showed no mercy you gave her up at Michaelmas? And you took Cupid to witness of that *rebel word.* Moreover, Scogan, Cupid will not take vengeance

On the, ne me, ne noon of oure figure;
We shul of him have neyther hurt ne cure,

we who are *hoor and rounde of shap.* But what really frightens me is that henceforth none of us gray-haired portly fellows will ever find success with the ladies. *Let the old Grisel joke and rime,* you say; but ... (and here is the point)—

> *Nay, Scogan, say not so, for I m' excuse—*
> *God helpe me so!—in no rym, dowteles,*
> *Ne thynke I never of slep to wake my muse,*
> *That rusteth in my shethe stille in pees.*
> *While I was yong, I put hir forth in prees;*
> *But al shal passe that men prose or ryme;*
> *Take every man hys turn, as for his tyme.*

It is not an affidavit, but it says plainly enough that, still near fifty, he has abandoned poetry; his Muse—and what a metaphor! —rusts peacefully in his sheath. Poetry is for the young. The Envoy sounds more emphatically the note of discouragement. Scogan is at Windsor where all good things are; Chaucer is at Greenwich, a wilderness, alone, forgotten.

> *Mynne thy frend, ther it may fructyfye!*

There may be some private joke in this, some temporary setback. But it does not sound so. The playful exaggeration about Scogan's blasphemies against Love, running through four stanzas, is only the excuse; it leads to a humorously sad admission of age and unshapeliness, with no more love, and then to the confession that he will write no more. One would not take this too seriously if it did not explain so much.

The chronology is still as vexed as the Bermoothes. The 'Book of the Duchess' and the 'Astrolabe' are fairly certain, 1369-1370 and 1391 or 1392. What came before the 'Book of the Duchess'? It may be "comparatively crude" but it is hardly the work of a beginner. And what came after 1391 or 1393? The *Troilus* is now generally put in 1385, but the arguments are not conclusive. The rest is a tissue of conjectures caught here and there with efforts to find and certify allusions to contemporary events, e.g., the marriage of Richard, or of one of John of Gaunt's daughters, or the death of Anne. Much of the discussion is necessarily comparative: this before or after that.

Chaucer's most settled years were 1374 to 1386, while he was living at Aldgate, broken only by the trips abroad; then after leaving the Customs he was perhaps not too busy; and then again in 1389-1391 he was heavily occupied with the business of Clerk of the Works. The writing of the General Prologue "is generally put in or about 1387 . . . and the *Prologue* was presumably written before the main body of the tales" (Robinson, p. 751). Some of the tales were already at hand and required only the links and a little touching up. These might be the Man of Law's Tale, the Clerk's Tale, the Physician's Tale, the Monk's Tale (except the modern instances), the Second Nun's Tale, the Manciple's Tale, and probably the Knight's Tale—leaving some 10,000 lines (besides the Melibeus and the Parson's Tale, which are translations) of the *Canterbury Tales* for the years from 1378 onwards. Now, Tatlock put the Melibeus and the Merchant's Tale in 1393-1394, and Lowes the Marriage Group (a little over 5000 lines without the Clerk's Tale) in 1393-1396; and apart from these no one has proposed any writing after 1396, save of course the Envoy to his Purse. Hotson's attempt to associate the Nun's Priest's Tale with the duel of Hereford and Norfolk in 1398 has found no favor. Skeat's "after 1389 the tales continued" and Robinson's 1393-1400 for the later Tales, including the Marriage Group, are obvious makeshifts.

For a rapid writer such as we take Chaucer to have been, there is nothing in these figures inconsistent with the assumption that in 1387-1389 and 1391-1393 ('Scogan') he could have brought the *Canterbury Tales* to such a state of incompletion as we now have it. He must always have composed when the spirit moved, and when it moved it moved swiftly. Very roughly speaking, 10,000 lines in four years is not too much. William Morris, who honored him and who as poet resembled him in many ways, once wrote seven hundred lines in a single day.

It makes very little difference, 1393 or 1396, seven years or four years of time in which to push on with, if not finish, the *Canterbury Tales;* and though the question is no doubt idle, it has to be asked: Why? For it tells something about the man which can throw a backward light. One thinks of 1612-1616 when the successful playwright, having turned out nearly thirty plays in twenty years, retired to Stratford. He had done enough. When the aging Swinburne was asked why he no longer wrote with the fire and force of *Atalanta* and *Poems and Ballads,* he answered simply that the *impulse* had ceased. It is easy to see why the 'Legend of Good Women' was left unfinished, apart from the relief at the Queen's death; or why the Monk's little tragedies never reached the hundred mark, if *that* was anything but a joke; or why the 'Hous of Fame' stopped just short of its climax, if it did; but why the *Canterbury Tales* was abandoned with only twenty out of the originally stipulated hundred and twenty— this remains a matter for thought. Somewhere along the way the plan of two tales from each Pilgrim was reduced to one; at I 25 the Host said to the Parson:

> *For every man, save thou, hath toold his tale;*

and there is nowhere a real hint of tales for the return to South- wark, though clairvoyant scholars have thought they saw such hints. It would be flippant to suggest that the solemn Parson, no longer the kindly sympathetic figure of the General Prologue, had blanketed the whole enterprise with his composite tract. The sun was setting;

> *But hasteth yow, the sonne wole adoun;*

and more than one good Chaucerian—Miss Hammond and Pro- fessor Lawrence, for example—have held that the *fructuous*

> *Moralitee and vertuous matere*

was all along in Chaucer's mind for a pious ending. Underneath his jesting gaiety our poet had his earnest substratum. It may be. Yet when the *disjecta membra* are laid out the certain points are too few for plotting a curve. It is true that the list of Pilgrims and the tales themselves begin with the Knight; and the list, as well as the tales, ended at first with the Parson (and his silent brother)—before Chaucer thought of adding five varied scoun- drels to be provided for. But the whole scheme was never finally fixed; that also is true.

Perhaps Chaucer came to recognize that the whole scheme was too ambitious. At the start it looked simple, as it grew it became more and more complex. To get on with it there would be not only wholly new tales to write, but no little readjustment of parts, more suitable stories for the Man of Law, the Shipman, and the Manciple, further development of the quarrels, loose threads to pick up, and more . . . more than he and his rusty Muse cared to undertake.

On the other hand, many improvements would readily occur to him, without attempting extensive or conclusive additions. These also were neglected. The question repeats itself, and the answers are but too obvious. There are no signs in the evidence of a long incapacitating illness. A failure of the spirit, then, rather than of the flesh is indicated. What we now call psychic disturbances should not be overlooked. The whole life of London had changed; the old Court for whom he had written in the eighties and early nineties had dissolved in confusion and tyranny; he no longer seemed a part of these disturbed affairs, nor cared to be. He had not so much lost favor as lost interest, zest, and zeal. Greenwich was not so much a solitary wilderness at the stream's end in reality as in his sensitive imagination. He was not forgotten, not at all, but what he remembered was more than what he anticipated with pleasure. His audience was gone. He had grown old and the world was no longer with him. He was ready to *flee fro the prees;* to say

> *That I have had my world as in my tyme.*
> *But age, allas! that al wole envenyme,*
> *Hath me biraft my beautee and my pith.*
> *Lat go, farewell! the devel go therwith.*
> *The flour is goon, ther is namoore to telle.*

No more Canterbury Tales. Let the muse rust: *if gold ruste, what shal iren do?*

III

It has long been an open question why Chaucer's poetry shows so little of the political life with which he seems from the *Life*

Records to have been so closely associated. He was in no sense what later generations called an 'interpreter of his age.' But there is not a single patriotic line in all his verse, as Legouis observed: "il n'a pas un vers de patriotisme, et c'est chose surprenante dans un temps où ce sentiment s'éveillait avec force dans l'âme anglaise, tour à tour exalté par les victoires et approfondi par les malheurs."[6] This has troubled many of his staunch admirers and gained him from some the name of Laodicean. He was a sharp observer and recorder of human weaknesses, and few of the characters he portrayed are wholly admirable, but he was discreetly silent about Court and political scandals which he must have known all too well. The contrast is striking and the reasons for it call for explanation, perhaps justification.

There is to be sure one simple explanation. A very large proportion of his poetry is conventional and derivative. He took his subjects and his models where he found them: Ovid, the popular French poets, Boccaccio, the fabliaux, and so on. A great deal is translation or adaptation. Some of the *Canterbury Tales*—the fabliaux and Canon's Yeoman's Tale notably—deal with the life of the common people, and of course the General Prologue and the links. For the rest, any opportunity for direct criticism of high life would have to be incidental or allusive.

By temperament he was not a reformer; his whole credo is in the Boethian 'Balade de Bon Conseyl': *Flee fro the prees,* avoid *envye* and *hir that turneth as a bal.* What he asked was *trouthe* (of which he saw so little round about him) and humble resignation—

> *That thee is sent, receyve in buxumnesse.*

It will not appeal to some as a lofty ideal, but it is honest—along with its slightly ironic smile in the refrain and the punning envoy —and is lifted above ground-level by its sincere though formal prayer

> *Crye him mercy, that of his hy goodnesse*
> *Made thee of noght.*

Perhaps the Host's adjective *elvyssh,* in spite of its humorous application to the elderly stout man, in spite also of that man's fluency and felicity of speech when occasion demanded, is truer to the real Chaucer than we generally suppose.

This charge of Laodicean has been met and partially answered by Professor Loomis,[7] first with "an array of testimony from some of the best critical minds united in the belief that Geoffrey Chaucer looked upon the stormy spectacle of English life with a smiling tolerance, was merely amused by abuses in church and state, was inclined to believe that this was the best of all possible worlds"; and then with some special pleading of his own for the defense. Those best critical minds include Lounsbury, Coulton, Root, Christopher Dawson, J. E. Wells, and Aldous Huxley; there are probably others who have not gone on record. They might not quite accept the terms of Professor Loomis' review but the idea remains: Chaucer was too aloof and took the miseries of mankind, the threats of outrageous fortune, and particularly "the great issues of his day," with too little seriousness. He never spoke out. And it is true: a good half-truth. But the other half need be neither apology nor extenuation, still less a plea of self-defense. The question "May not Chaucer have reasoned that, when there was so much wrong on both sides, there was no obligation to offer his career as a vain sacrifice to the cause of the oppressed?"[8] is a *petitio* with its own Laodicean stain. The answer is neither personal cowardice nor moral indifference. The answer is Chaucer's business as a writer of poetry.

There are in fact numerous incidental allusions to contemporary affairs which collected would make a fair show; but since they are nearly all incidental they are not impressive.[9] It is easy to make too much of them. In context they do very well for a quick point—a smile, a nudge, a silent 'I get it'; hardly more.

A passage in the Prologue to the 'Legende' (F 373 ff.; G 353 ff.) has frequently been taken as "a serious lecture on the duties of a king addressed to Richard II by Anne in the person of Alceste" (Robinson, p. 958). Whether Chaucer so intended it or not, the advice is there, quite explicit and firm, and it is paralleled by the address to Richard in the balade of 'Stedfastnesse.' The historical background of this advice has been fully set forth by Miss Schlauch as illustrating Chaucer's probable knowledge of theory and his interest in such a matter.[10] In the context Alceste is defending Chaucer from Love's charges against his followers; she urges that *a ryghtwis lord* should not be like the cruel tyrants of Lombardy—one of whom appears in the Monk's Tale—but must regard his liegemen, poor and rich, as part of his treasure and treat them with justice—

> *For, syr, yt is no maistrye for a lord*
> *To dampne a man without answere of a word,...*

and thus she brings her exhortation, which might else appear irrelevant, around to her main point. Chaucer must not be condemned unheard. The later G version adds a generalizing note which is a little less appropriate to Chaucer's situation and more appropriate to that of Richard: a king must remember that it is his duty to listen kindly to the complaints and petitions of his subjects. The G text was written after the Queen's death, when Richard's neuroses began to get the better of his judgment.

Another queen, in the Knight's Tale (A 1748 ff.), intercedes for the young knights in distress and urges her husband to show pity even at the expense of justice, and Theseus, with more good nature than the God of Love, says to himself:

> *Fy*
> *Upon a lord that wol have no mercy,*
> *But ben a leon both in word and deede,*
> *To hem that been in repentaunce and drede.*

These incidents have been thought to reflect Anne's softening influence on Richard's "unstaid youth," though the dates are not quite right. In a different, and less worthy, cause King Arthur's queen intercedes for the rapist knight.

The elaborate double-stopping of the 'Compleynt of Mars,' if there *is* a deadly parallel, is quite exceptional. The Envoy to 'Stedfastnesse' is the one significant exception. The underlying moral, along with a plethora of minor ones, of the Melibeus, its warning against the evils of war and revenge, is much the same on a vastly larger scale; but it is difficult to believe that Chaucer translated *Le Livre de Melibée et de Dame Prudence* and thrust it into the *Canterbury Tales* for 'himself,' just after Sir Thopas, in order to discountenance the Hundred Years' War, which was already lost.

Hence Chaucer's omission of commentary, to say nothing of satire, on the political scene is wholly understandable; nor should it be surprising. A mere glance at the troubled history of Edward's later reign and all of Richard's is enough to show that for a poet whose business it was to entertain the Court—in which he had grown up and to whose patronage he owed his position and his livelihood—any severe condemnation of public affairs would betray a lack of both gratitude and common sense. He was not by nature a Juvenal, and by 'predicament' he was excluded from the role of satirist. He was not by temperament a reformer, and by artistic endowment he was specially fitted for his chosen role of entertainer. Nevertheless, certain limitations are implied, which, if we presume to judge, must be recognized.

The charge of Laodicean should be directed not against his failure to condemn the public evils of his time, but where it belongs, against his moral attitude, his failure to represent the obliquity of human nature, the wickedness of mankind, with proper indignation and reproof. He constantly exposes, but seldom deplores. He preferred *delectare* to *prodesse*. And here too the answer, if we must answer for him, is much the same.

Charges of this lack of a serious attitude to life, or any sort of idealism or comprehensive view which would draw his fragments together have not been wanting; many of them are included in Professor Loomis' review. They may be readily elaborated, and exaggerated. Where does he look into the mysterious deeps of human character or where scale the heights of human aspiration? Where does he reveal any profound spiritual insight or concern with "the way of the soul"? It must be said of him as was said of a lesser poet: his "soul was not lit by sulphur, he did not, like Melville, measure himself against fate or walk on the sea-bottom, 'left bare by faith's receding wave', or wrestle with God, or hang, as Hopkins hung, on the dreadful cliffs of the mind." He did not "interrogate the universe." He never dreamed of Byzantium like Yeats or felt the burden of the mystery like Wordsworth. His language, brilliant and felicitous as it so often is, was never troubled by the incommunicable, never reaching for the unknown. He might never have heard of the Grail; he does not mention Percival, and his allusions to Arthur and Lancelot and Gawain are casual, without the high sense of glory or failure which is felt in the contemporary romances. He seems not to have known the tragedy of Tristram and Iseult.

There are writers, of poetry and prose, who touch us with the poignancy of the human lot. Chaucer is rarely among them. There are writers who by a word, a phrase, *tutto tremente,* break our hearts with the sudden revelation of our inadequacy, our futility, our tragedy, and also of our nobility (which haunts us though we fail), and of all the undulating beauty of mind and spirit. Chaucer is rarely, if ever among them. He neither raises nor answers the great troublesome questions.

This is so and must be set down, not in denigration but in fairness, not to take away what he never had or claimed to have, but to clear him of false praise. It is the obverse of his air of detachment, his habit of aloof observation, his way of recording without judging. It places him in the literary firmament and it is probably an index of his character. It is true, but it is not all. When we say that he seems not to feel strongly about sin and vice, the emphasis may well be on *seems.* He could in defense quote *Nolite iudicare, ut non iudicemini* or *Et dimitte nobis peccata nostra, siquidem et ipsi dimittimus omni debenti nobis.* He was of a charitable nature and felt that it is more blessed to forgive than to accuse. More than once he told us that

Pite renneth soone in gentil herte,

and he set the gentle heart above the inquisitorial temper. "Indignation," said Coleridge, "is the handsome brother of Anger and Hatred"; and thus Chaucer avoided one of the Deadly Sins.

If he had no roots very deep in a philosophical faith which he had won for himself, he had no branches exposed to false doctrine. If charity alone is no sufficient guide-line through the devious intricacies of life, it is at least a safeguard against the pitfalls of cynicism and hate. He had in abundance a natural buoyancy, which he communicates. He had a clear mind, which neither soared nor sank, a vivacity which carried him, and his poetry, over rough places. If we miss the depths, and the heights, we can enjoy with him the long fair level places. He could suffice unto his good and show us some of the way. He would have been at ease with Horace; he might have enjoyed Montaigne, though he lacked Montaigne's power of reflection and of looking over and under; for he was content without decisions. He betrayed most clearly his limitation by what he missed in Dante. Having both Dante and Boccaccio, he chose Boccaccio. His muse was the Comic Spirit; but not Meredith's Comic Spirit, which was something of a termagant.

On the other hand, he had no gift for tragedy, as the artistic failure of his most ambitious poem reveals. And this argues a want of depth in his character as in his poetry. His religion is sincere but conventional; when things went wrong in his stories he put the blame on Fickle Fortune not on moral weakness or deficiencies of character. Several times he airs the problem of fate and free will, but either lightly, as in the Nun's Priest's Tale, or straight out of Boethius, as in the *Troilus,* for artistic purposes. He lets Dorigen stir a novel difficulty, the cruelty of nature in the designs of a beneficent creator, and dismisses it with a feeble 'Let the theologians face it.' He always praised gentilesse, with or without a direct 'source,' yet all his moralizing is borrowed.

Thus it is the evasions when seriousness is expected which still trouble us. The Wife's Tale lies in fairyland and a rational solution to the peccant knight's situation would be out of place. But the Franklin's, though it be a Breton lay, presents a real moral problem along with a deliberate attempt to humanize what was originally an apologue, and Chaucer fobs us off with the dubious, in the circumstances, epigram of Arveragus, *Trouthe is the highest thyng that man may kepe,* and then leaves us with the impertinent question, *Which was the moste fre?* He ruins, either through carelessness or indifference, the tragic story of Virginia; with Dante before him he alters almost beyond recognition the story of Ugolino; he is inclined to laugh at the seductions of Jason and Theseus in his *glorious legende;* he turns aside the adultery of May in the Merchant's Tale with a comic trick; and chiefly, he allows his *litel tragedie* of Troilus and Criseyde to dwindle into pathos and then leaves us with a brusque apology for the hitherto moving tale of passion and loss. These are artistic failures, but they rest on that lack of high seriousness which Arnold has been ridiculed for recognizing.

There are, however, poems which have no part in this world, such as it is, poems which have only the merest touches of reality, hardly enough to warrant our suspension of disbelief, poems which describe the imaginary land in which he grew up poetically. This was the dream world of Guillaume de Loris' rose garden, which he never quite forsook, where only echoes of quotidian actuality penetrated, a world without real cruelty and bitterness and heartbreak; and the faraway world of Ovid's lovers. This gave his early poems an extra dimension, left the illusion of life still an illusion which called for no depth of thought or feeling. And it is remarkable how much this world was still with him through his later verse, partly as artistic convention, partly also as a natural convenience. The stylized formalities of Courtly Love, which you neither believed nor disbelieved, and the French borrowings, the exercises in Boethian paraphrase, the compleynts (when not burlesque) are purposefully unreal; the gaiety of the 'Hous of Fame' and elaboration of the Prologue of the 'Legende,' as well as its remote classical heroines, make no pretense of resembling such a world as ours. The Birds, half human as they are, are isolated by the beauty of their dream setting.

All this, be it understood, is not apology for Chaucer's Laodicean laxness. It is critical perspective. His worst characters, as well as those who belong in the land of dream, exist only on Chaucer's page. He made them and therefore he likes them, but it does not follow that he would like them in the flesh. That he seems to approve because he does not condemn is due to our faulty attitude. It is praise enough that we are sometimes betrayed into mistaking the image for the flesh, that we are confused by the poet's transmuting alchemy. Those repulsive characters "cease to be repulsive; they are, to use a transcendental metaphor, uplifted into the world of essences."[11]

Such a man then was Chaucer, or so it would seem, a mirror to the evil he saw so clearly, only a bright clean mirror. He smiled, he laughed, he did not take to heart the world's unhappiness and wickedness.

> *Swich is this world whoso it kan byholde;*
> *In ech estat is litel hertes reste.*
> *God leve us for to take it for the beste.*

(You can hear his voice. You can see the shrug: *whoso it* kan *byholde,* if a man can look at it and not blench.) Such at any rate he seems to be in certain of his poems, chiefly those later poems which we call realistic, written when his eye was on the ground, not on the rose-colored horizon of France. This escape from responsibility into humor, from severity into laughter, is certainly part of him, and if there is a reason we can only guess at it. "The more one suffers," said Kierkegaard, "the more, I believe, has one a sense for the comic. It is only by the deepest suffering that one acquires true authority in the use of the comic, an authority which by one word transforms as by magic the reasonable creature one calls man into a caricature." There is little sign of Chaucer's personal suffering in the official data and little elsewhere. That there were private disappointments and emotional crises, quarrels and heartaches must be assumed because no one is free from them. His satirical observations on the follies of womankind rest largely on literary convention, on sources. His overemphasis on Cupid's female saints and on men as lovers of *newefangelnesse* could also be conventional. These were subjects ready to hand, not the backspring of personal experience. But his marked sympathy for Criseyde's infidelity could be significant.

IV

There are other 'silences' besides the political if one need take account of them—"that roar which lies on the other side of silence." The visitations of the plague come in for passing allusion, though there is no reference in the 'Book of the Duchess,' where it might legitimately appear; there is passing mention of the Lollards, among whom Chaucer had good friends, but none of Wiclif, whom Lancaster had sponsored, once with serious consequences. There is nothing on the Great Schism, nor on the notorious Hawley-Shackwell sacrilege at the beginning of Richard's reign or the similar case of Tresilian in 1388; nothing on the famine of 1390 in the Midlands; nothing on Percy, the stormy petrel of the period and at one time an ally of John of Gaunt. There was a poem on the Duchess' death, but none on the Queen's a short while before, or on Edward's, or on the Black Prince's, or on Joan's (which is the more remarkable if credence is allowed to Miss Galway's persistent claims for his long romantic attachment to her), or on Richard's accession. There seems to be a sly allusion to Jack Straw and the murder of Flemings, but nothing on the Mile End or Smithfield incidents.

If it were not for the balade on 'Stedfastnesse,' where Chaucer did speak up, his omission of laureate verse would perhaps not be noticeable. Moreover, Chaucer could dash off a stanza on Adam his scrivener and write balades to 'Scogan' and 'Bukton' and to his 'Purse,' but his muse was not much given to such exercise. There is nothing like Dunbar's 'On His Heid-ake.' We speak of Chaucer's 'occasional' poems—the 'Hous of Fame' and the 'Parlement of Foules,'—but we are none too sure about the occasions. Why were all other occasions overlooked or neglected?

Another curious omission by a man who in his later years was connected with building and rebuilding is that of any reference to architecture. The King himself was much occupied with remodeling Westminster Hall (the work itself dates 1397-1399); there was constant construction going on at Ely, Exeter, Lincoln, Peterborough, Salisbury, Winchester, Worcester, and York. Wykeham's buildings of New College, Oxford, were of conspicuous importance. The Pilgrims never reached Canterbury, to be sure, but they came within sight of its towers—without seeing them apparently. Surely one would expect an intimation that Chaucer recognized the colored beauty of the windows and felt the structural beauty of nave and spire and buttress. Did he ever visit the Black Prince's chauntry chapel at Canterbury, or look at the Wilton diptych? In fact, is it certain that he looked attentively at real flowers and meadows and trees? There are some very fine passages about them, but the passages have a literary rather than an outdoor air.

There is another silence, reminding us how little we know about Chaucer.

This is not merely the omission of those infinite quotidian details of the life around him which a poet admired for his realistic observation might be expected to make note of and use of, and which the modern reader can find with a wealth of detail in Miss Rickert's *Chaucer's World*.

Chaucer had crossed the Alps four times—once in winter—and seen the blue of the Mediterranean, the beauty of Italian skies and Italian landscape. He had been to Florence and perhaps Fiesole. That he knew the Visconti libraries in Milan and Pavia is a possibility.[12] He knew the hardships as well as the rewards of long journeys in the fourteenth century. What trace have these experiences left on his mind and in his poetry?

With great learning and ingenuity Professor George R. Parks has traced, conjecturally, the routes which Chaucer followed in his two trips to Italy and back. Detailed information is meager, but the outlines, though dotted with *could* and *might,* with *if* and *or,* are valuable.[13] Few as are the known facts, plentiful as are the possibilities of speculation and of inferences, there is still enough reasonably certain for the present purpose.

Chaucer left London 1 December 1372 for Genoa and Florence, and was back 23 May 1373—twenty-five weeks. By Professor Parks's reckoning he would have reached Genoa early in January and therefore, assuming that the return journey took about the same length of time, he would have had thirteen or fourteen weeks in Italy on this first trip. We do not know how long his business in Genoa required—it was apparently unsuccessful—nor what business took him to Florence.

The all-sea route to Genoa is ruled out by considerations of time alone; and it is improbable, owing to the French wars, that he went down the Rhone to Marseille and by water to Genoa. Hence it seems as certain as such things can be that he crossed one of the Alpine passes in December, and this would be no slight experience. The various routes by which he could have reached Italy are five: (1) Calais, Flanders, up the Rhine to Basel, thence to Lausanne, up the Rhone to Martigny, over the Great St. Bernard to Aosta. This is favored by Parks for 1372. (2) As above to Lausanne, thence around the west end of Lake Geneva to Chambéry and over the Mont Cenis to Turin. Prince Lionel in 1368, during a lull in the French wars, proceeded with his huge retinue from Calais just before Easter, to Paris, thence to Dijon, Geneva, Chambéry, and over the Mont Cenis to Milan.[14] In 1393 Henry Bolingbroke returned from Milan over the same pass. To me it would seem more likely, in 1372, since Chaucer was accompanied by two Italians who would know the passes, that they would risk whatever chances of fighting there might be in Savoy and choose the Mont Cenis, which is a lower and safer pass for December. It is less than 7000 feet; the approach up the valley of the Arc is gradual, though the descent to Susa is very steep (5000 feet in less than twenty miles). (3) In 1368 Edmund Rose, one of Chaucer's fellow esquires of the King's household, left London 27 January and went via Paris and Dijon, but thence to Lausanne and Martigny and on up the Rhone valley to Brig and over the Simplon to Domo d'Ossola, Pallanza, and arrived at Pavia 20 March.[15] (4) As in (1) to Basel, thence to Lucerne and over the St. Gothard to Bellinzona, Como, and Milan.[16] This seems likely for the 1378 journey, which was in summer and Milan the destination. Chaucer left London 28 May with Sir Edward de Berkeley and nine others, was in Lombardy some six weeks, and returned to London 19 September.[17] (5) If Chaucer in 1372 was returning from Florence via Bologna and Padua, he could have continued northwards to Verona, Lago di Garda, Bolzano, Merano, across the Reschen-Scheideck, to Landeck, to Ulm, Stuttgart, Speyer, and down the Rhine, across Flanders to Calais. This was called the German Way.[18]

For the rest, we have only this little and our imagination. Chaucer crossed either the Mont Cenis or the Great St. Bernard in December of 1372; in summer he may have taken either of these passes on the homeward routes and he may have also crossed the Simplon and/or the St. Gothard; possibly also the Reschen-Scheideck. Many others at that time crossed the Alps, but only Adam of Usk left a record of his impressions: he was terrified by the experience. He noted Lucerne "and its wonderful lake, Mont St. Gotthard, and the hermitage on its summit, where I was drawn in an ox-waggon half dead with cold and with mine eyes blindfolded lest I should see the dangers of the pass, on the eves of Palm Sunday [9 March] I arrived at Bellinzona."[9] What Chaucer's feelings were we can only guess from his namesake's experience in the *grymme pawes* of the golden Eagle. To-day the road is exciting but not terrifying. It climbs from 1400 feet at Lucerne to nearly 7000 feet at the pass and descends to 760 feet at Bellinzona. Even in midsummer one sees the torrents below and hears the avalanches crash and thunder and watches the rain clouds on the Swiss side thin and turn to sunshine on the Italian side.

The great St. Bernard is equally exciting. From Lausanne the road follows Lake Geneva to its eastern end with fine views of the Dent du Midi, past the Castle of Chillon (13 c.) into the Rhone valley and up to Martigny, with the Savoy Alps on the right and the Bernese Alps on the left; then up to 8000 feet over the pass, and down again to Aosta (1910 feet). From Martigny to the pass the road climbs 6600 feet (nearly 3000 feet in the last eight miles) with gorges and precipicies and every kind of wild scenery. At Bourg-St. Pierre Chaucer would have stopped at the eleventh-century church and been shown the Roman milestone. Perhaps he spent Christmas at the wealthy monastery. If he knew the Roman name of Ferrara he must have known the Roman name of the pass; and if he did not light a candle to St. Bernard, he should have poured a libation to Jupiter Poeninus. From the monastery the descent is equally rapid; 4000 feet in the first twelve miles. At Gignod he would have noted the new tower, then in a few more miles the chestnut and walnut trees and the vineyards: twenty miles from winter to spring.

Since the fictive Oxford student and Canterbury pilgrim claimed to have got the Griselda story from Petrarch, at Padua, our Chaucerians have been gravely tempted to believe that their poet, having finished his business in Florence, moved north to Bologna and Padua, and there himself heard the Griselda story from Petrarch's lips. The Latin letter containing it, which we take as Chaucer's text, was not yet written in the spring of 1373, but Petrarch was fond of telling the story to his friends. The statement of the Clerk is of course not evidence; it tells us only that Chaucer knew of Petrarch's living at Padua. That he went there and talked with Petrarch cannot be proved or disproved; it remains an "unsettled possibility."[20] And if Petrarch, why not Boccaccio? Boccaccio returned from Naples in the early summer of 1371 to his home in Certaldo; he was poor and ill. Nothing seems to be certainly known of him in the spring of 1373, but in August of that year he was appointed to his professorship at Florence. In any case, whether they met in the flesh or not, Chaucer's failure to mention the name of Boccaccio is a remarkable 'silence.'

Now these conjectures, more or less futile in detail, are important for one thing. They crave the question: What did Chaucer learn from such varied experiences? What did he bring back except the manuscripts of Boccaccio and Dante and Petrarch and a knowledge of the language? (He certainly had manuscripts of Boccaccio at home; we assume that he had the others.) Praz suggests that Chaucer brought home a sense of the vividness of Italian life; "the Italians, have always appeared to foreigners as wonderfully lively beings . . . the wonderful thing Alfieri well expressed when he said that *la pianta uomo* grows more vigorous in Italy than anywhere else."[21] Did Chaucer thus learn from Italy the vividness which he gave us in the General Prologue? But what were his impressions of the hazardous Alpine crossing in December 1372, of the Italian lakes and valleys, the churches, all the strange sights and scenes? We do not know. Almost nothing shows through in his poetry. Skeat offered a faint guess that the ice mountain in the 'Hous of Fame' is a real reminiscence—

I wol yow al the shap devyse
Of hous and site, and al the wyse
How I gan to thys place aproche
That stood upon so hygh a roche,
Hier stant ther non in Spayne.
But up I clomb with alle peyne,
And though to clymbe it greved me, . . .

what he was most eager to discover was the composition of the rock itself. This is very little; it does not suggest climbing a real glacier, and the reference to Spain suggests the need of an easy rime. (Or could it echo some report he had heard from the men who crossed the Pyrenees before the battle of Nájara?) He had himself been among the highest ice-capped mountains of Switzerland.

Landscape, we know, had not much entered into literature by the fourteenth century. But if he had talked with Petrarch he might have learned about landscape something new and useful to a poet. Moreover, he had precedent at home in England. We can only guess what he thought of *Gawain and the Green Knight*, if he had read it. His Parson's slighting reference to alliterative verse need not imply his own adverse judgment. In any case, we have a contemporary illustration of the valid use of real landscape description. First, here is the coming of spring:

Bot þenne þe weder of þe worlde wyth wynter hit þrepeȝ,
Colde clengeȝ adoun, cloudeȝ vplyften,
Schyre schedeȝ þe rayn in schowreȝ ful warme,
Falleȝ vpon fayre flat, flowreȝ þere schewen,
Boþe groundeȝ and þe greueȝ grene ar her wedeȝ,
Bryddeȝ busken to bylde, and bremlych syngen
For solace of þe softe somer þat sues þerafter
bi bonk.

Ȝeferus, which also brought in the spring of the Canterbury pilgrimage, is only a few lines farther on. And then dusty autumn, when

> *Wroþe wynde of þe welkyn wrasteleʒ with þe sunne,*
> *Þe leueʒ lancen fro þe lynde and lyʒten on þe grounde,*
> *And al grayes þe gres, þat grene watʒ ere.*

Then the winter scene in Wirral—

> *a forest ful dep, þat ferly watʒ wylde,*
> *Hiʒe hilleʒ on vche a halue, and holtwodeʒ vnder*
> *Of hore okeʒ ful hoge a hundreth togeder;*
> *Þe hasel and þe haʒþorne were harled al samen,*
> *With roʒe raged mosse rayled aywhere,*
> *With mony bryddes vnblyþe vpon bare twyges,*
> *Þat pitosly þer piped for pyne of þe colde.*

Then the carefully detailed description of the castle and its surroundings (contrast the general description of the dream castle in
the 'Hous of Fame'), topped off with a figure:

> *So mony pynakle payntet watʒ poudred ayquere,*
> *Among þe castel carneleʒ, clambred so þik,*
> *Þat pared out of papure purely hit semed.*

These passages are not meant for invidious comparison. Each
man works with his own media. They show, however, a lively
interest in realistic description.

Chaucer has one passage which hints at a similar interest, the
grisly feendly rokkes blake off the Breton coast which so obsessed
Dorigen and produced her remarkable query why *a parfit wys
God* had created such *a foul confusion Of werk*. Similar thoughts
would certainly occur to one whose life had been spent in the flat
country around London, when he first made his way up the Great
St. Bernard pass. Was there a connection in Chaucer's mind?

For further details of Chaucer's various impressions of Italy
one can only draw a bow at a venture. Imagination would reel at
the effort to reconstruct Alta Italia in 1372 and 1378. The fighting
among the city states can be followed—Professor Parks has done
it thoroughly in an attempt to establish the possibility that Chaucer *could* have met Petrarch at Padua or Arquà—but there is so
much else. Manly opined that Chaucer took a side trip to Saluzzo
in the interests of his Griselda poem; but the dates are not right,

unless he had had Petrarch's letter before he left England. Did he pass through Vercelli? What did he *see* at Genoa? Perhaps not much besides the harbor, to compare it with the Thames reaches. Later, when he had his Dante open before him at *Inferno* XXXIII, when he was doing the Ugolino story for the Monk's tragedies, he would see what Dante had said of the Genoese—

> *Ahi Genovesi, uomini diversi*
> *D'ogni costume, e pien d'ogni magagna,*
> *Perche non siete voi del mondo spersi?**

At Florence he would certainly visit S. Maria Novella, which was completed only some twenty years before; S. Croce, the Duomo, and Or San Michele were still building; Giotto's Campanile was unfinished, but Andrea Pisano's door of the Baptistery was at least in place; he should have looked at Fra Angelico's angels in the monastery of San Marco; and he would not have missed Giotto's portrait of Dante in the Bargello. He may well have gone up to Fiesole.

Milan would have impressed him as so much larger than London, and the lavishness of the Visconti was greater than anything he had ever beheld. Beyond these cities we have to guess. In Pisa there was the Campo Santo and the group of white marble Duomo, Baptistery, and the leaning Campanile. If he crossed the Apennines to Bologna there was another leaning tower which he would recall when he read *Inferno,* XXXI; for there Antaeus, leaning down, takes Vergil and Dante in his arms,

> *Qual pare a riguardar la Carisenda.*

It is not the details after all that matter, but the whole effect on a sensitive agile mind of strange sights and strange people in a different setting of beauty from anything he had even seen or read about. They should have affected him profoundly, but when he sat down with his Muse they vanished without a trace. Or so it seems. For even when he was translating Boccaccio he added no little touches of his own which betray a recollection of what he had gathered from contact with Boccaccio's country. An addi-

---

* Oh, Genoese, men perverse in every way, and full of every foulness, why are you not driven from the earth?

tional word about *Mount Vesulus in special* would have been natural in the Clerk's Prologue; for Monte Viso (12,615 feet) is one of the most beautiful of all the Alps and is celebrated for other reasons than being the source of the Po.

There are many gardens in Chaucer, but they are picture-book gardens, more like manuscript illuminations than real gardens studied from nature. Or could perhaps that garden near Dorigen's castle contain a reminiscence of something he had seen in France or Italy?

> *This gardyn ful of leves and of floures;*
> *And craft of mannes hand so curiously*
> *Arrayed hadde this gardyn, trewely,*
> *That nevere was ther gardyn of swich prys,*
> *But if it were the verray paradys.*
> *The odour of floures and the fresshe sighte, . . .*
> *So ful it was of beautee with plesaunce.*

It hardly seems so.

It is not that one expects Chaucer to have moved ahead several centuries and found a place in his narrative poems for Byronic descriptions of the Alpine scene or for Shelley's mingling of natural and mental phenomena or for something like Wordsworth's loving pictures of the English lakes. Yet there were opportunities where a touch of nature here and there might have found a response in his audience; and some vivid vignette—he could have learned about this from Dante—of the extraordinary Swiss scenery or the trials of travel might well have astonished or amused the court of Richard. His friend Edmund Rose would have recognized such details, or any of those who had been in Lionel's entourage or in the suite of Sir Edward Berkeley, or of the many others who had traveled on the Continent. He was not so timid as Adam of Usk, but there was matter for a Canterbury Tale in some such incident, or at least some allusion to be added to the Wife of Bath's journeyings.

Much of this may be vain surmise, but it has a point.

V

What has been called (I suppose facetiously) *Chaucer and the Woman Question* has the same pitfalls as other Chaucer problems.

Chaucer begins his ostensible defense of 'good women' by insisting on his *feyth and ful credence* in books, and when he makes his selection of examples (such as they are) they come not only from books but from the remote past. This might imply that he knew of no real modern instances, or simply that he preferred, in contrast to the Wife of Bath, *auctoritee* to *experience*. As his Eagle explained the matter, Jupiter felt pity

> *That thou so longe trewely*
> *Hast served so ententyfly*
> *Hys blynde nevew Cupido,*
> *And faire Venus also,*
> *Withoute guerdon ever yit,*
> *And never-the-lesse hast set thy wit—*
> *Although that in thy hed ful lyte is—*
> *To make bookys, songes, dytees,*
> *In ryme, or elles in cadence,*
> *As thou best canst, in reverence*
> *Of Love, and of hys servantes eke,*
> *That have hys servyse soght, and seke;*
> *And peynest the to preyse hys art,*
> *Although thou haddest never part;*
> *Wherfore, also God me blesse,*
> *Joves halt hyt gret humblesse,*
> *And vertu eke, that thou wolt make*
> *A-nyght ful ofte thyn hed to ake*
> *In thy studye, so thou writest,*
> *And ever mo of love enditest, . . .*
> *Although thou maist goo in the daunce*
> *Of hem that hym list not avaunce.*

Jove considers all this, and also that you have no present news of Love and lovers at home or abroad;

> *For when thy labour doon al ys,*
> *And hast mad alle thy rekenynges,*
> *In stede of reste and newe thynges,*
> *Thou goost hom to thy hous anoon;*
> *And, also domb as any stoon,*
> *Thou sittest at another book*
> *Tyl fully daswed ys thy look,*
> *And lyvest thus as an heremyte,*
> *Although thyn abstynence ys lyte.*

The Eagle's final fillip is beautifully ambiguous: a text for the Devil when he feels like quoting Scripture; and the picture of Geoffrey Chaucer exhausted by his day's work at the Customs going home to his wife at their 'mansion' over Aldgate and sitting in stony silence over his books all evening is very precious.

So he dreams in his legendary arbor on the May morning that the God of Love and his consort find him watching the *resurrection* of the daisy and he sings (or hears sung) a Balade in praise of his Lady (or Alcestis).[22] The God attacks him, a very *worm,* as the mortal foe of lovers, whereas *My seruants,* He says, *ben alle wyse and honourable.* The dreamer, who is easily recognized as Chaucer, has been so stupid as to teach that those who love *paramours, to harde and hot* are proper fools; witness his translation of the *Roman de la Rose* and his book of Troilus and Criseyde, in defiance of his sixty books with stories of clean women. Alcestis intercedes for him on the ground that he wrote merely from habit, *gessyng no malice*—or perhaps someone commanded him to write those offensive things. On the other hand, he *has* written the 'Hous of Fame,' the 'Book of the Duchess,' the 'Parlement of Foules,' 'Palamon and Arcite' (which all presumably glorify sacred love?), and many a hymn for Love's feast days—not to mention sober works like the translations of Boethius and Pope Innocent, the life of St. Cecilia, and Origen on the Magdalen. At this, the God of Love handsomely forgives Chaucer, who, in thanking Alcestis, starts to defend himself and so brings down on his head the lifelong commission of *a glorious legende Of goode wymmen*. The penalty is severe and Chaucer soon breaks under it; 1072 couplets seemed penance enough.

Now who can take this at all seriously, considering the nature of the charge and of the defense, the kind of logic which Alcestis uses, and the tone of the Legends themselves? It is all playful, and if it implies some puritanical criticism from Chaucer's contemporaries it may help to explain the apologetic Epilogue to the *Troilus*. Assuming that the Legends were composed in the order of their appearance, it would seem that Chaucer started well and in the right spirit: Cleopatra and Anthony, Pyramus and Thisbe are each an honor to the God of Love. Then the scene changes: Dido was too trusting; Hypsipyle and Medea too forward; Phaedra and little Ariadne too eager; Phyllis too simple; Lucretia and Philomel were victims of lustful men, and Hypermnestra a victim in another sense. The subject is not any longer good women but bad men.

What else? There are first the women he knew personally and about whom we know so little: his wife Philippa and her sister Katherine, Cecilia Chaumpaigne, and no doubt many more who are nameless. His wife has been suspected of adultery. Of her sister we know enough and to spare, not much of it favorable. In court circles there are Blanche, the Duchess of Lancaster, and Queen Anne, good women both; but against them are Alice Perrers, Joan of Kent (in her youth at least; she was not quite certain that her marriage to the Black Prince was legal), Anne's Bohemian attendant Agnes Launcekron (who carried on an affair with the King's favorite, Robert Vere, Earl of Oxford), John's one mistress known by name, Marie de Saint Hilaire, a demoiselle of Queen Philippa. The chroniclers have a rich selection,

> *And evere an hundred badde ageyn on goode*

(to reverse the text, G 277). If he looked in his heart before writing of women he would see a dark picture. He gave us some of it in the 'Hous of Fame':

> *And of Loves folk moo tydynges,*
> *Both sothe sawes and lesinges;*

> *And moo loves newe begonne,*
> *And longe yserved loves wonne,*
> *And moo loves casuelly*
> *That ben betyd, no man wot why,*
> *But as a blynd man stert an hare;*
> *And more jolytee and fare,*
> *While that they fynde love of stel,*
> *As thinketh hem, and over-al wel;*
> *Mo discordes, moo jelousies,*
> *Mo murmures, and moo novelries,*
> *And moo dissymulacions,*
> *And feyned reparacions; . . .*

Such are the tidings of Love's people he could expect in the home of all tidings, both true and untrue as the case might be, with the balance against honor.

When in turn we look into the women of his fiction the proportions are about the same. There is no ideal woman, like the worthy Knight or the perfect Parson. They all belong in their own tales, the tales which he chose to tell. The women in the fabliaux of Miller, Reeve, and Shipman are where they belong; we must accept them with their situation and so leave them, with the wife of Phebus in the Manciple's Tale. They do not count here, for or against, though Chaucer makes them all rather engaging hussies. Virginia hardly counts; at least he could no nothing with her beyond wringing the soft heart of the Host. St. Cecilia hardly counts; she had anyway a touch of spiritual pride. Nor Custance, for she also is a saint, though uncanonized. Nor Prudence, who is an allegorical figure. Griselda is in her different way a symbol, out of märchen-lore, of Christian fortitude, and for real life pointing an impractical moral. Canace is too young and Emily too colorless, though she looked

> *fressher than the May with floures newe—*
> *For with the rose colour stroof hire hewe.*

The May of the Merchant's Tale is what would now be called a little bitch; just what January deserved, but no ornament to her sex. Chaucer, however, with characteristic kindness gives her a gentle pat on the shoulder (which is a warning to all of us) and lets her say:

> *Ful many a man weneth to seen a thyng,*
> *And it is al another than it semeth.*
> *He that mysconceyveth, he mysdemeth.*

The others, who seem to have form and pressure, are Dorigen, the Prioress, the good Wife, and of course Criseyde. Dorigen is a special case. She comes alive at moments, when her neuroses about the rocks and her single-minded Arveragus take command, and when she sets out to the garden to keep her foolish promise. But she is too submissive to her husband at the crisis and too obedient to the plot when she makes her rash promise, to be a true woman. At best she is a warning to faithful wives. The Prioress is a study in ambiguities, portrayed with delicate skill as no doubt a competent manageress of a ladies' convent, but somewhat wanting as a religious. When she comes on the scene with her pathetic miracle Chaucer still shows her a little out of focus. The Wife is a very special case, a paragon of female virility on the verge of breaking. Chaucer uses her with the greatest dexterity to exemplify and repudiate all the faults of her sex; admirable in her vulgarity, but not a woman Chaucer would bring forward for our admiration or one by whom we could estimate his regard for her sex. With Criseyde we tread burning ground. She has her followers, including her creator, and her detractors. With all her brightness she is pitifully weak. She suffers from her heredity— Benoit and Boccaccio—and she also has to obey the plot. Fate and Fortune are against her. Hardy might have called her, as he called Tess, a pure woman, loving and erring. When under strain she proves herself her father's daughter and her uncle's niece. She is Chaucer's one female character; she may well be his typical woman, lively and tender and amorous, and weak when strength is demanded. Chaucer may have seen her in real life more than once; she may have been drawn from the life more truly than we can know; one often fancies that the Criseyde of the first half of the poem (at least) owes something to Philippa Chaucer.

If these few specimens in Chaucer's poetry are not enough to reveal surely his judgment of womankind, there is another part of the garden where better fruit may be found, namely, the chances of love and marriage in the narratives themselves. Whatever the origin of the tales, they seemed to Chaucer worth telling, though he cannot be held responsible for their contents. The evidence of the Nun's Priest's Tale is oblique: Chanticleer is devoted to Pertelote, the oversolicitous wife, but he has his paramours, like so many husbands. The unfaithful lover is described in 'Anelida and Arcite' and in the Falcon-Princess episode of the Squire's Tale. The 'Mars' celebrates adultery. The marriage of Griselda and the Marquis had every promise of being successful; but Walter was obsessed with a passion for testing. The reconciliation is part of the impressed moral, but it is true that after Walter was satisfied and Griselda martyred they lived long *in concord and in reste*. It is the same with Palamon and Emily: their bond

> *That highte matrimoigne or marriage*

turned out well finally; only it was, at the end, a political marriage engineered by Theseus and his barons. Arcite worshiped War and lost, thanks to the machination of Saturn; Palamon worshiped Love and won, thanks to the public policy of Theseus. Emily remained a pawn, but so also were her two lovers the instruments of a game. All sides are represented in the 'Parlement,' which is dedicated to Love, its *hard* attempts, its *sharp* successes, and its *dredful joy, alwey that slit so yerne*. The lesser birds each gets its mate or mistress happily. The three noble suitors however and the formel are granted a year's delay: is this a warning against hasty marriage in high life? There may be allegorical adjuncts in the background, but the point still is that the *homme moyen sensuel* must have his way. Such anyway was my dream, says the poet, after falling asleep over Cicero and Macrobius, and it was disappointing. The marriage of Ceyx and Alcione was happy while it lasted and Alcione followed her husband even to death; the love of John and Blanche was also a happy one—marriage is not considered in the poem—till death

intervened, but the later life of John was different. The marriage
of Arveragus and Dorigen seems to be ideal and is set before us
as the perfect balance-of-power between man and wife; but it is
only saved from the rocks by the lucky last-minute gentilesse of
a squire hitherto passionately urgent. Arveragus gave command,
Dorigen obeyed, Aurelius withdrew: is this the formula for success in marriage?

These are to be sure mere straws, but such as they are they
underwrite the moral of the *Troilus,* that in this world there is
litel hertes reste. Whether Chaucer's own experience and his
considered judgment confirm it deponent saith not.

What Chaucer thought of womankind can hardly be deduced
from occasional remarks in their narrative context. The reported
slanders of the Wife's Prologue cancel out, and also the pros and
cons set forth in the Melibeus. There are good women and bad;
in the G prologue of the 'Legende' Alceste insists that Chaucer
knows both kinds. Sometimes they are

> *ful of innocence,*
> *Ful of pite, of trouthe, and conscience,*

but they yield too easily to importunate men. The Falcon in the
Squire's Tale recognizes Canace's sympathy as

> *Of verray wommanly benignyte.*

Theseus asks Emily at the end to manifest her *wommanly pitee.*
And Proserpine, condemning that Jew Solomon for never finding
a good woman, asserts that other men have found many

> *Wommen ful trewe, ful goode, and vertuous.*

Women are inclined to tearfulness: Theseus was sorry for them
for they wepen evere in oon; and when Palamon and Arcite were
caught fighting alone, Queen Hippolita *for verray wommanhede,
Gan for to wepe.* They are also sentimental; the Nun's Priest
ridicules them because they *holde in ful greet reverence* the book
of Lancelot of the Lake. They can show moderation; at least
Canace went to bed early, for

> *She was ful mesurable, as wommen be;*

but this from the Squire does not quite ring true. The Wife of Bath has her ideas of what women most desire: the obvious things, but chiefly flattery, and above all mastery of their husbands and lovers. Their advice is not to be trusted:

> *Wommenes conseils been ful ofte colde;*

thus the Nun's Priest, but Chanticleer might have done better to heed his wife's.

As for marriage, the Wife could speak knowingly of its woes and tribulations, but she managed pretty well for herself. On the other hand, that *worthy knight* of the Merchant's Tale, though he had both sides explained to him and at first called it *a ful greet sacrament* without which a man is helpless and desolate, later came to grief deservedly. The Marquis of Saluces thought of marriage as *servage,* the very opposite of freedom; but his son's marriage was fortunate. Custance, setting out on her devious and troubled wanderings, cried pitifully:

> *Wommen are born to thraldom and penance,*
> *And to been under mannes governance.*

The Franklin, however, speaking in dead earnest and possibly with the Wife of Bath in mind, for *maistrie* was her word also, knew that

> *Love wol nat been constreyned by maistrye....*
> *Love is a thyng as any spirit free.*
> *Wommen, of kynde, desiren libertee*

and not to be thralls. It is a nice distinction, and like his epigrammatic juggling phrase,

> *Servant in love and lord in mariage,*

guaranteed to satisfy both parties. The Wife of Bath could smile.

Finally, there is the cynical couplet spoken by the perfect Knight but perhaps canceled by Chaucer,

> *For wommen, as to speken in comune,*
> *Thei folwen alle the favour of Fortune.*

This is no compliment to the sex, though it does well enough for the aloof Emily, and is quite unworthy of the Knight. That Chaucer wrote it and then meant to drop it is a fine example of ambivalence; and this word, so far as we can read the evidence, sums up Chaucer's attitude towards women.

VI

Is is of the first importance to remember that Chaucer's life came between two worlds, one dying, the other still unborn. It seems almost fitting, because it suited his temperament, to find him at the end of a great period, "when the vitality had departed from medieval culture," when chivalry was more than a memory yet not altogether real, when scholasticism had done its work, when the Church was divided against itself, and when the commons were beginning to make themselves felt in education, wealth, and power; before the collapse of the fourteenth century in England and also before humanism had reached England in any strength. It was a moment of autumnal decay, when the colors still seemed bright and the sword of winter had not fallen—the most fitting time for Chaucer's brightness and gaiety, his sense of beauty with a touch of the all-too earthy; for his laughter, in a word, which could be sympathetic without falsification by sentimentality, and his smile which was tolerent without quite condoning iniquity—a moment of delicate balance congenial to his spirit. He witnessed the great schism of the papacy and seems not to have known it. He lived in a period of great building, cathedrals remade or finishing, colleges founding; and he seems to have taken no notice. He lived through a great insurrection, and made two or three fleeting allusions to it. He lived at the corrupt court of one king and through the tyrannies of another. He praised Queen Anne; he said nothing of Alice Perrers. Through three decades of political and social confusion at home and of disastrous wars abroad his muse was devoted chiefly to a gentle policy of entertainment; her satire was without indignation.

Yet Chaucer was the coeval of William Langland (if that was his real name), who saw these same distresses, felt them earnestly, and wrote of them in English vigorously. The moment of decay produced both *Piers Plowman* and the *Canterbury Tales*. It produced also a man whose name we cannot even guess, who wrote a golden elegy of faith and a golden romance in which chivalry, with its old true religious feeling, brightened with fine humor, came back for an instant of poetry. The Knight's Tale is a small thing beside *Sir Gawain and the Green Knight*.

He was to be sure a civil servant and had his position to maintain. He was neither all for Apollo nor all for Dionysus; he made token offerings at both altars, bowing and smiling to each. His world did not banish him, but he his world. One can hear him say: "They complain that I took no interest in current affairs because I have so little to say about them in my verses. That is unfair. It is my poetry, not I, which for the most part was unconcerned with the contemporary scene. Poetry is not a record but a reflection. You should not look to me for history; those monks who write chronicles in Latin will have to serve you there. Why does one write poetry at all?" Thus Chaucer was excluded from dealing with certain subjects by his temperament, which inclined him to a cheerful view of both good and evil, and by his surroundings, which encouraged if they did not wholly induce him to write for a special audience. What he felt and kept to himself is not for us to know.

Nevertheless we persist in making inquiries, in peering between the cracks. "To know an author, personally," said Trelawny, "is too often to destroy the illusion created by his works." We may think that a man's poetry tells us more of the truth about him than his letters, his friends' talk, all the accumulations of an intimate biographer; but it is a dangerous assumption. The poet is an amalgam, difficult to analyze, of a human being and a voice. The two often speak a different language. We might argue that a man who could draw such a wily and shifty character as Pandarus must have had many of the same traits, the same skill in persuasion, the same gift of gab, the same ability to deceive as well as to be a faithful friend; and the impression remains with ever so many readers that Pandarus is in some sense, even if unconsciously, a partial self-portrait. We might argue that the creator of the Wife of Bath must have known and enjoyed such company; that the author of the Miller's Tale and the Reeve's Tale must have liked dirty stories and probably knew a great many more; and also the man who had translated Boethius and was so familiar with the text that he could add a suitable patch here and there to whatever he was writing, would also himself be saturated with the spirit of the *De consolatio;* that . . . . But to form a picture from such fragmentary inferences is to ignore both the complex inconsistencies of human nature and the subtleties of imaginative experience.

Note on Cecilia Chaumpaigne

On 1 May 1380 Cecilia, daughter of the late William Chaumpaigne (or Chaumpeneys)[1] and his wife Agnes, gave Chaucer a full and formal deed of release from all charges "de raptu meo." The witnesses to the document were Sir William de Beauchamp, brother of the Earl of Warwick, Sir William Neville, and Sir John Clanvowe, all three of the King's household and known in other ways as Chaucer's friends— together with Sir John Philipot, collector of Customs while Chaucer was controller, and one Richard Morel.[2] Evidently Chaucer was well-protected. Now *raptus* in fourteenth-century legal terminology had two meanings: abduction *(raptus heredis)*[3] and rape *(concubitus violentus)*. Since Cecilia was able to sign the release, she was not a minor, nor a ward, and therefore not kidnaped for a forced marriage. If she had been a ward, the release would have been signed by her guardian. If the charge against Chaucer was rape, which was a felony, why was he not prosecuted? It seems clear from three documents of the following months—a release to Chaucer by Richard Goodchild, a cutler, and John Grove, an armourer; a release to Goodchild and Grove by Cecilia; and a recognizance by Grove of a debt of £10 to Cecilia— that the case was compromised out of court by a money settlement; and that the sum was considerable has been inferred, perhaps incautiously, from the fact that Chaucer sold his father's house in St. Martin's in the Vintry a year later. (It has also been inferred, if the three later documents are related to the *raptus* release, that Chaucer may have abducted Cecilia to save her from attack by Goodchild and Grove.) But Chaucer's friends at Court may have brought influence to bear or some new facts may have come to light which induced Cecilia to modify or withdraw her charge. For instance, she may have become pregnant; and under mediæval law, conception was taken to mean consent. Or indeed she may have consented and then repented. Perhaps both parties were not altogether innocent and therefore they did well to settle by compromise. One thing *seems* clear: the accusation of *raptus* meant rape and not kidnaping.

An interesting possibility, usually left as a guess, is that the *lyte Lowys my sone* for whom Chaucer wrote his unfinished 'Astrolabe' was Cecilia's son. Nothing else is known of him and the conjecture that he was Chaucer's godson may be dismissed. The dates are about right, for the 'Astrolabe' was apparently compiled in 1391, when Lowys was of the *tendir age of ten year*.

Where so much is obscure and uncertain, even speculation may be unjustified. Yet considering how little we know about Chaucer's private life and about his marriage, and how much we do know about the immorality of the Court under Edward and Richard—it would be easy to compile a *chronique scandaleuse* for the period—it hardly seems necessary to be squeamish. Most of the legal tangles would be less tangled if Chaucer had seduced the lady, if she then lost her temper and threatened suit for rape and then under pressure compromised by releasing him for certain considerations. Legally of course it remains a case not proven, but there is no reason except Christian charity to whitewash the poet. Two legal minds have wrestled with the problem, without much conclusive result.[4]

Other poets before (e.g., Dante and Boccaccio) and since have been guilty of irregularities. Chaucer need be no exception; he had abundant contemporary precedent. But more interesting are the literary implications. Chaucer's frequent denial of a personal knowledge of love is of course partly a literary pose. It would, however, take on an effective irony for contempory readers if the opposite were well known to be true. For example, when Troilus wishes to abduct Criseyde after the exchange was announced, the audience would recall with a smile the *raptus* of Cecilia. Pandarus, we know, urged Troilus to run away with Criseyde—

> *Go ravisshe here ne kanstow nat for shame?*

(*Troilus* IV, 530. The word is repeated in this sense at ll. 637 and 643.) Troilus replying uses the same word *ravish* for the abduction of Helen (l. 548), which had brought on the whole war, and rejects the advice. But Pandarus counters (l. 596):

> *It is no shame unto yow ne no vice.*

Here Chaucer first wrote:

> *It is no rape in my dom ne no vice.*

Both words bear the same meaning, to carry off by force, and in the context the revision has no point—in fact *rape* serves the argument of Pandarus better—unless to avoid the suggestion of *raptus* in its legal sense of *concubitus violentus* and a possible reminiscence of Cecilia. (Elsewhere in Chaucer *rape* is the other word meaning haste.) Then when Chaucer circulated the 'Legend of Good Women,' his mock-palinode to the *Troilus,* with its furious attacks on male seducers, there would be more ironic laughter. In the Prologue the poet insists that he had written Criseyde's story

> *To forthren trouthe in love and yt cheryce,*
> *And to ben war fro falsnesse and fro vice;*

but Alceste charges him with the obligation to make *a glorious legende Of goode wymmen*

> *And telle of false men that hem bytraien,*
> *That al hir lyf ne don nat but assayen*
> *How many women they may doon a shame;*
> For in youre world that is now holde a game.
> And thogh the lyke nat a lovere be, . . .

(If, as has been contended, Alceste is the Princess Joan, the irony would take a fresh twist.)

These are but two of many instances which would titillate an audience, the poet concurring, if he were known for amorous dealings. They add a fine gesture to the literary pose of one who dared not pray directly to the God of Love

> *So fer am I from his help in derknesse.*

And Alceste says to the God of Love:

> *Whil he was yong, he kepte youre estat;*
> *I not wher he be now a renegat.*

('Legende' G 400 f.; not in F.) This is richly ambiguous. Such allusions are certainly not evidence in the Cecilia Chaumpaigne case; though that also, whatever the facts, guilty or innocent, would unquestionably enhance the deprecation. In sum, then, while we can have a reasonable interest in Chaucer's private morals and even a wholly suspended judgment in the *raptus* affair, the real, the prime interest is in relation to his poetry, its origins and its overtones.

CHAPTER II. CHAUCER AND THE SCHOLARS: THE PARDONER

"IF Chaucer has suffered much at the hand of copyists," said Mario Praz, "he has suffered more through the misguided zeal of scholars and would-be scholars." One is told sometimes that the younger generation of Chaucerians are falling away from this error, but the signs are still not clear; for though their path is not the path of Cook and Root, of Kittredge and Manly, and those other "noble clerkes," they have branched out in new directions. Now we hear of æsthetic distance and "cultural relativity" in the *Troilus,* and of the "tapestry" of the General Prologue with its "two voices" (*pace* Tennyson), of the "phallicism of the opening lines" (*pace* Freud) and "a designed togetherness" of the portraits. No one has yet speculated on the failure of Criseyde's marriage or on Chaucer and the Nicene Creed, but the Church Fathers have been approached, and only a short while ago (1929) we were told that in the Knight's Tale and in the *Troilus* Chaucer "became interested in the deeper problems of life to which he was able to see no solution except through religion." The moral Chaucer as a companion to *moral Gower.* We are still trying to correlate the Pilgrims' Tales with the topography of the journey. We are still seeking a unifying principle in the humorous medley of the 'Parlement'; and just recently (1957) the principal lovers have been identified, on Baconian lines, as Prince Lionel and Violanta Visconti. We are discovering profound aspects of anarchy and "cosmos" in the Knight's Tale; and when one scholar takes up eighteen pages of *PMLA* to show that the Tale was revised in 1390, another has to rebut them three years later in eleven more pages. In 1929 a "would-be scholar" came to Criseyde's defense in *PMLA* and in the same year he was refuted by two better men, one in *PMLA,* the other in *SP.* Somewhat earlier an eminent Chaucerian offered a theory that Chaucer first planned to begin the *Canterbury Tales* with the Melibeus, spoken by the Man of Law, but was dissatisfied and substituted the 'Palamon and Arcite.'   In 1935-1938 there was a curious flurry on Chaucer's "Wreched Engendring" by four scholars in six articles in three learned journals.   In 1947 a British scholar tried to reintegrate, to the advantage of Chaucer's sublety, the Theseus as a *noble duc* in the Knight's Tale and the Theseus as a deceiver of women in the 'Legend of Good Women.'   When Chaucer changed his mind about the St. Cecilia poem and neglected to change the text, we are informed that *unworthy sone of Eve* was no unusual description of a nun in the fourteenth century.   Manly saw the Monk as a "sad-faced pedant" and "a gloomy and uninteresting person"; but Tatlock saw in him a "combination of force, cultivation and high self-respect."   And so on.   These are but random *ensaumples*.   The old road is strewn with such parry and thrust, expostulation and reply.   Hypothesis begets hypothesis. We have a passion for explaining everything and when no explanation is at hand we invent one.   Interpretation begets interpretation and so runs into progressions, arithmetical, geometrical, and harmonic.   Welcome strictures occur occasionally, such as Lumiansky's observation: that Chaucer gave us in the Franklin's Tale his view of the perfect marriage is "a theory which comes from Professor Kittredge rather than from Holy Writ."   (Professor Lumiansky is not a Harvard man; but, see below, his eye is not without its beam.)   As long ago as 1803 there came from Charles Lamb, writing to Chaucer's biographer Godwin, a protest which was also prophecy: ". . . a conjecturing spirit, a fondness for filling out the picture by supposing what Chaucer did and how he felt, where the materials are scanty."

Evidences, good and otherwise, of this accumulation of exegesis will occur in later pages, but first a rather special case, that of the poor Pardoner, will serve as a prime exhibit of the scholars collaborating with the poet.

The Summoner and the Pardoner are introduced together at the Tabard Inn but get separated on the road to Canterbury, when the Summoner is paired off against the Friar and the Pardoner is brought in to follow the Physician.   The Pardoner is first described with persistent irony and sarcasm.   He is *gentil,* a friend and peer of the most repulsive of all the Pilgrims; he has come straight from Rome with his false relics and he is singing a love duet with the Summoner, who bears him a *stif burdoun,* a base accompaniment. He looks like a gelding or a mare.[1] But in his profession he is a complete success; that is, the better the worse. With his preaching he fleeces the country people, and in church he sings the offertory like a master, for his own profit.

When next we see him he makes a display of himself by rashly interrupting the Wife's Prologue. He says, jokingly, that he is planning to marry, but her remarks have frightened him. She replies: Wait till I have finished my story of marital tribulation; and he quickly subsides, with mock courtesy. The passage is almost a draw. Then when the Physician has ended his sad tale of Virginia, with its moral on the 'merit' of sin and the worm of conscience—

Forsaketh synne, er synne yow forsake—

the Host, sentimentally heartbroken by the tragedy, makes his clumsy comment and turns to the Pardoner for *som myrthe or japes* as comic relief.[2] The Pardoner agrees, but asks for time to eat and drink *at this ale-stake.* At this the *gentils* seem to fear something ribald coming (what else would they expect from him, by this time?) and insist on *som moral thyng;* and so the Pardoner obliges. These lines have begotten several variations, but they need signify no more than Chaucer's readjustment of the situation when the Pardoner tells the story first meant for the Parson. For the Tale *is* an *honest thyng* and is made dishonest only by the Pardoner's devastating Prologue.

We were hardly prepared for the Pardoner's exposure now of his own debasement. Nothing in the General Prologue suggests this kind of rascal and in the Wife's Prologue we learned only that he could gratuitously make a fool of himself. Hence another variation. But there is perfect consistency between the fact that he deceived the country people and the account of his methods. Only his brazen display of the methods is surprising.[3]

Having thus advertised himself as *a ful vicious man,* the Pardoner proceeds with his moral tale, by which he is accustomed to get liberal contributions from his audience. He begins with the Flemish rioters, inveighs against drunkenness, gluttony, gambling, and swearing in no very orderly manner—was he therefore drunk?—and then gets to his story of the Three Rioters, which he tells with great skill. (The voice is now the voice of Geoffrey Chaucer.) Then, at l. 889 the problems set in. These difficulties *exact* interpretation, as Mr. Sedgewick will tell us. First there is the reference to Avicenna on poisoning. The Parson might have made it, for he was a learned man, a clerk. It is certainly unexpected from the Pardoner. But we may frankly label it "Auctor" as in the Ellesmere manuscript, and let it pass.[4] Next is the fine oratorical outburst on the cursed sins of the tavern, so called: a grand climax for the Parson in one sense and for the Pardoner in another. Then the Pardoner speaks clearly: Now, good people, beware of avarice and obtain my pardon by your generous offerings. This has been his exhibition sermon, which he marks beyond any question by turning to the Pilgrims with his *And lo, sires, thus I preche.* Probably each reader has his own interpretation. As for Chaucer, did he with deliberate malice leave it completely ambiguous, laying a trap for future commentators? Or did he think it was all plain enough?[5] The rest is fairly simple, though open to secondary explanations. The Pardoner has slipped, tries to recover by another brazen display, and boisterously congratulates the Pilgrims on having a Pardoner at hand for any emergency. He goes further, applies directly to the Host as *moost envoluped in synne*—an easy jest—and the Host loses his temper and his sense of decency. The Pardoner is speechless with anger. The worthy Knight intervenes, everybody laughs, and the opponents kiss anon, all passion spent.

Thus far Chaucer's Pardoner. Now the critics' Pardoner.

Hardly an item in Chaucer's account has escaped elaboration, but the present review will try to cover only the principal points.[6]

There has never been any question of the historical accuracy of Chaucer's picture. Jusserand, in his Chaucer Society Essay, "Chaucer's Pardoner and the Pope's Pardoners," showed, as Skeat restated it, "that Chaucer has not in the least exaggerated; for exaggeration was not possible."[7]   But in his *English Wayfaring Life* Jusserand indulged in a "classic fantasy" on the pardoner, which coupled with a realistic touch of Chaucer's started a train of misstatements. Said Jusserand, giving his imagination wing, but not without an eye on Chaucer's text:

> On the tavern bench the pardoner is still seated. There come Chaucer, the knight, the squire, the friar, the host—old acquaintances. We are by ourselves, no one need be afraid to speak, the foaming ale renders hearts expansive; and the unseen coils of that tortuous soul unfold to view; he gives the summary of a whole life, the theory of his existence, the key to his secrets. What matters his frankness? he knows that it cannot hurt him; time and again has the bishop brought his practices to light, but the crowd always troops around him. And who knows if his companions—who knows if his more enlightened companions, to whom he shows the concealed springs of the automaton—will, to-morrow, believe it lifeless? (English Transl. p. 189).

This is so patently Jusserand's picture that no charges may be laid against the author. But Chaucer had let his Pardoner say *heere at this ale-stake/I wol bothe drynke, and eten of a cake.* Without explicity telling us, Chaucer pretends that the Pilgrims have paused in front of an inn. The inn is there—you recognize it by the ale-stake. And it is not there, because Chaucer omitted to mention it. Such simple reasoning, however, did not satisfy Professor Gerould. First in 1935 and again in 1952[8] he brought forward the picture of the Pardoner's friend the Summoner—

> *A gerland had he set up-on his heed,*
> *As greet as it were for an ale-stake;*
> *A bokeler had he maad him of a cake.*

But this was back in the General Prologue (666-68) at the Tabard Inn. There Chaucer gave us the Summoner both in Southwark (*in that place,* 623) and also riding with the Pardoner (669): Professor Gerould takes the ale-stake from its first appearance in a simile, creates it anew, and contributes to the *Canterbury Tales* this piece of low comedy: "So the Pardoner, making his little joke about the ale-stake, leaned over and broke off a bit of his companion's buckler."[9]

But this is not all. Tupper maintained that the Pardoner told his story *in* a tavern,[10] and Brown agreed;[11] and Legouis said, "il est entré dans la taverne";[12] and Robinson said (p. 834), "apparently . . . at the tavern" and then "in a tavern," to give emphasis, as Tupper claimed, to "the humor of the situation." At least, says Robinson, "there is no indication that they take the road before the Pardoner begins"; nor, in fact, any indication to the contrary. None was needed, for it is part of the fiction—unrealistic as that may be—that the Pilgrims all told their tales as they rode. If the scene must be filled in, since Chaucer did not, one may imagine that just as the Host called on the Pardoner the cavalcade was approaching an inn; the Pardoner, pointing up at the ale-stake, said: Wait here while I have a drink and a bite; then they proceed on their way. Well, the ale-stake, which is all that Chaucer gave us, implies an inn, and it would of course be outside the inn. The rest is unnecessary embroidery.

The "Flanders heresy" (Sedgewick) is no more than a suggestion that "through the Pardoner, a professional moralizer," Chaucer was "warning his King and country" against contemporary conditions in Flanders.[13] There was reason enough, to be sure, but there is also the *exemplum* of Thomas of Cantimpré which begins "In marchia Flandrie" and another in the same collection which has "interesting correspondences" with the Pardoner's Tale.

The Tale itself has two main parts, one of them, a kind of introduction—Chaucer was given to long introductions—is the tavern scene laid, for local color, *In Flaunders whylom* with its homiletic attack on the Sins of the Tavern; the other is the *exemplum*. The transition is abrupt, but need not be called clumsy (Sedgewick, p. 439), and has bothered some because in Flanders, at the outset, there was a whole company of rioters and now only three *of which I telle,* i.e., I am about to tell.[14]

These are small matters. The 'sermon' is more serious, and has brought forth various surmises. The first thing to recognize is that the Tale, both parts of it, is, as the Pardoner says, a discourse which he regularly uses to extract money from his hearers: *I preche no thyng but for coveitise.* He starts with the Flemish revelers as a sort of text and a pretended audience, for greater vividness; and having softened up his hearers (not the Flemings, needless to say) with a rousing picture of their sins, drunkenness, gluttony, gambling, and so on, he proceeds to the *exemplum* which brings home to them the particular vice of avarice, and, for our amusement, the Pardoner's also. This is plain enough, only it was misleading to call the first discourse a 'sermon' and then test it for the six parts of a typical sermon as prescribed by the mediæval treatises.[15] It is still worse to say that the sermon "contains nothing designed to induce the congregation to come forward and offer to his relics. Has he, for the time being, completely forgotten salesmanship?" The question is already answered.

Professor Gerould's interpretation is quite different and very appealing: the Pardoner was already drunk and having bitten off some of the Summoner's cake he

. . . started to think of some 'honest thing,' and succeeded in pulling out of his befuddled brain the text of 1 Timothy vi, 10. This set him off, with drunken shamelessness, on an account of his scandalous way of life. The discourse, which is roughly in the form of one of his sermons, suggested to him ensamples and brought back to his mind the tale he had to tell.[16]

This theory, which explains so much, is elaborated with restrained eloquence in the *Chaucerian Essays;* I will not mar the fuller form by excerpts. It explains the erratic incoherence of the sermon,[17] and above all it accounts for the blatant exposure of the Pardoner's depravity, which without the aid of alcohol would have been incredible. It poses, however, another kind of credibility: whether Chaucer would agree; whether Professor Gerould's empathy has assigned to the poet the skilful execution of a sublety outside of his habitual methods.

Others have taken the indecent exposure more or less for granted. Ten Brink said simply, the Pardoner "unmasks his trade and practices with the shamelessness and bare-faced frankness which the atmosphere of the Canterbury Tales requires," without justifying the requirement. Sedgewick undertakes to justify the exposure by a circuitous route. When the Pardoner asked for time to drink before he starts his Tale the gentles utter a "swift cry"—

> *Nay, lat hym telle us of no ribaudye—*

which

has a double importance. On its surface it recalls the portrait of the rascal as he has appeared in the respectable part of the Pilgrimage: too clever to be predictable, physically abnormal, disturbingly contradictory, scoundrelly beyond words, a clear candidate for interdict. Even the Wife of Bath has eyed him darkly. [So far we agree.] As for the bawdry which the Miller has already uttered in their hearing, they had expected he would tell 'his cherles tale in his manere,' and they had known the worst he could do before he began. [This allows too little for the brightness of the Miller's Tale, and nothing for the bold bawdry of the Reeve's.] But they were troubled by the Pardoner's duplicity: altogether too visible on the one hand, and on the other a quite unknown quantity. If the inevitable fabliau came from the visible side, no doubt they could stand it; it was the other quarter they feared. *Ignotum pro horrendo.* This, I believe, is a possible reading of the gentles' mind, or of what Chaucer thought would be there.

So they ask for *som moral thyng* and this command "the Pardoner knows he dare not disobey." It is "a galling choice," because to tell a moral tale *as such* would be out of character; "since he is known to be a charlatan, he can prove he is the cleverest of his kind." He pauses for his drink.

But only for a moment. We can easily imagine his rapid thinking as he swallows his ale: 'I have it! The Wife made a hit with her confessions. Why shouldn't I follow her example and give an exhibition, with running comment, of my technique? They have asked for morality and they shall have it; but it will be morality with my special difference, from the mouth of a dark horse. There can be no risk. Here and now I am perfectly secure.'

Much of this, Mr. Sedgewick admits frankly is "naked 'assumption,'" but "By the device of the 'protest' Chaucer jockeys his Pardoner into a corner . . . . The charlatan's self-revelation is therefore, not only 'credible' on other grounds, it is as near to dramatic inevitability as it can be made."

This is subtle and ingenious. As special pleading it may not seem cogent, but as private supplementation it is richly imaginative. The objection to it is that it needlessly imputes to Chaucer

an elaborate justification for a simple proceeding. The Pardoner
was a noble ecclesiastic and proud of his successes; he welcomed
an opportunity to show off before his fellow pilgrims; and Chaucer, knowing also that confession was a recognized literary device, gave him free rein. If he had anything up his sleeve, it
was the grand climax in which the Pardoner is led from one
excess to another and then to complete deflation.

Professor Gerould put his finger on a tender spot when he
spoke of the "complexities" of the Pardoner's "personality," and
in the same paragraph called him "a murky figure." In truth,
the pardoner whom Professor Manly saw, who "must have been
nearly as familiar to Chaucer's readers as was Rouncival itself,
which they passed daily as they journeyed between London and
Westminster,"[18] may very well have had a complex personality
and Chaucer may have known him very well, even to his "secret"
deformity. But the Pardoner of the Canterbury pilgrimage is
only what Chaucer made him. The description of him is so
circumstantial—his shrill voice, his beardless face, his sparse yellow
hair—as to suggest a living model; and it would seem that a
pardoner of Rouncival with such a marked appearance should
have been easily recognizable. But Chaucer never said that his
Pardoner was a *eunuchus ex nativitate* and Chaucer's readers
journeying between London and Westminster would not be
likely to know that he was, however often they passed him. We
have actually confused two figures, Chaucer's Pilgrim and his
possible model: one an extraordinary fiction, the other, in so far
as he existed, an unusual human being; and only Chaucer knew
how much alike the two were. This would seem to be simple and
obvious. We must admit then that we know only the Pardoner
of our text and we know about him only so much as Chaucer
reported. It may be a quibble to insist that a fictional character
has no "personality," but however adroitly genius may mingle
appearance and reality the distinction stands; however skilfully an
author may create the illusion, the man remains a fiction with no
existence off the printed page; and the most we can say is that
Chaucer's Pardoner resembles a complex personality according to
those data which Chaucer provided. So we avoid the risk of

fallacy if we ask merely whether those data afford a simplex-complex which is self-consistent and also consistent with our experience of human beings. The Pardoner has no private life except in our imagination guided by Chaucer's hints, and our imagination requires strict surveillance in such matters. We know, for example, that the Pardoner was the kind of man who would boastingly display his worst qualities, but we cannot be sure, nor do we need to be, that he was as black as he chose to paint himself. He had certain evil characteristics which he revealed, but it does not follow that he was a drunkard or that having paused to drink while he recalled a good story he was so drunk he could not keep his wits about him—until the poet pushed him aside (as he "pushed his tankard aside") and soberly told his story for him, only to let the intoxication return when the story was done.

Would Chaucer accept this interpretation? Is there good ground for supposing that Chaucer meant to depict the Pardoner as drunk and expected us to recognize his intention? This may be a hard question to answer, but surely it is uncritical to evade it. In his chapter on "The Pardoner's Secret" Professor Curry is careful to anticipate such a question. "Before we can grasp the full meaning of the poet's purpose . . . it becomes necessary to acquire as nearly as possible the point of view with which the fourteenth century Englishman looked upon the world" (p. 56). Then, however, he states his thesis guardedly, that Chaucer's "selection of both form and feature given to many of his characters is determined in large measure or at least influenced, I believe, by" the books on physiognomy. The next step is to show from those books, always assuming that Chaucer was acquainted with them, that many of the features of the Pardoner reveal him as a *eunuchus ex nativitate;* and from here it looks like an easy step to the position that Chaucer intended to represent the Pardoner as recognizably a eunuch. The textual evidence is

I trow he were a geldyng or a mare;

which is plain enough to be no secret, the other details being corroborative, but not plain enough to prove eunuchism. It need only mean: 'it is pretty obvious that he was very effeminate.'[19] To go beyond this is interpretation,[20] and nothing that follows requires us to go further. It is amusing to fancy that Chaucer really knew that his Pardoner was a eunuch and took pleasure in saying so with a metaphor, but it is only an amusing fancy. Harry Bailey (who of course had not read the General Prologue) did not think so (C 952).

The climax, the endlink in which the Pardoner addresses the Pilgrims and provokes the Host's wrath, has tempted the interpreters beyond their strength. Only Carleton Brown refused to be drawn: "His tale once concluded, the Pardoner, like the Clerk, relaxed into a mood of pure raillery" (p. xxxv). He noted Kittredge's version and Sisam's observation that it does not take account of the formal purpose of the closing prayer. He dismissed Curry's version with a remark which might be writ large over what now follows: "The obvious difficulty with this explanation is that it must be read into Chaucer's text."

Kittredge's version is itself a kind of climax. It goes back to his *Atlantic Monthly* article of 1893 and was reproduced as the grand finale of his Johns Hopkins lectures.[21] It is entirely consistent with his enthusiastic dramatizing of the *Canterbury Tales,* but I have reason to believe that he was not himself taken in by it. Like the Pardoner, Kittredge had "the histrionic temperament." The Pardoner's cynical self-portrait was "dramatically inevitable, a forestalling of the Pilgrims' judgment"; and he "is willing to pass for a knave, but objects to be taken for a fool."[22] Then after the display of his pulpit oratory, "suddenly, unexpectedly, without an instant's warning, his cynicism falls away, and he utters the solemn words: 'May Christ, the physician of our souls...' ... and now, under the spell of the wonderful story he has told, he suffers a very paroxysm of agonized sincerity." Then follows the equally sudden reaction and the Pardoner "takes refuge from himself in a wild orgy of reckless jesting." Finally, "nobody but Geoffrey Chaucer divined the tragic face behind the satyr's mask"—nobody except G. L. Kittredge, who made a blank verse line for it. This is real divination; one is delighted to read it; but it is not Chaucer.

Yet Chaucer left the door open and we can all walk through. If he had an interpretation of his own he kept the secret. Robinson simply summarizes Kittredge (p. 837); Lowes follows: "a single sharp moment of revulsion."[23]   Curry calls this "a pleasant but unconvincing" solution of the problem, and adds his own. The turning point is

only a preparation for his proposed master-stroke of deception. . . . To hypnotize the Pilgrims into buying relics after he has declared their worthlessness and his own perfidy, would constitute the crowning success of his career. Turning suddenly to them, he says in effect: 'Lo, sirs, this is the way I preach to *ignorant* people. But *you* are my friends; may God grant that *you* may receive the pardon of Jesus Christ; I would never deceive you! Come, now, and kiss this relic.' This is, moreover, the correct manner in which to conclude a well-constructed oration; having no customary audience, he is compelled to make shift with an appeal to the Pilgrims themselves. But he reckons without his Host![24]

Sedgewick rejects the solutions of both Kittredge and Curry. The benedictional ending is conventional and also "a thoroughly sincere expression of personal feeling"; for the Pardoner means: "I have proclaimed myself a charlatan but I would not have you think me a heretic." The rest is "ironic banter" or "impudent horseplay." "Only an utter fool would *seriously* ask the Knight and the Monk, not to speak of the Host, to kneel down or else give money 'at every miles ende.'" But here the Pardoner overreaches himself; for "Chaucer, it seems to me, has made up his mind that this lofty rogue should take a fall . . . . At any rate, the fall was arranged." "I imagine," continues Sedgewick,

that a hush had fallen over the pilgrims as the Pardoner brings his "sermon" to a close. No one, not even the Host, has a word to say. True, there is no basis for this assumption in the text except that a shift is plainly indicated. The preacher evidently *intends* to stop, does stop in fact—and then goes on. . . .

Professor Gerould has a fresh variant, with several surprises coming after his first remarks on the Pardoner's "personality." With the end of the Tale "his intoxication, whether with ale or with his own acting, appears suddenly to end." His words about

Christ's pardon "are words of truth and soberness, and puzzling words" as coming from the Pardoner. But

we should be unwise to assume that they are "out of character." The Pardoner is Chaucer's creation . . . . His unexpected and momentary exhibition of decency must be accepted without reserve, since his author attributed it to him . . . . One may guess that Chaucer put the words in his mouth because he meant him to be a human being. He was a very wicked man, but no devil.

And in a moment Professor Gerould says: "the Pardoner is so amusing that he fails to shock us by his wickedness."

This adds two new problems: because Chaucer did it, is it therefore right? and are we amused? The former is fundamental to nearly all Chaucer criticism; the latter concerning the Pardoner, has already received contradictory answers. Professor Patch says: "His companionship with the horrible Summoner in the song 'Come hider, love, to me' is the most violent satire in all Chaucer's poetry. The insinuation shows the poet's hatred" (p. 164). This puts the worst possible construction on what may be only reckless levity. If true, it shows the Pardoner as even more brazen than his later revelations do; it makes him flaunt his homosexuality before all the Pilgrims. Sedgewick thinks Patch's language too strong and comments that "The Pardoner would be quite capable of explaining that he learned his ditty from the Pope." And how can we be sure that Chaucer hated the Pardoner? No doubt he disapproved of the contemporary practices which his character illustrates; but this is not the same as hating the character he created. One remembers Chesterton's quip that the poet was himself "a gentle pardoner." It is hard to think of Geoffrey Chaucer as capable of hatred. But on the æsthetic side, has he made his Pardoner, the pilgrim invented for the Canterbury journey, a revolting figure? There may not have been any moment of agonized sincerity, but the man had his good points. He seems to have been honest in giving himself away, and his evident vitality is almost enough to save him from our censure. Both he and the Wife of Bath are artistic creations, not real people. And the crowning incident of the final episode is: *Anon they kiste,* the bluff hearty Host and the dreadful vicious Pardoner. A beautiful benediction.

There are more of these critical exchanges, and probably not all the permutations and combinations have yet appeared in print. Let one more suffice. Professor Lumiansky has conjectured that the Pardoner has joined the pilgrimage—of course the Pardoner had no choice in the matter; he is there because Chaucer put him there—

with the definite purpose of extracting money from his travelling companions by a refinement of his usual methods of salesmanship among the peasants, directs his actions and words throughout toward that end and fails, after almost succeeding, because he reverts to those usual methods at the crucial moment.[25]

This long report of clashing views would be unwarranted without a moral. The imagination is free, though enthusiasts may sometimes mean license when they cry liberty. There is even room in a crowded world for many "damnable heresies," if they lie along the pilgrim's way to St. Truth. One recalls the now dead controversies over a stanzaic 'Palamon and Arcite,' over the priority of the F or G prologue to the 'Legend of Good Women,' over the schematic treatment of the Seven Sins, and the search for a key to the three suitors of the 'Parlement'; even the disturbances over the character of Criseyde have abated.

The Pardoner problem may some day be solved or a general agreement reached, if certain distinctions are observed. For there are levels of the glorious art of glossing, with varying degrees of justification or merit. At the lowest and safest is the exercise of restating in the language of exposition what is actually in the text—the method of parallel lines. Above this is the development or elaboration of what is in the text, from the mere explanation of hard words and historical background to the use of these for illustration and clarification—a method of rising spirals. Further, there is a critically intuitive extension of the text—in parabolic curves—supplementing, enlarging the picture (without distortion), and adding perspective depth. Lastly, there is a purely tangential kind of interpretation in which the critic, spider-like, spins out of his own substance impertinent contributions of his own, supplanting the text. Between these levels are many gradations whereby one merges into another, and perhaps the critic himself cannot always say what he is trying to do. Some of these methods involve what Bacon calls the vanities of learning. Often there seems to be a tacit assumption that Chaucer did not know what he was about and therefore is in need of the modern commentator to supply a native deficiency. This extends from filling in what Chaucer only sketched to the critic's pitting his own skill against the poet's, apparently hoping that we shall enjoy his new set of variations as much as we did the original theme. The most daring and not the most uncommon method is that of divining what was, or must have been, in Chaucer's mind when he wrote, though he failed to make it clear, and seeing deeper into Chaucer's purpose than was apparent to other critics or even to Chaucer himself. The most unfortunate, because so obviously uncritical, attempt to *explain* Chaucer rests on an assumption that the King can do no Wrong, that Chaucer was always perfect and needs only our patience or ingenuity to make everything artistically neat and tidy. The reasons behind this attitude are sometimes defensive and sometimes genuinely admiring; defensive when they imply a band of the initiate and devout who must maintain the dignity of the cult, and even among the genuine admirers a passion for justifying their poet at all points at all costs. But Chaucer has merits enough to support a few charges of error. It would be more decent and more sane to acknowledge the faults rather than obscure them.

Most of all this confusion came of what Chaucer had left undone. Since the *Canterbury Tales* is an unfinished work, it stands to reason that the Pardoner is an unfinished 'character.' Who knows what plans Chaucer had for him before the Pilgrims were reseated at the Tabard Inn, or what might occur to Chaucer's fertile mind for subsequent development or clarification? The still incomplete pieces may be fitted together in different patterns; but what business have we to arrange them according to our limited knowledge and pretend that such or such must have been the poet's intention? The line between legitimate and illegitimate speculative supplementation may be hard to draw, but the futility of enlarging upon Chaucer's hints without proper reserve or caution is well illustrated by the scholars' toying with this Pardoner, some of it ingenious, some of it absurd, and very little of it necessary. One makes a clever guess; another challenges it; and *voilà,* a problem, a controversy, and more learned articles.

CHAPTER III. THE CANTERBURY TALES

1. THE CANTERBURY FELLOWSHIP

THE General Prologue, so-called by modern editors, is first of all an introduction to the Tales: it gives the preliminary setting, presents descriptively and analytically the dramatis personae, and sets the dramatic machinery in motion; and it does all these things supremely well, with admirable conciseness and clarity. It is consistently admired and has been called Chaucer's greatest achievement. But it has certain peculiarities which illustrate Chaucer's way of writing elsewhere.

The most striking characteristic, at the very outset, is his mingling or contrast of a formal style and the friendly, almost casual, manner, which looks like carelessness; and so cunningly are the two interwoven that one is often at a loss to distinguish between the artless and the well concealed artistry. There are times when as one reads—not only in the General Prologue but throughout the *Complete Works*—one feels that Chaucer is merely extemporizing; and there are other times when both the style itself and also the manuscript evidence show careful workmanship and revision. The best and the less good are so frequently in close juxtaposition as to make one wonder if what one sees is really there.

Nothing could be finer than the opening sentence of the General Prologue. Its description of spring is both conventional, with a long history,[1] and fresh; the sentence is neatly balanced on the *when—then,* and the *then* part is divided into general and particular; and its formalism is relieved by little parentheses and asides. *Zephirus* eek *with his* sweete *breeth* balances *Aprille with his shoures* soote. The prose order of *pilgrimages . . . To ferne* is varied by an intruded but parallel clause: *And palmeres for to seken straunge strondes.* It all starts with a metrical *attaque* on the stressed first syllable, it ebbs and flows and subsides on the sound of *seeke* echoing *soote*. It has the breath of spring and it is brightened, to offset a little the conventional mode, with hints of humor. Zephyr inspires the tender buds figuratively and breathes literally on them. The little birds, so moved by the vernal impulse, both sing all night and sleep all night (with one eye open) or seem to. It sharpens the attention to get just the right meaning of April's sun having run its half-course in the Ram. Yet with these and other excellences there are bothersome details.

The abstract figure of April piercing the drought of March hardly prepares us for the apparently literal figure of bathing every vein; and *veyne* must be transfigured to the sense of root, rootlet. Moreover,

> *in swich licour*
> *Of which vertu engendred is the flour*

is so condensed as almost to defy syntax. It must mean 'in such a liquid as that by whose power or virtue the flower is begotten,' with a subtle suggestion of insemination (if the word is not too modern); but the correlatives *swich . . . which* are not clearly handled and if *Of* means 'by' it must be used twice to make *which* become 'whose.' No one misses the general sense, but it is an extremely elaborate way of saying that April showers bring May flowers; and the grammar is less than perfect. Any poet may do slight violence to language; but is it here a conscious forcing or a small carelessness? And are we to understand that pilgrims visit the Becket shrine chiefly because the saint has helped them in recent illnesses? and that each of the twenty-nine to follow is in some sort gratefully convalescent? Why an emphasis on this particular reason for a pilgrimage to St. Thomas of Canterbury?[2]

Now the style changes. The first carefully constructed sentence of eighteen lines is followed by one only half as long and loosely constructed: 'It happened that one day at that time of year at night a group of fully twenty-nine miscellaneous persons had arrived at the inn, people who had come together by chance, being all pilgrims on their way to Canterbury.' This is informal truly.

'And to be brief about it, by the time the sun had set [it was already night, eight lines before, when they arrived at the inn] I had become so well acquainted with them that they invited me to join their party.' Are we to understand that twenty-nine, a very precise number, sundry persons had united themselves into a *felaweshipe* before they reached the Tabard? Then the poet says—

> *ther as I yow devyse.*
> *But nathelees, whil I have tyme and space,*
> *Er that I ferther in this tale pace, . . .*

The first *I* is the fictive Pilgrim whom we think of as Chaucer though he is never so named, and who is going to tell us about the whole journey; the second both is and is not.[3] *Whil I have tyme* to give you a description of each of the twenty-nine implies that Chaucer the Pilgrim will spend the rest of the night setting down his impressions of the previous evening, but it really says that Chaucer the poet thinks it appropriate to describe his characters before the action of his story begins. This may be and probably is a humorous confusion, but the reader must look sharp to recognize it. Again, when the portraits are finished, the same ambiguity returns.

> *Now have I toold you shortly, in a clause,*
> *Th'estaat, th'array, the nombre, and eek the cause*
> *Why that assembled was this compaignyne*
> *In Southwerk. . . .*

It is the author speaking; but he continues:

> *But now is tyme to yow for to telle*
> *How that we baren us that ilke nyght,*

and the author and Pilgrim are reunited. The Host is introduced, the compact agreed upon, and the next morning they are all on their way.

In between is the long *clause* containing the famous series of vignettes. We soon discover that the *aventure* which brought these divers folk together was of the poet's own making. There are first a Knight, his son, and his Yeoman, a Prioress, a Monk, and a Friar: a natural selection and arrangement; but notice that as they descend the social scale they also diminsh in *moral vertu*. Next is the Merchant, a somewhat sinister figure, loosely attached to the Friar in that the latter's name is given at the end of his description and the Merchant's withheld. Next is the Clerk, a contrast. Then come, higher up the scale, the Man of Law and the Franklin together; but their companionship is not mentioned again. Then the five burgesses and their Cook, and so on. There is order, but it is not too obvious. We share the friendly atmosphere of that first meeting at the Tabard.

It seems to me, Chaucer begins the series,—

> *Me thinketh it accordaunt to resoun*
> *To telle yow al the condicioun*
> *Of ech of hem, so as it semed me,*
> *And whiche they weren and of what degree,*
> *And eek in what array that they were inne.*

Al the condicioun is thus distributed under three heads: general character, rank, and appearance. The first *And* is epexegetical.

For the Knight these three, plainly labeled, appear in due sequence, but there is some irregularity in the listing of his campaigns; they do not follow a geographical pattern nor are they (so far as they can be identified) in chronological order; they begin with the capture of Alexandria in 1365, shift to Grenada and Algezir in 1343 and 1344, and then back to the 1360's with the lord of Palatye. For the Squire the order is: general statement, appearance, age, height, physical powers, youthful exploits, appearance, musical accomplishments, general statement, appearance, horsemanship, other accomplishments, zeal as a lover, and finally his courtesy, humility, and—with a nimble twist dwindling the showy young man—usefulness:

> *And carf biforn his fader at the table.*

Altogether a most effective disorder, though more like a bright miniature in a manuscript than the description of a real person.

The fillip for a last line is duplicated in the next: after a total picture of a professional woodsman—

A forster was he, soothly, as I gesse;

and a little later, with variation, closing the accounts of the Friar and the Merchant: *I noot how men him calle,* that is, I'd better not name him. A signal specimen of the method of alternation, of separating details one would expect to find together, already seen in the Squire, occurs at the end of the Franklin's portrait: he was lord at sessions and often knight of the shire, a dagger and a pouch hung from his girdle, he had been a sheriff and a *countour;* and even more strikingly in the Miller's: his nostrils were black, he carried a sword and buckler, his mouth was big.

The tripartite formula, applied carefully for the Knight, abandoned for the Squire and the Yeoman, is taken up again with the Prioress, save that it begins with her smile and her favorite oath; and the last twelve lines, one fourth of the whole, are devoted to her appearance. For the Monk, however, the method is different: the revealing line is

And I seyde his opinion was good.

Thus we are permitted to hear the narrator conversing with the Monk, exchanging views and drawing him out. The effect is to remind us of the earlier line,

So hadde I spoken with hem everichon,

and to confirm our impression that the descriptions were based on personal interviews:—although we had not assumed that the Knight told him about all those campaigns or that the Prioress displayed, on first introduction, some of her personal weaknesses. The device used for the Monk recurs when we learn that the Friar was better acquainted with inn-keepers and barmaids than with the sick and the poor, because, as he said—

> For *unto swich a worthy man as he*
> *Accorded nat, as by his facultee,*
> *To have with sike lazars aqueyntaunce.*
> *"It is nat honest,"* [said he,] *it may nat avaunce*
> *For to delen with no swich poraille.*

And there are other slight indications of this conversational method, as with the Merchant:

> *His resons he spak ful solempnely,*
> *Sownynge alwey th'encrees of his wynnyng:*
> *He wolde* [he said] *the see were kept. . . .*

The Squire's surcoat like a meadow

> *Al ful of fresshe floures, whyte and reede,*

is one thing, his father's gypon

> *Al bismotered with his habergeon*

is quite another. We are not to wonder, for example, where the Knight landed when he *was late ycome from his viage,* and why he was in such haste to reach the shrine of St. Thomas, or where and when his son met him dressed in all his finery, or why he had with him his Yeoman fully equipped for his business of woodcraft. These and many more such matters are not so much left to our imagination as not to be considered at all.

So with the other portraits. We hear almost as much about the wives of the burgesses as about them, and nothing about them individually; the *array* of the Cook is limited to his mormal and of the Plowman to his tabard; the Manciple's is omitted altogether. Each portrait has its special merit. Variety is the guiding principle. The formula was introduced only to be neglected.

In short, Chaucer uses in alternation or in combination three methods as he finds them convenient, that of personal observation, that of question and answer, and that of the omniscient author. Realistic reporting alternates with literary convention.

Still a different point of view results from the blend of Pilgrim-narrator and omniscient author. It was natural to describe the Knight as having good horses and the Monk as having a brown palfrey with jingling bridle and the Merchant as sitting high on his horse, for these are generalizing details. But when we are told (at l. 287) that the Clerk's horse was as lean as a rake, we must look ahead from the gathering at the inn to the fellowship on the road: the Clerk would not have a horse while pursuing his studies at Oxford. This shift, this double use of time, continues in the pictures of the Man of Law, the Wife of Bath, and the Plowman, who rode a mare. We are both at the Tabard and on the way to Canterbury. Then the method seems to change again, this time with a real difference.

After presenting the first twenty-one—the Prioress had a Nun and three Priests with her, but they are only mentioned in passing—Chaucer pauses to draw breath. The list is already almost too long and varied for easy absorption by even a very attentive reader, to say nothing of listeners. Clear, concise, brilliant as the portraits are, the pace has been so rapid that the final effect, except after repeated rereading, is in danger of becoming confused. Recognizing this, Chaucer pauses at l. 542, reassuringly, as much as to say: **we are nearing the end,** there are only five more—

> *Ther was also a Reve, and a Millere,*
> *A Somnour, and a Pardoner also,*
> *A Manciple, and myself—ther were namo!*

But this is not all. Long ago Miss Hammond gave us the hint, often neglected, that Chaucer's first plan included only those foregoing Pilgrims. He later added the final five when he saw the opportunity to enliven the pilgrimage by the interplay and quarrels of five rascals. As the fragments now stand, she observed, the Miller's and the Reeve's tale come at the end of A (barring the unfinished Cook's), the Pardoner's at the end of C, the Summoner's at the end of D, and the Manciple's is a fragment by itself. Equally striking is the fact that in the General Prologue the Miller is described as leading the cavalcade *out of toune* and the Reeve as bringing up the rear. Similarly, in the Miller's Prologue we are advised, in Chaucer's second 'apology,' that both the Miller and the Reeve told *harlotrie*. Nowhere else do the signs point ahead; the method is to describe events as they happen. It seems likely then that the Miller and the Reeve were added to the original plan, and probably with them the Summoner; and it is these three whose tales are of the conspicuously fabliau type. The Pardoner's Tale is a special case, since it seems to have been first intended for the Parson. The Manciple's is early work and run in as filler; it is far from appropriate to this Manciple; and we are still in doubt why the Manciple is in the company at all, unless Chaucer had a private reason.

Thus we are permitted to watch the plan develop as the methods change. It looks as though the first plan was static, and therefore the 'dramatic' conception of the pilgrimage, for which Chaucer receives most praise, was an afterthought. Moreover, the suggestion recently offered by Professor Lawrence, that the general idea of a pilgrimage sprang from Chaucer's desire to experiment with the fabliau as literary material, with the addition of *moralitee and holinesse* for variety and makeweight, loses credence. This is not the only instance of new developments as fresh ideas came to mind.

There is another kind of variety in these descriptions. Each figure is in its way a type and also an individual: a type in the dual sense that he is not a fully developed character, but a sketch suitable for larger development, and that he may stand for a group; and an individual in that each is given particular marks: the Cook's ulcer, the Franklin's coloring, the Shipman's barge, the Reeve's identification with Norfolk, the Pardoner's with Rouncivale, and so on, all with Chaucer's "deep regard for the concrete." By a graduating process some of the Pilgrims approach portraiture, as Manly and others following him with greater and lesser success have shown. Harry Bailey and Roger of Ware were real persons, perhaps others also, whom Chaucer could expect his contemporary readers to recognize. But for us there will always be uncertainty and what looks like literal detail may be Chaucer's literary art. The methods of creative artists are often mysterious to themselves and the element of coincidence, warned against in so many modern novels, is always present. (Meredith had something to say on the subject. There is also Henry James's distress, in the letter to his brother over the supposed resemblance of Miss Birdseye in *The Bostonians* to an actual, still living Miss Peabody, with the concrete and confessed detail of her misplaced spectacles.) In the General Prologue, as in the 'Parlement of Foules,' the 'Mars,' and elsewhere, Chaucer could rely on the attractive possibilities of identification to stimulate interest while honestly denying any intentional portraiture. The Wife of Bath stands out above all the rest: she inherited something from the *Roman de la Rose,* but how much of her is due to an actual weaver from near Bath we shall never know. The Knight's campaigns are listed with remarkable fulness, yet part of the effect, and doubtless the purpose, is owing to the accumulation of remote and romantic sounding names. Put beside the knights in Froissart's *Chronicles,* his activities are certainly not typical of English knighthood in the fourteenth century, yet he has most of the chivalric virtues.[4] The Parson may resemble the poor priests of Wiclifite persuasion, but he is not representative of the contemporary priesthood any more than his brother of the peasantry as we know them from other sources. About the Manciple there is some question. He was the accomplished purchasing agent of *a temple* and also a *lewed* man; but half of the lines devoted to him are curiously indirect. He had thirty masters, of whom a dozen were capable of managing the affairs of *any lord* and he deceived (*not* was capable of deceiving) them all. When he reappears later he is played off against the drunken Cook with the implication of some business relationship between them and hence perhaps with the Cook's Guildsmen; but his Tale is not what we should expect of a *lewed* man and its warning against talking too much requires no little subtlety to fit it to his character. There may be therefore something in the suggestion that Chaucer had a particular manciple in mind.

Chaucer's selection of just those twenty-nine Pilgrims has been a matter of speculation. They are often said to constitute a cross-section of life as he knew it. Certainly they are *sondry* enough, but realistically they form a surprising fellowship, as Crabbe was among the first to note. The Prioress and the Wife of Bath, the Knight and the Pardoner, the Clerk and the Summoner would not mix too well. About a third are drawn from the clergy, not many of whom have the narrator's *ful devout corage;* and from what we know of Chaucer he was not specially interested in the clergy. The rest are from the lay ranks, ranging from the worthy Knight to the simple Plowman; but few of these are remarkable for moral virtue and some from both groups are downright unpleasant, even vicious. Would it do to imagine that they are just the sort of motley who would come together *by aventure* and a little guidance from the poet, for a holiday pilgrimage? Professor Hulbert has put the usual view in a rather extreme form:

The sketches were devised to provide representatives of the chief classes of English society under the higher nobility . . . . The result therefore is a conspectus of mediæval English society; it would be possible to use the prologue as a basis for a survey of fourteenth century English life. . . .[5]

Some of the Pilgrims do represent a class, but very unevenly. There were knights and squires and monks and prioresses, and so on; some of the individuals may well be typical of their functions in England of the late fourteenth century, others not. Society is too complex to be generalized so easily.

As the portraits are arranged in a pleasantly casual order, so they differ in size, not according to importance or intrinsic interest but as the poet found ready materials for them. The largest is the Friar's (62 lines), and the next the Parson's (52 lines), the Prioress' (47 lines), the Pardoner's (46 lines), the Monk's (43 lines). The Knight, the Reeve, the Physician, and the Wife are done in 36, 36, 34, 32 lines respectively; the Clerk in 24, the Shipman in 23, the Squire and the Man of Law each in 22, the Franklin and the Manciple in 20, the Yeoman in 18, the five burgesses (and their wives) in 18, the Merchant in 15, the Plowman in 13, the Cook in 9. These statistics are useful as a corrective to one's impression; for the vividness, sublety, penetration, even the fulness of description, is independent of the size of the picture. The Prioress is more distinct than the Friar, who gets a third more lines, and the Cook with his nine lines is as memorable as the Parson with his fifty-two.

There they are, then, his nine-and-twenty men and women, about to wend their way, with purpose and cross-purpose, to Canterbury. Yet as we know so well they never arrive; and that is a lesson in itself. What with illness or indolence or preoccupation the poet's muse went *rusty* in the sheath.

The pilgrims never reached Canterbury and therefore never returned: we may fancy them still as wraiths in their limbo, harried by scholars and critics, in perpetual suspense. Their quota of tales was reduced from four to two, then to one or two (F 657-58), and then to one (I 25). Some never had a chance; and St. Thomas still waits. But actually its whole object was entertainment by the way, of which there was plenty—and the grand climax, to *knytte up wel a greet mateere* was, in spite of the Parson's long treatise, to be a convivial supper, for Harry Bailey's profit, at the Tabard Inn.[6] And if all *had* been said and done, we should still have been in the Field full of Folk, still busy "abouten the mase," with no vision and no promise of one.

For the two Prologues invite and defy comparison. Langland's was composed not long after 1362 and was expanded but not otherwise altered in revision. It is therefore some twenty-five years older than Chaucer's, but the social conditions it reflects had not greatly changed except for the worse in those twenty-five years. Most of the parallels are superficial. Many of the same people appear in both, notably the clergy, with emphasis on their shortcomings; but Langland has no Prioress, and Piers himself, a more vigorous counterpart of Chaucer's Parson, comes in later; nor any Franklin nor Clerk of Oxford, nor any Wife of Bath. His figures are not introduced by set-piece descriptions; we see them in motion rather than hear about them in advance; they come and go as in a dream, "a merueilouse sweuene." What strikes us as we read the two Prologues side by side is, after the differences of dialect and meter, the earnestness of the one and the detachment of the other. They are equally bright and vivid, equally clear about the folly and wickedness of mankind, equally alive to the humor, especially the low humor, of the people they contain; but Langland is not amused. His sense of humor is as keen as Chaucer's, but unlike Chaucer's it is often bitter and barbed; it does not titillate. It exposes the comic and ridiculous without smile or laughter. Even its indignation (which Chaucer hardly shares) is without overemphasis. But after the courtly and polished language of Chaucer his speech seems rough and crude. He is too interested in his subject to lavish much embellishment; yet when he choses he can be poetical enough.

> *In a somer seson   whan soft was the sonne,*
> *I shope me in shroudes   as I a shepe were,*
> *In habite as an heremite   unholy of workes,*
> *Went wyde in þis world   wondres to here.*
> *Ac on a May mornynge   on Maluerne hulles*
> *Me byfel a ferly   of fairy, me thouȝte;*
> *I was wery forwandred   and wente me to reste*
> *Vnder a brode banke   bi a bornes side,*
> *And as I lay and lened   and loked in þe wateres,*
> *I slombred in a slepyng   it sweyued so merye.*
> *   Thanne gan I to meten   a merueilouse sweuene,*
> *That I was in a wildernesse   wist I never where;*
> *As I bihelde in-to þe est   an heigh to þe sonne,*
> *I seigh a toure on a toft   trielich ymaked; . . .*

This will surely stand comparison with Chaucer's spring flourish.

But the reason for setting the two Prologues side by side is not to disparage one or exalt the other; it is to suggest the great difference between two contemporary revelations of the same world and to show the different purposes of the two pilgrimages which they introduce.

In spite of the help of many contemporary chroniclers, each writing with his particular, and undisguised, bias, and of the many modern historians who have reinterpreted for us the complex story of Edward's declining years and Richard's tempestuous reign, it is still difficult to understand with any confidence that unhappy period. The weakness of Edward and the power of his mistress, the temperament of Richard and the influence of his favorites, the shifting allegiances of the Court parties, the Lancastrian faction and the anti-Lancastrians and the character of John himself, the Appellants and the counter-Appellants, the French wars and the Spanish campaigns, the Despencer fiasco in Flanders, the threats of invasion, the financial troubles, the rivalries of the guilds and mayors and bishops, the wealthy tradesmen from one side and the Commons from the other encroaching on the regalities, the 'Protestant' tendencies of Wiclif and his followers, the good and bad Parliaments with their promulgations and retractions, all the forces which culminated in the Peasants' Revolt—all these and much else have yielded a rich opportunity for confusion and prejudice and misjudgment among both the contemporary witnesses and the modern interpreters. If then it is asked how fully Chaucer portrays and reflects this manifold complex of social and political and military 'history,' the answer can only be: Not at all fully. If the same question is asked of the other great poets of the time, the Pearl-Poet, Langland, Gower, the answer must favor Langland and Gower in his *Vox Clamantis.* It has even been set down as a merit that Chaucer's muse was unblemished with topicality, though a few eager searchers, feeling no doubt the want of such matter, have discovered contemporary allusions here and there in his verse. But Chaucer was not like Tennyson, a professed interpreter of his age, and the subjects he chose for poetry were not either his personal affairs nor the public business. His interest was in people and their strange ways, not in life with its great aims, its troubles of the spirit, and its "tragical mysteries." Is there one of all the characters in all his poetry who seems to have a soul and to be concerned about it? One notes this, not in complaining spirit, but only to set the accounts straight. The ways of God to man were not his province, but the ways of man to man, and he finds them amusing, sometimes pathetic and often deplorable, but men being what they always are, no worse than should be expected.

Chaucer begins his human comedy—as broken and unfinished as life itself—with *Whan that Aprille. . . ;* Langland begins his great poem, in its way also confused but finished finally after thirty years of writing and rewriting, with *In a somer seson. . .*—the one when winter has passed and the restlessness of spring has come; the other when summer is at hand and the labor of sowing and reaping not far off. Chaucer's pilgrims, assembled by chance at a Southwark inn, set out over the roads of Kent, and to lighten the journey,

> *For trewely, confort ne myrthe is noon*
> *To ride by the weye doumb as a stone,*

told their various tales of morality and harlotry. If they were greatly interested in "seynt Thomas of Caunterbury" who

In sauacion of mannys saule   in holychurche was sleye,

they give little evidence of it. The Host says beforehand, with covert irony,

The blisful martir quite yow youre meede!

Langland has his own view of pilgrims and palmers who

pliȝtet hem togidere
To seke seynt Iames   and seyntes in rome,
Thei went forth in here wey   with many wise tales, . . .
Heremites on an heep   with hoked staues,
Wenten to Walsyngham   and here wenches after.

(There were no such wenches among Chaucer's pilgrims.) But Piers, when he had gathered his pilgrims, led them to the shrine of Saint Truth. He was not concerned to shorten the way with amusing or improving stories, but to know the good from the evil in the world, the temptations and sufferings of the poor, the malpractices of the ruling class; all culminating in the successive visions of Do-well, Do-better, and Do-best. The contrast of the two works hardly admits of comparison, but what is significant is that to enliven his series of narratives Chaucer selected the framework of a pilgrimage, a pilgrimage with only a nominal religious intent, a pilgrimage which never arrived—a holiday pilgrimage, a literary convenience, a mockery of devoutness thrown into imbalance by the Parson's *ersatz* finale. *Swiche is this world;* such it certainly is: one set of pilgrims lost in speculation, the other foundering in incompletion. To say this darkens in no way the transcendent success of Chaucer's Prologue, it merely draws attention to the kind of subject Chaucer chose to undertake.[7]

2. THE SURPRISE GROUP

THE *Canterbury Tales,* usually spoken of and carelessly thought of as one work, is nevertheless a heterogeneous miscellany of nineteen or twenty Tales, besides two long translations and the Monk's Tragedies, with prologues and links here and there. Parts of it are 'early' work, parts 'late.' Each part has its problems and even the intended order is uncertain. Manly's study of the manuscripts proves, as nearly as such things admit of proof, that the various arrangements "are due to editorial efforts of the early scribes (or their directors) or to later disarrangements caused by accidental shiftings."[8] But three fragments, DEF, are commonly regarded (following Miss Hammond and Kittredge) as a kind of unit presenting the pros and cons of marriage—with two unrelated interludes. Another fragment, B[2], Robinson's VII, seems also to be a kind of unit, well supported by the manuscript evidence. If it was so designed by Chaucer, it is worth examining as such, even at the risk of creating some new problems.

Of this Fragment Robinson says simply, "Within the group there seems to be no principle of arrangement save that of contrast or variety" (p. 11); whereas Kittredge, who penetrated farther into the dramatic structure of the *Tales* than most readers and expressed himself with greater certainty, lays it down:

Two acts in Chaucer's Human Comedy are so completely wrought that we may study their dramatic structure with confidence. One of these is the group of tales beginning with the Wife of Bath's Prologue . . . . The other is the group that begins with the Shipman's Prologue. . . .[9]

It is unnecessary to repeat his summary of the action as he saw it; his clue is Chaucer's delicate and subtle interplay of character. But there is another sort of unity in the Fragment: I should call it the Surprise Group.

The assignment of the Shipman's Tale to the Shipman was defended by Kittredge; others prefer to call it "frankly unprofessional." As an introduction to the group it is ambiguous; it prepares us, if we have not learned anything from the sequence Knight-Miller, for more of the same sort, against which Chaucer had disarmed criticism in the General Prologue, that is, for more *vileynye*. But Chaucer immediately fools us in the broadest fashion with the Host's *But now passe over* . . . . The Host was thoroughly pleased with the Shipman's bawdry—Root stigmatized it as "essentially more immoral" than the Miller's or the Reeve's Tale—and then turned, with what Robinson calls "without exaggeration the politest speech in English literature," to the Prioress for the next tale. The Prioress replies with one word, *Gladly*.

The Prioress begins with a short prayer to the Virgin, humbly comparing her powers of expression with those of *a child of twelf month oold, or lesse,* and beseeching the Mother of God—

Gydeth my song that I shal of yow seye.

This *song* has almost always been accepted at its face value. It is an "infinitely pathetic legend" (Kittredge); it "breathes the spirit of heart-felt religion" (Root); the workmanship is "flawless," and Chaucer's "humor was held completely in abeyance and the story is told in the spirit of consistent pathos" (Robinson). But many years ago Brandl, in the first edition of Paul's *Grundriss* (II, 1, 680), summarizing rapidly the *Canterbury Tales,* remarked that "Selbst die Priorin, obwohl sittig bis zu Zimperlichkeit, bringt nichts Säuberlicheres vor als die Legende des stommen Knaben Hugh von Lincoln. . ."; and to this unsympathetic judgment Brandl added: "Jetzt greift der Dichter ein. Auf die unmittelbar vorgehende Verspottung kindischer Legenden. . . ." This section of the *Grundriss* was not reprinted, but Miss Hammond (*Manual,* p. 287) quoted the last phrase, and Professor Robinson (p. 840) says severely: "For the opinion, certainly mistaken, that Chaucer meant the Prioress's Tale as a satire on childish legends, see A. Brandl" etc.; and in another place (p. 12) "surely that criticism is perverse which maintains that Chaucer wrote the *Prioress's Tale* as a satire on childish legends." The opinion, the criticism, was expressed by Brandl only in those three words "Verspottung kindischer Legenden," but apparently they have sufficed. It may be an exaggeration, but still it is pregnant of direction. At any rate, there can be no harm in suggesting that we may have missed something in the text, and so I shall run through it with tentative comment, emphasizing—and of course for the moment over-emphasizing—the little touches by which Chaucer hints that the story of Litel Clergeon may be read as something less than completely serious. It is not that Chaucer meant to farce the story or to ridicule the Prioress or to make light of the miracle; it is rather that he wrote it with his usual "keen sense of the ridiculous" and with a twinkle which he trusted us to catch.

The tale is localized in Asia, among the Asiatic Christians, in a city which has a street open at either end. Somewhere along this street is a ghetto maintained *for lucre of vileynye,* and at its farther end is a school for Christian children where *swich manere doctrine* as obtained there (among the Asiatic Christians) was taught to the children, namely, to sing and read. Though the topography is not altogether clear, we know that the seven-year-old Clergeon and his friend have to pass through the ghetto on their way to and from school.

Through the first ten of the twenty-nine stanzas the tone is carefully pitched; it is neither too high, like the aureate style of the Prioress' Prologue, nor too low. If we read alertly our suspicions may be aroused, but there is no overt humor; the mask of perfect gravity has not moved. We may note in passing the extreme delicacy of the Prioress' allusion to St. Nicholas' *reverence* (513-515) in contrast to her plain language in l. 573; and we may be touched by the lad's willingness to accept corporal punishment for neglect of his studies while devoting himself to memorizing the hymn, and at the same time wonder a little that at his age he should have such difficulty in committing to memory a comparatively short poem; and we may be struck by the fact that having learned it he sang it aloud only when he was passing through the ghetto:

> *Twies a day it passed thrugh his throte,*
> *To scoleward and homward when he wente.*

Then with the startlingly mixed metaphor that Satan the serpent, who had his wasp's nest in the Jews' heart, swelled up, *then* we begin to wonder, and the innocent innuendoes of the preceding stanzas become cumulatively effective. Suddenly the narrative leaps forward—

> *This cursed Jew hym hente, and heeld hym faste,*
> *And kitte his throte, and in a pit hym caste;*

and the smiling Prioress, who exerted herself

> *to been estatlich of manere*
> *And to been holden digne of reverence,*

astonishes us by continuing:

> *I seye that in a wardrobe they hym threwe*
> *Where as thise Jewes purgen hire entraille.*

After the fine stanza, *O martir, sowded to virginitee,* with its fragment of the apocalyptic vision and its emphasis on the virginity of those who follow the Lamb, we are told that the poor widow, *This newe Rachel,* who is Litel Clergeon's mother, after a long night of anxious waiting, inquires about her missing child and learns that he was last seen in the ghetto; but she still continues, distraught, to look for him everywhere and at last among the cursed Jews (596-99); and finally Jesus directs her to the pit, where she finds him, this emerald of chastity (aged seven), this ruby of martyrdom, lying on his back his throat cut, singing the *Alma Redemptoris*

> *So loude that* al the place *gan to ringe.*

Christian passers-by now

> *In coomen for to wondre upon this thyng;*

the processes of civil law are brought into action, and all the Jews *That of this mordre wiste* are drawn by wild horses and then hanged.

Meanwhile, Litel Clergeon is placed before the High Altar and as soon as the mass is finished

> *the abbot with his covent*
> *Han sped hem for to burien hym ful faste.*

This abbot is, as we are twice told, a holy man; but the Prioress cannot refrain from adding, *As monkes been, or elles oghte to be,* perhaps, as Kittredge says, with a slant at the monk in the Shipman's Tale, or perhaps with a hard look at her fellow Pilgrim; yet he has an inquiring mind and wishes to know why the boy continues to sing,

> *Sith that thy throte is kut to my semynge.*

Litel Clergeon answers with three stanzas of explanation: he admits that according to the laws of nature he should have died long since, but—and so far in this brief interval has his education progressed—

> *But Jesu Crist, as ye in bookes fynde,*
> *Will that his glorie laste and be in mynde.*

And when the young martyr gives up the ghost all the convent fall weeping on the pavement of the church, then rise,

> *And in a tombe of marbul stones cleere*
> *Enclosen they his litel body sweete.*
> *Ther he is now, God leve us for to meete!*

In closing, the Prioress draws attention to the parallel martyrdom of Hugh of Lincoln *but a litel while ago* (about a hundred and thirty years), asking him to

> *Preye eek for us, we synful folk unstable,*
> *That, of his mercy, God so merciable*
> *On us his grete mercy multiplie,*

but forgetting, naturally enough, that no mercy had been shown to the Jews. Wordsworth could speak of her "fierce bigotry."

Does it not look as though Chaucer, in choosing this tale for the Prioress and in writing it down with her in mind, meant to preserve the same balance between *game* and *ernest* that he manifested in his description of her in the General Prologue? Just as there he smilingly reveals her little pretensions to elegance and her amiable little weaknesses without malice and without discourtesy, just so he renders her story of the martyred little boy, with appropriately smiling gravity which, without altogether sacrificing its moving pathos—

> *Whan seyd was al this miracle, every man*
> *As sobre was that wonder was to se—*

enhances the characterization and the dramatic moment by letting us into the delicate play. The poet touches us with his sympathetic understanding of the Prioress and his gentle handling of a pious story, and he amuses us with his artistic detachment. It is only because he has caught so nicely the tone and effect of a simple miracle that he can by deft touches of slight exaggeration here and there produce that precarious ambiguity of *simplicité* and *simplesse* which allows us to have it all one way, if we wish, and which matches the reverent raillery of our first introduction to the Prioress.

When the Prioress has finished, the company are all *sobre* of course—till the Host reacts quickly with his characteristic jesting and, addressing 'Chaucer,' asks for *a tale of murthe* forthwith, and Chaucer produces the Rime of Sir Thopas. About the intention of Sir Thopas the scholars and critics have shown little doubt. Attention has centered on identifying the particular romances Chaucer may have had in mind and on the possibility of socio-political satire against the Flemings, which is at best a very subordinate motif. The parody runs from broad burlesque to an almost loving playfulness, a display of the minstrels' weaknesses as well as of their literary vices. It is the high comedy of criticism, intellectual yet sympathetic laughter. The Melibeus, however, has been somewhat gingerly treated by both scholars and critics. They have hesitated between condemning it as dull and tiresome to the modern reader and condoning it as a form of uplift both palatable and gratifying to mediæval taste. As Ker put it: "Chaucer's whole literary career shows him emerging from the average opinion and manner of his contemporaries, and coming out from the mediæval crowd to stand apart by himself, individual and free." As an implied defense of the Melibeus this is shrewd and probably sound. The piece itself, said Ker, speaking frankly from the modern point of view, "is perhaps the worst example that could be found of all the intellectual and literary vices of the Middle Ages, bathos, forced allegory, spiritless and interminable moralizing"; but he felt bound to admit with a smile that "there is nothing for it but to believe that Chaucer found some interest in the debate of Melibeus and his wife Prudence." That is, when he translated the work Chaucer had not yet emerged "from the mediæval crowd." But Ker went further. He offered the suggestion, which he denominated "desperate" and immediately withdrew, and which has since been quoted with disapproval, namely, that "sometimes one is tempted to think that the *Tale of Melibeus* is a mischievous companion to the *Rime of Sir Thopas,* and meant to parody a worse kind of 'drasty speech.' "[10] In similar vein Coulton said: "The monumental dulness of this [Melibeus] . . . is no doubt a further stroke of satire, and Chaucer must have felt amply avenged in recounting this story to the bitter end."[11] The language of Ker's desperate suggestion may be too strong, but it points a direction. Chaucer could still be mediæval enough to have translated *Le Livre de Melibee* with approving enthusiasm and at the same time when he thrust his translation into the *Canterbury Tales* he could have felt sufficiently emergent and "apart" to recognize some of its "bathos, forced allegory, spiritless and interminable moralizing" and use it for comic purposes, just as he saw the faults of the minstrel ballad romances and parodied them for similar effect. In this case, however, it was unnecessary to make his own parody, for he found one ready to hand—or something still better, a serious piece with the germ of parody latent in its very bloodstream. He might well have appreciated its cardinal weakness, which is not the extent but the falsity of its moralizing, its "exalting expediency over right."[12]

It is part of the humor, moreover, though sometimes misunderstood, that Chaucer insists, with an oath, that he cannot avouch for the accuracy of his text; he offers the parallel of the Synoptic Gospels (including John) and implies that the modifications will be noted by the company, who are probably familiar with some version. But the signal comedy of the situation is that the brighter piece was speedily interrupted, thus saving Chaucer from the danger of overplaying the joke, whereas the other piece was allowed to continue to its triumphant end. Just as it was "much more modest, and vastly more humorous" (Root) for Chaucer to offer his fellow pilgrims not a masterpiece of narrative but the deliberate burlesque of Sir Thopas, so he "gave proof of consummate tact and taste . . . in assigning to himself . . . nothing more ambiguous than a version of a popular discourse—half narrative, half homily—in prose."[13] Harry Bailey liked it no doubt, and there is no sign in the following link "that the pilgrims regarded *Melibeus* as a penance." True, but to argue that "A prose tale of [more than] 16,000 words forms a pretty extensive practical joke" (Tatlock) rather misses the point. For the modern reader it may seem like a kind of jest that the Melibeus and the Parson's Tale are included among the stories recited along the Canterbury road; Chaucer as artist may even have regarded them as slightly amusing misfits. If Sir Thopas and the Melibeus had no serious appeal they would miss fire as comedy. They had to be good in one sense in order to produce their special kind of comic catharsis.

The Host, who impercipiently exposes his bourgeois taste by decrying the downright vulgarity and foul language of Sir Thopas and asks for *som murthe or som doctryne* in prose, is answered with the Prioress' word *Gladly,* here accompanied by an oath to tickle his palate. He gets *a litel thyng,* a trifle (says Chaucer), which not only pleases him but provokes a surprising domestic revelation. Then he turns to the Monk and in words which recall the Monk's characterization in the General Prologue offensively bids for another bawdy tale like the Shipman's. The Monk, however, suddenly reacts with dignity; he will not be put upon by a man like the Host; or perhaps he "takes all his [Host's] broad jesting with the good humour of a man who is used to it" (Coulton). He offers to relate two or three stories, including the Life of St. Edward, or first some of his hundred tragedies; and after an apology for their arrangement he begins the series, without waiting for the Host's or the company's approval. Having finished the seventeenth, he pauses to repeat the already repeated definition of tragedy—when the Knight interrupts, adding his own repetition, and is seconded by the Host. It is significant now that the Host, confident in his own judgment, requests a hunting story from the Monk; significant because it betrays Chaucer's recognition of the fact that the worthy *prikasour* ought naturally to have told a hunting story; in other words, that the assignment of the tragedies to the Monk was comic business. One may turn back to *The murye wordes of the Hoost to the Monk* and see that the Host's ebullient language about the Monk's valor with *Venus paiementz* was merely the poet's prepared joke in order to palm off the tragedies on the *fair prelaat* who *lovede venerie.* Both he and the Host knew that from the *prikasour* was expected *somwhat of huntyng.* The poet and the Host thus connive to deceive the reader, for a moment, and the Monk compliantly falls in line. As with Sir Thopas, the Monk's Tale had to be acceptable to serious-minded readers or there would be no fun in having it interrupted; and the point is barbed by making the Knight his agent of interference. The Knight, who is both worthy and wise, has thus his own limitations.[14]

The Host's saying

> *Youre tale anoyeth al this compaignye.*
> *Swich talking is nat worth a boterflye*

is mere excuse. If any inference is to be drawn from allowing the Melibeus to be heard entire, it is probably that the translation was already at hand; whereas Sir Thopas was composed with the purpose of having it cut short and the Monk's tragedies were inserted when Chaucer saw the humorous opportunities of their taking off.[15]

Thus the scene of Fragment VII (B²) opens suggestively with a fabliau from the Shipman. The Host is immensely pleased, but to right the balance turns courteously—Tatlock's word is "obsequiously"—to the Pilgrim least likely to follow in the same strain. The Prioress obliges with a pious Prologue in the best aureate manner and her simple and touching story of the little martyr. This is not quite what we expected, for we were prepared for something more *estatlich of manere,* something to signalize both her function as a nun and her claims to a superior social position. Her tale reveals her sensitivity more than her worldly ambition, and it contains a slight—*unnethe it might be lesse*—element matching the ambiguous description of her in the General Prologue. The Pilgrims are not supposed to see this; the poet dangles it before the reader. Her story, which followed the undulant line between pathos and bathos (Oliver Wendell Holmes called it "grisly"), left the Pilgrims in a sober frame of mind, none more so than the pilgrim Chaucer; and the Host, seeing an opportunity to relieve the tension by making this Chaucer the butt of his easy humor, jocularly calls for something equally fine: *Som deyntee thyng*. Chaucer has his mild revenge by producing a bit of satire too delicate for the Host to understand; and when he is interrupted for his *verray lewednesse* and *drasty speche* retaliates in the opposite direction, with his *litel thyng in prose,* full of proverbial wisdom heavily underlined by repetition, entirely within the Host's comprehension. Offered the alternatives of *som murthe* or *som doctryne,* he obliges with a trifle which is of doctrine all compact. The Host is naturally pleased, and as simple folk will takes the lesson home to himself: would that his wife could have heard this story of Prudence! So we have it both ways: some are gratified for one good reason, some for another, the poet watching with amusement from his point of vantage. And now *unbokeled is the male*. The Host, as though compensating for his indiscreet personal revelations, calls on the Monk, who had earlier missed his turn because the Miller was overcome by the ale he absorbed while not listening to the Knight, all but demanding a dirty story, and the Monk is or pretends to be offended; and he has *his* revenge by launching into his hundred tragedies. It is the same hoaxing formula which had put the delicacy of Sir Thopas after the delicacy of the Prioress' Tale and then the complete Melibeus from the elvish Pilgrim after the broken Sir Thopas. But even the Knight is finally bored and betrays his common humanity by demanding comedy. The Host enthusiastically supports him and begs the Monk to continue with a hunting story, which is just what we had expected in the first place, before the Host provoked him to a punitive recital of tragedies. But the Monk is both firm and courteous in his refusal to continue; so the Host, blocked there and seeking another victim, addresses the Nun's Priest with rude boldness and this time gets really the *tale of myrthe* of which he had been defrauded since the Prioress finished her miracle of the Virgin. The wheel has now completely revolved and the Fragment ends as it began, in the best of humor. Why the Nun's Priest chose not to be offended is a question outside our knowledge: we had hardly heard of him before. But he must have looked like a cheerful fellow and he fully justified the Host's hope.

It is not merely contrast, then, which unites the Tales of this Fragment. There is an element of surprise and reversal running throughout. The Shipman's fabliau called for something to follow which would please the less vulgar Pilgrims; the Host addressed the Prioress and she surprised both the Pilgrims with her sensitive miracle, for they expected something more in harmony with her courtly ways, and also the reader, who sees through Chaucer's double-dealing with her pathos; the Host, pretending to expect something equally dainty from Chaucer, is surprised and not a little baffled by a parody which is over his head (and possibly the reader expected from Chaucer a superior piece of a different sort); the Host surprises the Pilgrims by interrupting Chaucer, who in turn surprises the Host, pleasantly, with a lengthy treatise of moral proverbs, and the reader, less agreeably, with his *moral tale vertuous;* the Host surprises first the Pilgrims by exposing his domestic troubles and then the Monk by bearing down on his *lust in engendrure;* and the Monk in his turn surprises everyone by his complaining tragedies; the worthy Knight, otherwise *as meeke as is a mayde,* surprises us by interrupting; and finally the Host surprises the reader by calling on the hitherto unknown Priest—whose Prioress must have been a little surprised by the Chantecleer story and by the Host's comment.[16]

3. THE KNIGHT'S TALE

THE Knight's Tale has generally been held in high esteem, but there is still a division of opinion over the grounds on which it is to be praised and enjoyed. For a time it seemed to have lost favor, owing to disagreements about various aspects of the poem. In recent years, however, critical emphasis has been directed to Chaucer's 'intention' particularly, and a valiant effort has been made to pull the discordant views together.[17] Now, without attempting a formal review of these conflicting opinions, I propose to re-examine the Knight's Tale *as it is,* and then proceed to a critical synthesis.

For a start, some of the poems's shortcomings should be recognized. First to be noted are the elaborate language here and there, which Chaucer perhaps regarded as essential to his noble theme, and the cue for which he got from Boccaccio; and with this the unrealistic pictures, which he perhaps thought of as equally natural for such a subject. Theseus returning from his victory over the Amazons meets

> *A compaignye of ladyes, tweye and tweye,*
> *Ech after oother, clad in clothes blake,*

kneeling beside the highway (with the Temple of Clemency in the background) and loudly lamenting their plight;

> *And of this cry they nolde nevere stenten*
> *Til they the reynes of his brydel henten.*

The eldest of these ladies, having swooned (and recovered), acts as spokesman and when she has finished they all *fillen gruf and cryden pitously.* Theseus is sympathetically touched, alights from his horse,

> *And in his armes he hem alle up hente,*
> *And hem comforteth in full good entente.*

This curious situation is followed almost immediately by the extravagant description of Theseus' banner:

> *The rede statue of Mars, with spere and targe,*
> *So shyneth in his white baner large,*
> *That alle the feeldes glyteren up and doun.*

Thus the tone is set. When Arcite has been freed and Palamon is still in captivity

> *Swich sorwe he maketh that the grete tour*
> *Resouneth of his youlyng and clamour.*
> *The pure fettres on his shynes grete*
> *Weren of his bittre, salte teeres wete.*

Later, when Palamon recognizes Arcite in the forest,

> *For ire he quook . . .*
> *As he were wood, with face deed and pale . . .*
> *And seide: "Arcite, false traytour wikke, . . ."*

There is an element of boyish bluster and violence in his language;

> *I wol be deed, or elles thou shalt dye*

has a touch of Almanzor in it. And Arcite replies: I should slay you at once if you were not sick and mad for love, and unarmed, but I will bring you weapons tomorrow—

> *And ches the beste, and leef the worste for me.*

(Arcite's promise to provide food and bedding for the night is apparently not fulfilled.)

This is followed by a rhetorical outburst from the "auctour,"

> *O Cupide, out of alle charitee! . . .*

in the best high style; and a few lines later by another on *The destinee, ministre general* to account for the coincidence of Theseus hunting just when and where the two lovers are fighting; and then by a sort of footnote,

> *This mene I now by mighty Theseus.*

The same high style accompanies the account of Arcite's death:

> *Swelleth the brest of Arcite, . . .*
> *Shrighte Emelye, and howleth Palamon,*
> *And Theseus his suster took anon*
> *Swownynge . . .*
> *Infinite been the sorwes and the teeres. . . .*

The descriptions of Lygurge and Emetreus are certainly elaborate and colorful and such exaggerations as there may be—the red and yellow eyes of Lygurge, the bright *citryn* eyes of Emetreus;

the twenty-odd white wolf hounds, *as grete as any steer,* with the one and the tame lions and leopards with the other—are well within the bounds of legitimate picturesqueness.

Over against these samples of fine language must be set others of a less elevated style. Arcite's compleynt (1223 ff.) contains, apropos of our ignorance of the divine prescience, four lines about the man who is as drunk *as a mous.* At the beginning of Part III Chaucer addresses the reader (or hearer) colloquially: I think it would be regarded as negligence if I forgot to tell how much Theseus spent on the erection of the amphitheatre. And presently, having named the three altars and oratories (which at once become full-sized temples) he says he almost forgot to describe the details. And having finished his account of the Temple of Venus he goes on: Why should I not tell you about the pictures in the Temple of Mars. And finally: Now I will hurry on to the Temple of Diana. Here he is somewhat colloquial about *Calistopee,* who was turned into a bear and then into the lodestar—believe it or not—

> *Thus was it peynted, I can sey yow no ferre.*

Her son is also a star, he adds. Next he sees *Dane* and brightly explains: I mean the daughter of Penneus, not to be confused with Diana the goddess. And after describing the *statue* of Diana, with a woman crying out in childbirth, he notes

> *Wel koude he peynten lifly that it wroghte;*
> *With many a floryn he the hewes boghte.*

These specimens are all within the space of two hundred lines. There are of course many others.

A different kind of stylistic ornament is first met in l. 1026.

> *He took his hoost and hoom he rood anon.*

(Thus the Ellesmere manuscript; Robinson and Manly read *rit* for *rood.*) And with similar effect:

> *O persone alone, withouten mo,*

which brings with it

> *And haryed forth by arme, foot, and too.*

The most studied example occurs in lines 1809 ff.—

> *She woot namoore of al this hoote fare,*
> *By God, than woot a cokkow or an hare!*
> *But all moot ben assayed, hoot and coold;*
> *A man moot ben a fool, or yong or oold,—*
> *I woot it by myself ful yore agon,*
> *For in my tyme a servant was I oon.*

In 1076 we get *square as any sparre;* in 1331 *Thebes with his waste walles wyde*—a bit of rum-ram-ruf.

By way of transition from grave to gay one may cite this lively example of *occupatio:*

> *Who koude ryme in Englyssh proprely*
> *His martirdom?   for sothe it am not I;*
> *Therefore I passe as lightly as I may.*

But how the grand manner can be made, no doubt deliberately, to *sink* is most clearly shown where the two lovers are fighting. One like a lion, the other like a tiger and both like wild boars—

> *Up to the ancle foght they in hir blood.*
> *And in this wise I lete hem fightyng dwelle,*
> *And forth I wole of Theseus yow telle.*

Or if this is not plain enough, take the manifest burlesque of

> *Ne who sat first ne last upon the deys,*
> *What ladyes fairest been or best daunsynge,*
> *Or which of hem kan dauncen best and synge,*
> *Ne who moost felyngly speketh of love;*
> *What haukes sitten on the perche above,*
> *What houndes liggen on the floor adoun,—*
> *Of al this make I now no mencioun.*

The origin of this astonishing anticlimax is not far to seek. At the beginning of Book VI Boccaccio tells of a period of reconciliation and high festivity while the warriors are gathering for the grand tournament:

> *Altro che canti, suoni e allegrezza*
> *nelle lor case non si sentia mai,*

e ben mostravan la lor gentilezza;
a chi prender volea davano assai;
astor, falconi e can di gran prodezza
usuvano a diletto, né giammai
erano in casa sanza forestieri,
*conti e baroni e donne e cavalieri.**

This was the seed: but who would have guessed the flower it would bring forth?

After recognizing this descent we can have no hesitation in singling out the passages of forthright humor, not to say joking, in the poem. There is for example the point—for those who could not see it, it was explained for modern readers by Professor Emerson—in *opie of Thebes fyn* (1472) by which Palamon's jailer was put to sleep—the other Thebes, of course. There is the playful echo (or if not an echo, a very curious parallel) of the opening lines of the General Prologue when Palamon set out to the Temple of Venus to offer up his prayer—

> *With* hooly *herte and with an heigh* corage,
> *He roos to* wenden on his pilgrymage
> *Unto the* blisful *Citherea benigne.*

This is closely followed by the pointed

> *Up roos the sonne, and up roos Emelye.*

And there are the amusing innuendoes in the poet's hesitation to describe the ceremonial rites performed by Emily, and the false reference to Statius as a source. A little later, when just before the tournament, people are commenting on the different warriors:

> *Somme helden with hym with the blake berd,*
> *Somme with the balled, some with the thikke herd.*

The first is of course Lygurge—*Blak was his berd.* The last is similarly Emetreus—*His crispe heer lyk rynges was yronne.* But

---

* Their houses were never without singing and music and joyfulness, and well they showed their gentilesse; they enjoyed themselves to the utmost; goshawks, falcons, and dogs of great prowess they had for their pleasure, and among the guests there were but counts and barons and ladies and knights.

had any one been described as *bald?* Two of the epithets fit so
neatly that before you get the point you have to turn back and
see. And finally there are the two well-known extraordinary
lapses into facetiousness. When Arcite is dying—

> *And certeinly, ther Nature wol nat wirche,*
> *Fare wel phisik! go ber the man to chirche!*

and when he is dead—

> *His spirit chaunged hous and wente ther,*
> *As I cam nevere, I kan nat tellen wher.*
> *Therfore I stynte, I nam no divinistre;*
> *Of soules fynde I nat in this registre,*
> *Ne me ne list thilke opinions to telle*
> *Of hem, though that they writen wher they dwelle.*
> *Arcite is coold. Ther Mars his soule gye!*

(His spirit moved away to a place where I have never been; I
cannot tell where it was. I have no competence in divinity or
divination. I find nothing about souls [after death] in my index
and I don't care to report the opinions of those who have sent
back a written record from where they are. Arcite is dead: let
Mars take his soul). But Arcite in his dying words had just
prayed devoutly—

> *And Juppiter so wys my soule gye, . . .*
> *So Juppiter have of my soule parte.*

Such things as these are not to be measured by the space they
occupy but by the shadow they cast. Their infelicity is enhanced
by the serious context in which they stand, and rather than try to
explain them away, one must recognize them as examples of a
fault into which Chaucer's cheerfulness may at any moment betray him. It is pleasanter to turn to some illustrations, so obvious
that they need little pointing, of the legitimate humor which
lightens the poem. At the end of Part II, the decision of Theseus
to settle the lovers' quarrel by a tourney is greeted with an effusive-
ness of gratitude which suggests rather comedy than romance—

Who looketh lightly now but Palamoun?
Who springeth up for joye but Arcite? . . .
But doun on knees wente every maner wight. . . .

Theseus himself is marked throughout by a strong sense of humor. His handling of the bereaved ladies and his later devotion to Diana, after Mars, as shown by his *appetit* for hunting are but hints. Better is his acceptance of Palamon's confession ("This is Arcite, my enemy and yours, and I Palamon am also your enemy: we both deserve to die"): "You have put it very briefly," says Theseus. "There was no need of torture to extract this confession from you. You shall both die." But the Queen and all the women, including Emily, thought this was a *Greet pitee*—

And no thyng but for love was this debaat.

So Theseus was immediately softened—

For pitee renneth soone in gentil herte—

though he could be stern enough towards the two errant young knights. He told himself by way of extenuation that it was proper to make distinctions, but aloud to the company he made light of love and all its works:

The god of love, a, benedicite!
How mighty and how greet a lord is he! . . .
Who may been a fool, but if he love? . . .
Se how they blede! be they noght wel arrayed? . . .
But this is yet the beste game of alle,
That she for whom they han this jolitee
Kan hem therfore as muche thank as me.

And he goes on to say that he has himself often been caught in Love's snare. The lovers are both worthy enough, he says, but obviously they cannot both have her—not now anyway (and the irony of this is as pointed as the jest)—and therefore he proposes the tournament. All of which is in Chaucer's best comic manner with proper lightness and without forcing the note.

After Arcite's death old Father Egeus does more to lessen the pathetic tension by his noble platitudes than the poet's flippancy about the destiny of Arcite's soul. Even the most careless reader has felt this.

There are a number of needless inconsistencies in the poem. For example, Palamon escapes from prison *By helpyng of a freend* (1463), but there had been no intimation that Palamon and Arcite were attended (as they were in Boccaccio) by friends and servants during their captivity. And afterwards Palamon says that he escaped *by grace* (1592) rather than by getting his jailer drunk. On the morning of the single combat the poet says,

> *Cleer was the day, as I have toold er this,*

but there had been no mention of the weather. Emily is clothed in green when she goes on the hunt with Theseus and when we first saw her she was described as fairer than the lily on its green stalk; but green is the color of infidelity, as Chaucer well knew; and Chaucer seems not to have been troubled, as Boccaccio was, by Emily's willingness to marry either suitor. Arcite when he returned to Thebes is laid waste by the Malady of Hereos, but as soon as Mercury suggests his return to Athens, he rises, so disfigured by disease as to be unrecognizable, goes *the nexte way* to Theseus' gate and offers his services *To drugge and drawe,*

> *For he was yong and myghty for the nones.*

In their prayers before the tournament Palamon bluntly asks for *possessioun* of Emily regardless of the outcome of battle which is to decide the issue, and Arcite bluntly asks for victory regardless of Emily's affection. Just before *the grete fight* Theseus declares against *mortal bataille,* though one of the opponents might (perhaps accidentally) *sleen his make;* he wishes *no destruccion of blood,* though he must have expected plenty of bloodshed; yet Arcite attacks Palamon with the fury of a tigress who has been robbed of her cubs and Palamon is as eager *to sleen his foo Arcite* as a hunted lion is eager to have the blood of his prey. At ll. 2910 ff. Emily appears

> *With fyr in honde, as was that tyme the gyse*
> *To do the office of funeral servyse,*

but seven lines below Chaucer begins his long anaphoristic list of what he will not record with *how the fyr was maked*. But the most curious lapse is the location of the pyre. The amphitheatre stands on the ground where the two lovers were discovered in single combat, but after Arcite's death Theseus, having given long and careful consideration to the matter, decides on the same spot as most appropriate for *the sepulture*.

Many or even most of these are inconsistencies which perhaps need not concern a writer of romance. Some of them spring from Chaucer's hurry to get through Boccaccio's long poem, others may be trivial; but altogether they argue a want of attention to detail. The relation of the gods to the characters of the story is, however, a somewhat more serious problem. Palamon, who is the first to catch sight of Emily and be smitten by her, fancies she may be Venus herself and offers a little prayer to the goddess. This is of course as it should be, though later he complains, rhetorically, that Venus is slaying him with fear and jealousy of Arcite. Palamon is throughout a follower of Venus and in the end has his reward. On the other hand, Palamon complains that he is imprisoned through the jealousy of Juno and Saturn and Arcite complains of the hostility of Juno and Mars—

Alas, thou felle Mars! allas, Juno!

Juno is explicable in terms of the Theban story, but why should Arcite accuse Mars, who is the special deity? and why should Palamon accuse Saturn, who is, astrologically speaking, the patron of his chief warrior Lygurge (if Professor Curry is right) and who causes Pluto to introduce the *furie infernal* which destroys Arcite? It is Saturn who occupies the ambiguous position. He is apparently inimical to both Palamon and Arcite and he is represented as umpire of the Gods; yet he sides with Venus against Mars though he is described in a vivid passage which, though astrologically correct but inappropriate here, reads almost like a replica of the horrors of war as they are depicted in Theseus' newly constructed Temple of Mars. This is an inconsistency which is not beneath the attention of a storyteller; and it cannot be explained as a cynical treatment of pagan deities, for the gods are a necessary and integral means of resolving the main conflict of two equal suitors.

Such then are some of the shortcomings of the Knight's Tale; a number of inconsistencies, some trivial and some serious, and a most extraordinary mixture of styles, some high and some very low, with humor legitimate or misapplied as a kind of connective. It would be convenient to regard the Knight's Tale in its earlier form as written before Chaucer had quite learned his trade. Whether it was composed soon after his first journey to Italy and he had presumably read Boccaccio for the first time, say between 1372 and 1376, or if he obtained his Boccaccio manuscripts only after the second Italian journey, 1378, the case is much the same. Certainly, his use of the *Filostrato* is vastly superior to his use of the *Teseida.* Thus the comedy and jocular language might be accounted for as crudities not unnatural to a beginner, especially to a beginner wholeheartedly devoted to the Comic Spirit rehandling an elaborate quasi-epic. But such a conjecture, entirely plausible in itself, does not allow for Chaucer's revision of his early poem for the Canterbury series.

At the end Chaucer seems to depart significantly from his source. After the burial of Arcite and the funeral games he says he will turn *shortly to the point,* and thus he omits Boccaccio's long description of the temple built by Palamone for Arcita's ashes and the closing stanza of Book XI in which by way of epitaph Arcita says:

> *e per Emilia usando il mio valore*
> *mori': dunque ti guarda da amore.**

Book XII begins with Emilia's mourning:

> *Ma poi che furon più giorni passati*
> *dopo lo sventurato avvenimento.†*

The Greeks agreed by general consent that Palamon and Emily should marry. Chaucer however lengthens the period of mourning:

---

* And displaying my valor I died for Emily: so beware of love.
† But then more days passed after the unfortunate event.

> *By processe and by lengthe of certeyn yeres,*
> *Al stynted is the moornynge and the teres*
> *Of Grekes, by oon general assent.*

(This is the usual punctuation; the Italian seems to favor the punctuation adopted by a few editors: a period after *teres* or a semicolon after *Grekes*.)

Whereas Teseo has gathered the barons about him, Theseus summons a parliament to consider, among other things,

> *To have with certein contrees alliaunce*
> *And to have fully of Thebans obeisaunce.*

Theseus sends after Palamon—and with his formal speech Chaucer picks up Boccaccio again. When Palamone comes

> *non sappiendo esso però la cagione,*

it is one thing; when Palamon is sent for,

> *Unwist of hym what was the cause and why,*

it is quite another; in either case Palamon might have divined—for it appears that Chaucer's wise duke is not only rounding out the story as already forecast by the oracle of Diana (more than three hundred lines back) and ratified, as it were, by the council in heaven, but taking shrewd advantage of the opportunity to confirm the subjugation of Thebes (which he had already razed two thousand lines back). This is truly supererogatory. Is it an alteration of Chaucer's earlier 'Palamon and Arcite' poem mentioned in the Prologue of the 'Legend of Good Women' with an oblique allusion to the marriage of Richard and Anne, or simply an expansion of Boccaccio's hint of the gathering of barons to include a formal parliament with ulterior political motives? If the latter, we can only note one more demerit in the poem; if the former, we face the whole question of a larger revision than is now generally assumed when the early poem was assigned to the Knight in the *Canterbury Tales*.[18] But either way, the marriage appears to be rather a political maneuver than the foregone conclusion of the preceding story, and Chaucer has risked the charge of twisting his material in the interests of a courtly gesture: of sacrificing art for favor. One then recalls Arcite's little fable of the dogs and the kite: the dogs *foughte al day, and yet hir part was noon;* and his cynical moral:

> *And therfore, at the kynges court, my brother,*
> *Ech man for hymself. Ther is noon other.*

The symmetry of the Knight's Tale is always and justly praised. It inheres in the plot, which may be diagrammed as a double isosceles triangle, with Palamon and Arcite at the common base and Theseus at one peak and Emelye at the other. There are two equal lovers, blood cousins and sworn brothers, discovered *by and by* when they first appear. They fall in love almost simultaneously. They make parallel compleynts. Each of them has his divinity, Mars and Venus, and each wins according to his desire, one martial glory, the other a wife, at the end. Each has a conspicuous chieftain in the tournament with his hundred followers. The outcome of the jousts is a draw: Theseus so declares it. The story moves on two levels, human and divine—the rivalry of Palamon and Arcite for Emily's hand, and the rivalry of Venus and Mars in heaven; and as Theseus presides over the one, so does Saturn over the other. As the amphitheatre is provided with three temples—that of Venus at the East gate, that of Mars at the West gate, and that of Diana at the North gate, described in this order—so the two heroes pray to their divinities in prayers of equal length (one is 50, the other is 49 lines) and Emily to hers in an appropriately shorter prayer, though the order of their prayers, being determined by astrological considerations, is different: Venus, Mars, Diana—Palamon, Emily, Arcite. Of the two heroes, Arcite is mentioned first, and so wins Emily first; but Palamon sees her first, is smitten first, and declares his love first, and thus is appropriately rewarded on the grounds of precedence, though only at the end. Similarly, before the tournament, Palamon's chieftain Lygurge is described before Arcite's chieftain Emetreus.

Thus balance and symmetry are scrupulously observed. But for variety there are elements of imbalance. Perotheus is a special friend of Arcite, though one might have expected him to be equally devoted to Palamon. Palamon however does have a friend who helps him escape from prison. Arcite suffers conspicuously from the *loveris maladye Of Hereos,* whereas Palamon, who is a worshiper of Venus and is ultimately successful in love, does not. Diana is a poor third in every case. The description of her temple is less than half as long as that of Mars; Emily's prayer is shorter by one third than the prayers of Palamon and Arcite; and at the council in heaven she is not so much as mentioned. All which is quite as it should be.

For whatever reasons, there seems to be a special emphasis on the martial interests. The description of Emetreus, the chief of Arcite, is twice as long as that of Lygurge, Palamon's leader; and the description of Mars's temple is more than a third longer than that of Venus. The account of the lists, the prayers before battle, and the battle itself take up one third of the whole poem, and commencing as they do about midway occupy the climactic position; and when the death and funeral of Arcite are added, the total is nearly half of the whole poem. About half of the poem therefore is devoted to the predicaments of the two lovers, and half—the more lively half—to the grand tournament and Arcite's end. In a word, the affairs of Venus and the affairs of Mars are about evenly balanced, spatially, but in descriptive and narrative brightness and color Mars seems to be favored, perhaps by way of compensation for his defeat.

The search for imbalance in the two figures of Palamon and Arcite has brought out conflicting results.[19] Yet when all the details have been gathered and paired off, revealing Palamon as this and Arcite as that, it remains an assumption that Chaucer intended to differentiate the two more than the outline of the story required. The small contrasts add a gentle liveliness to each one, but anything like 'characterization' is certainly beside the point. Emily is by all counts but a lay-figure, a necessary convenience to the plot, and a subject for two playfully cynical comments on the eternal feminine.

Perhaps a little more can be said of Theseus. Though he in some sense dominates the action and his function is to be the *executant of destiny,* he exhibits certain traits which make him almost a real person. He is a great warrior and ruler: he has conquered Femenye and carried off Ypolita as his queen; he defeats Creon and razes Thebes: he is inclined to laugh at love, having now put all that behind him *(in my tyme a servant was I oon)* and he laughs at Palamon's confession of wrongdoing when the two are discovered at their duel and condemns them both to death. But he has a softer side. He has pity on Creon's victims; although he has refused to ransom the young captives, he yields to the request of Perotheus to release Arcite; he is properly angered at the two for fighting their duel in secret, though he takes no offense at Arcite for his long imposture as Philostrate; when the queen and her women deplore the fighting of the two lovers, he ordains a grand tournament to *darreyne* Emily, and mitigates the risks of *mortal bataille* by forbidding unnecessary slaughter; he constructs an elaborate amphitheater, he entertains the guests handsomely, and after the tournament gives Arcite a splendid funeral; and at the end he marries Emily to Palamon, reconciling them with a dignified formal speech, but makes a political occasion of the marriage. These contrasts are easily reconciled and his sense of humor gives him an attractive human quality which the other figures lack.

In truth, throughout the Knight's Tale there is implicit understanding between poet and reader that this is a *story* and therefore somewhat unreal. This is not because the scene is legendary Athens, a place which exists only in books, for there is plenty of minute realism of a sort in the details,[20] and the never-never land of romance is close enough to the chivalric ideas which Chaucer knew directly. It is because the characters are *dramatis personae*. There is no pretense that they are human beings. There is no attempt at the illusion of real life, for they are not *felt* as human beings. Rather, they are amusing figures of a pictorial representation meant to be decorative and unreal. And this is not so much detachment or aloofness as a principle of artistic procedure. Chaucer's treatment of the story and its characters is purely literary.

The critical problem of the Knight's Tale has still to be faced. What, in a word, is its "central conception"? Why has the poem raised so many questions, brought out such disparate answers, and left so much uncertainty? Could the fault lie with the modern critics, or possibly with the poet himself?

In postulating a *moral* for the Knight's Tale one might well recall Mrs. Barbauld's comment on 'The Ancient Mariner' and Coleridge's reply that "It ought to have had no more moral than the Arabian Nights' tale of the merchant's sitting down to eat dates. . ." (*Table Talk,* 31 May 1830); and then add Miss Bodkin's discovery in it of the pattern of rebirth and Professor Tillyard's view of it as a spiritual adventure of crime and repentence and the inexorable suffering which pursues other men even after the criminal has repented. Of such is Professor Muscatine's conviction that the Knight's Tale represents the conflict of chaos (Palamon and Arcite) and order (Theseus) and Professor Frost's similar view that the descriptions of the temples "symbolically extend the misfortunes and grief of the central characters," that the picture of Mars and Saturn, "chaotic and hideous enough," is offset by the presence of the gods to give "a degree of order" to human life. For good measure, Emily is seen as "the emblem of vernal innocence." And further, against the "conflict of an ethic of battle and an ethic of love," appear the figures of Theseus, Ypolita, and Perotheus "as an emblem of the two kinds of value reconciled and in accord." Mr. Frost's position is put a little less vividly earlier in his article. The Knight's Tale, he says, "develops from three widening concentric circles of interest: the merely human interest of the rivalry between two young heroes. . . ; the ethical interest of a conflict of obligations between romantic love and military comradeship; and finally the theological interest attaching to the method by which a just providence fully stabilizes a disintegrating human situation."

On a more mundane view the moral is simply that somehow things come right in the end and even passive love is triumphant; Arcite, who put his trust in Mars, is rewarded by victory in battle and a fine funeral, but the astuteness of Palamon, who put his trust in Venus, is ultimately justified. This is perhaps not very edifying, but it has a Chaucerian flavor.

More restricted is the view of the Knight's Tale as "an *exem-*

plum of the power of love which overrules all fellowship, even that of the truest of knights and devoted friends." It was suggested long since by Pater, was repeated by Mather (1899), is held now by Professor Wilson. Another critic finds no grand philosophical solution; for the Knight's Tale is "a tragedy, an irony of existence whereby virtue has been arrayed, not against vice and evil, but against an equal virtue; . . . a hero had died so as to make way for another hero. Why a merciful providence had permitted this might well have continued to puzzle Chaucer's audience even after an exposition of Boethius. . . ."

Those seeking a loftier position have noted that the conflict of loyalties between Palamon and Arcite is raised to a supernatural level, but they can find little satisfaction in the choice of Saturn as umpire, a malignant figure who boasts of fostering the very same calamities as those depicted in the temple of Mars. Others might be content to understand the debate in heaven as a bit of decoration (only forty-five lines long) carried over from Boccaccio's epic machinery.

It is true that the gods seem to decide the contest of Palamon and Arcite: they were consulted in the three prayers, and their decisions announced oracularly, before the case was laid before Saturn. But Chaucer was hardly concerned with classical theology. There is however a sense of predestined happenings throughout this poem, as elsewhere in Chaucer; but here it is less likely than elsewhere that Chaucer means to certify or illustrate his personal belief in Divine Providence. Arcite asks why people complain of the *purveiaunce of God, or of Fortune,* which often does better by them than they could do for themselves. Palamon in his parallel *compleynt* is more bitter. The gods who rule the world are cruel, he says, and he is openly cynical in his question—

> *What governance is in this prescience*
> *That giltelees tormenteth innocence?*

But he dismisses the problem, as Chaucer usually does, by leaving the answer *to dyvynys.*

These are of course dramatic speeches. The most conspicuous appearance of

The destinee, ministre general
That executeth in the world over al
The purveiaunce that God hath seyn biforn

occurs when the threefold coincidence has to be accounted for, when Arcite goes a-Maying and Theseus a-hunting to the very place and at the very time when Palamon is lurking in the forest near Athens. In the formal closing speech of Theseus, which is a composite of Boethius and Boccaccio, when the grand harmonizing of all oppositions takes place, the words are *Firste Moevere* and *Prince* and *Juppiter the Kyng* together with *purveiaunce* and *grace;* and the general sense is that all things are ordained by divine order and we should thank Jupiter *of al his grace* and *make of sorwes two O parfit joye,* that is, the wedding of Palamon and Emily. This fine speech, moreover, is not a model of reason but a display of eloquence—else we might wonder at the curious remark that Arcite was fortunate to die young rather

Than whan his name appalled is for age.

The occasion calls for fine language, not logic, and Theseus rises to the occasion. If Chaucer meant us to see here a sign of the loving kindness of Providence rather than merely the happy ending of his story, one can only admit that he leaves a great deal to interpretation. For the final outcome is properly provided by the answers of Mars, Venus, and Diana and by Arcite's dying wish, to say nothing of the Athenian parliament.

One small point remains. At the end of Pars Prima the poet addresses *Yow lovers* with the question: Which of the two heroes was in worse plight, Palamon, who could at least see his lady from the prison window, or Arcite, who was out of prison but could never see his lady? No more is made of this *demande* later in the tale—it may have been only a device for ending a chapter—but we do not forget it. When the story is finished we rephrase it: Which of the two equal suitors should win? The answer is: both won. We are then more than half persuaded that the whole tale, in this form which Chaucer gave it, exists for its ambiguity and its ingenious solution.

There is general agreement on the many fine qualities of the

Knight's Tale, ranging from single lines to considerable passages, lyrical, descriptive, and narrative. The poem's appeal is in large part due to these: the young prisoners in their tower with Emily singing in the garden beneath their window on a May morning; the formalized arguments, the stylized compleynts, the particularized prayers, the two battle pieces, one a single combat, the other a grand tournament; the elaborate amphitheater with its three temples and their ornamentation; the one emotionally moving scene of Arcite's farewell; the funeral ceremonies; and above all the plight of the young knights, sworn brothers, both in love with the indifferent Emily, with the courtly but genial Theseus as master of ceremonies. The setting, the figures, the situations are all *romantic* to the last degree. That the combination of these elements is somewhat artificial does not lessen their attractiveness. But that their effect is mainly decorative and picturesque should be recognized fully and made the starting point of a sound criticism; and the additional elements which enthusiastic readers have discovered in the poem, the characterization of Palamon and Arcite and the profound moral significance should be regarded with caution.

Another great merit of the poem is its atmosphere. The setting of the love story is ancient; but the décor of the foreground is pure Chaucerian modern, or only faintly in the recent past with only hints of historical distance. The background of chivalry, which Chaucer himself saw as passing, is described with a clear sense of its departing splendor, with exaggerated emphasis on the variety of armor, and the overcolored accessories of Lygurge and Emetreus. The grand tournament and the knightly virtues are represented with that slight artificiality of conscious revival, or deliberate retention, which he himself witnessed only a few years later, in the two tournaments at Smithfield, a pageantry which suited admirably the romantic remoteness of ancient Thebes and Athens, touched, like that of Malory for us, with the nostalgia for a glory that was slipping away.

What now will account for the excellence of the parts alongside the shortcomings and the want of general coherence? Suppose that in the early or late 1370's, that is, soon after he had been to Italy and discovered the *Teseida,* Chaucer felt moved to make over the Italian poem for himself.[21] He would no doubt have been impressed by it and recognized its attractive features as well as some which were to him less attractive; but it was rich in material. He might not be too clear at the outset just what he could make of it, but he would discard most of the epic machinery and concentrate on the main episode of the two sworn brothers and their love of the disinterested heroine. He begins with a rapid sketch of Boccaccio's opening—in 400 lines he disposes of the first three books, 2500 lines—and incorporates some of the grand style of his model. This grand manner, however, strikes him as slightly comic in its high-flown exaggerations; and his own sense of humor insistently craves indulgence. Instead therefore of treating the material as a noble love story in the artificial fashion of Boccaccio he will see what can be done with the curious situation of two equal lovers who each win the lady though in different ways. This is actually an amusing situation, the more so because Emily was not emotionally involved and neither of the lovers was in a position to approach her directly—a love story without any lovemaking, a love problem which can be solved in two ways at once, a serious subject with opportunities for his natural proclivity towards the lighter vein. Along with this he finds of course all the richness of decorative description and the whole chivalric background as of the present with the antique flavor of a distant unfamiliar past: Scythia and the Amazons, ancient Thebes and Athens. So he continues to the end, regardless of apparent difficulties and possible inconsistencies—regardless because his enthusiasm (which he communicates) carries him along. When it is all done he admits its faults; he cannot claim for it any great unity either of conception or of handling, but it is full of variety and color and incident, and certainly a variety of interests, grave and gay. It has a love story, one rather different from those other romances; it has war and knightly combat on a large scale; it has temples full of bright pictures; it has a moving death scene and the ancient burial celebration; it has supernatural adjuncts (the omens and the scene in heaven, in which for a moment the very gods are baffled); it has coincidence of event requiring double explanation by the powers of Destiny and the divine foresight; it has surprises enough, including the specially satisfying surprises about which there needed to be no suspense or concealment, illustrating how both suitors can win. His people are not very real in themselves, and do not need to be: the passive heroine and the dual hero, two young knights so nearly alike that one can hardly tell them apart yet sufficiently unlike to give the impression of difference, and a king,—the Duke of Athens who had himself had a checkered past (of which nothing is to be said) and has now a mellow humor along with fine instincts for statecraft and speech making. For all this abundance the reader will be grateful, without looking anxiously or hypercritically for minor flaws.

So there it is, an imperfect poem, an early work. It will of course find a place in the *Canterbury Tales* and while not altogether suitable for his Pilgrim Knight, who had devoted most of his long life to the service of the Church Militant in foreign lands and who would not be much concerned with a *demande d'amours* or any sort of love tale, still it will do. (It would have done better for the Squire perhaps.) Yet, to go back and revise it, to harmonize the styles to one level, to iron out the inconsistencies, even to remove some of the blots of his pupil pen, might destroy its peculiar qualities. Therefore, let it stand, with only the insertion of a few lines to place it among the pilgrim's narratives.

4. REALISM AND TALES OF THE SUPERNATURAL

CHAUCER liked to picture himself as a bookish fellow. His Clerk might have been content with twenty books of Aristotle and his lore; Chaucer himself had, towards the close of his life, sixty—

> *Yis, God wot, sixty bokes olde and newe*

about Greek and Roman women alone. He was a constant reader

what for lust and what for lore, and he read hopefully to acquire *al this newe science that men lere,* and also confidently:

> *Than mote we to bokes that we fynde . . .*
> *And to the doctrine of these olde wyse*
> *Yeve credence, in every skylful wise.*

Sometimes on a May morning his worship of the daisy would get him away from his books, but for the most part they kept him from daily contact with the practical business of life, so that he knew almost nothing of the love affairs all around him

> *Ne of noght elles that God made.*

What with his accounts at the Customs and his devotion to books he got no rest and no knowledge of *newe thynges;* he was becoming a recluse, a hermit; and it took Jupiter and the eloquent Eagle to free him from this bondage—if free him they could. For even when the Eagle had brought him into the very presence of the stellified birds and fish and beasts of the Zodiac and the constellations,

> *As the Raven, or eyther Bere,*
> *Or Ariones harpe fyn,*
> *Castor, Pollux, or Delphyn,*
> *Or Athalantes doughtres sevene*

(alack, his books betrayed him on that last name), he stubbornly persisted in refusing such intimacies:

> *"No fors," quod y, "hyt is no nede.*
> *I leve wel, so God me spede,*
> *Hem that write of this matere,*
> *As though I knew her places here. . . ."*

Actually, he tells us, he is already (at the date of the 'Hous of Fame') too old to learn any more—

> *"Wilt thou lere of sterres aught?"*
> *"Nay, certeynly," quod y, "ryght naught."*
> *"And why?"   "For y am now to old."*

How close to the letter we are to accept all this need not be seriously asked. But certainly he grew up as a page to Prince

Lionel's wife and as King Edward's esquire, he had seen fighting in France, had crossed the Alps, had dealt with the men of big business in London. In truth we find touches of realism in his earliest work, even in the 'Book of the Duchess,' which is a distillation of his reading in French poetry. For example, with all the conventional description of the Duchess's manners and person he devotes half a dozen lines to her fair throat (939 ff.)—it had no unbecoming *boon ne brekke;* it was not hollow, the collarbone was not visible. The bright and original picture of the dreamer's room is also a mixture of real and unreal. Skeat felt it necessary to remark that since stained glass was expensive the windows depicting the whole story of Troy were dream windows; but the poet was careful to say that they had no cracks in them. The streaming colors on his bed come from observation, but when he takes his horse and rides out of the room, that is pure dream. A little later Chaucer turns to the *Roman de la Rose,* where he reads:[22]

> *Mais li arbre, ce sachiez, furent*
> *Si loing a loing come estre durent;*
> *Li uns fu loing de l'autre assis*
> *Plus de cinc toises ou de sis.*

This he had translated:

> *One from another in assyse*
> *Fyve fadome or sixe I trowe so*
> *But they were hye and great also,*

and then remade it in the 'Book of the Duchess':

> *And every tree stood by hymselve*
> *From other wel ten foot or twelve,*
> *So grete trees, so huge of strengthe,*
> *Of fourty or fifty fadme lengthe.*

For the marvelous forest of his dream the trees had to be closer than thirty or thirty-five feet, so he set them only ten or twelve feet apart (*twelve* for the handy rime), and he gave them also an extraordinary height—two hundred forty to three hundred feet

> *Clene withoute bowgh or stikke*

before the branches began. To confirm the unrealism, these branches, he says, met to form an impenetrable shade, as in the *Roman,* for the comfort of the numberless animals there. Then, to indicate how many these were, he picked up from a very different context in the *Roman* and 12,500 lines away, the Argus-Algus figure and gave the whole his comic twist: there were so many animals that even *the noble countour* could not reckon up all the marvels of his dream.

The realistic details, descriptive and analytical, in the fabliaux and the comic Tales need no pointing; a few more, out of many, in less likely places may be noted. Troilus, to forestall comment if he is missed during the nocturnal meetings with Criseyde, gives out

> *Ther-while he was aboute this servyse,*
> *That he was gon to don his sacrifise,*
>
> *And moste at swich a temple allone wake,*
> *Answered of Apollo for to be.*

This is not in Boccaccio and it is more than many modern novelists condescend to. It looks ahead also to the irony that later Pandarus actually finds him in such a temple wrestling with his anguish over the exchange. In case of any disturbance that might arise if Troilus decides to run away with Criseyde, Pandarus pledges active support,

> *Theigh ich and al my kyn, upon a stownde,*
> *Shulle in a strete as dogges liggen dede.*

This is also not in Boccaccio. It recalls the line where Thisbe finds her lover

> *Betynge with his heles on the grounde*
> *Al blody.*

Throughout the *Troilus,* with all its airs of remoteness in religion and manners, *of payens corsed olde rites,* there is so much contemporary realistic detail that Chaucer, even after casting as much blame as he could on one Lollius, felt the pressure of criticism and tried at the end to recant.

Chaucer had no theory of realism; the theory is a modern invention. What we see in him of this sort runs to the purely reportorial founded on acute observation, especially of English low life—the Cook's ulcer, the Miller's wart, the Squire's carving, the Knight's dirty tunic—and analytical insights of motive or action—the Merchant's *chevisaunce,* the Friar's sophistries, the Reeve's cunning. The old widow, we recall,

> *Thre large sowes hadde she, and namo,*
> *Three keen, and eek a sheep that highte Malle.*

This is the very acme of realism. With such accuracy he had to combine the conventional abstractions he accepted from his early models. Sometimes they will cleave but not incorporate, as with the feet of Nebuchadnezzar's statue. His Custance, Griselda, Dorigen are graduated examples, his Criseyde the most complex and difficult. For the delicate touches by which she comes alive disassociate her from the simple role in which she was originally cast, of amorous fickle young woman. At Chaucer's best the abstractions are blended with "the rich substance of concrete things." At his best, furthermore, the exactness is enhanced by imaginative strokes which yield not only verisimilitude but the image of life itself (though that too is an abstraction).

Realism is of two kinds. One is that which is confected for the common reader, who has no imagination and little memory, who asks no more than that what he is given should resemble what he knows. This is the kind which panders to the secondary merit of recognition, provided the language is vivid enough. It is preoccupied with the phenomenal world, not the real world. The other kind reaches higher, towards the universal by way of the imagination. "Je dis une fleur," said Mallarmé—and Chaucer would not follow him here, but perhaps he would vaguely feel what is meant—"Je dis une fleur et . . . musicalement se lève, idée même et suave, l'absente de tous bouquets." Just so: for Chaucer's unreal meadow of flowers white and red is nothing that he reports from observation and memory, but an ideal Platonic meadow. His Chanticleer and Pertelote are not barnyard fowl, nor human beings slightly disguised; and by a sort of magic fallacy the illusion transcends concreteness. The concrete elements are a means given and absorbed. In this sense Chaucer sometimes achieves the higher realism, beyond the empirical, and along with it comes that detachment and amoral attitude which refuses to be embroiled with moral judgments, which makes his weak characters pardonable and his villains companionable.

One touch of nature can be very deceptive. Its purpose may be to deceive, and it may be no more than a single detail which is willingly accepted as validating the whole. So the Knight's *gipoun Al bismotered* seems to make him more real than all his campaigns in heathendom. Yet he never becomes a person; he is as much a painted figure as his son. The Squire is described full length, with an accumulation of pictorial and characterizing detail, yet he remains a picture; he never *acts* like a human being moved by parts and passions from within. And this is true of all his people, save the three pre-eminent exceptions. It places Chaucer as a mediæval on the verge of the Renaissance. So in painting and sculpture St. Mark had his lion, Luke his heifer, John his eagle, and this sufficed, with only the simplest likeness to the human figure; even the lions, heifers, eagles did not pretend to be very lifelike. But by the late fourteenth century and the early fifteenth something like portraiture has begun. When King Richard in the Wilton diptych is shown adoring the Virgin, the angels are done with conventional faces, John the Baptist is at the same time symbolic and human, but Richard himself is almost certainly a portrait, and the two kings, St. Edmund and St. Edward the Confessor, are so individualized in costume and in feature as to suggest contemporary originals.

Chaucer's realism is a paradox. His descriptions of people and things are conventional but often raised "for the moment" by shrewd, well-placed brush strokes to the third dimension of seeming reality—the cat driven from the ingle bench, January's sagging jowls, that gay popelote the carpenter's wife, the friar kissing Thomas' wife, and a hundred more. Perhaps this was obvious, so obvious as to be overlooked. On the other hand, there are the three people to whom Chaucer allotted time and space for portraiture, as though Nature spoke for him—

> *lo! I, Nature,*
> *Thus can I forme and peynte a creature,*
> *Whan that me list—*

the Wife of Bath and Pandarus and in part Criseyde. Beside these the Clerk is thin, the Prioress pale, the Pardoner merely a rough diamond, and the others nowhere. Those others have their moments, Dorigen, for example, but for the most part they are movable types.

Much of Chaucer's admired realism is a matter of vivid imagery. There is a picture of Jovinyan

> *Fat as a whale, and walkynge as a swan.*

The swan could be from observation, but had Chaucer ever seen a whale? There is Chanticleer singing:

> *He wolde so peyne hym that with bothe his yen*
> *He moste wynke, so loude he wolde cryen,*
> *And stonden on his tiptoon therwithal,*
> *And strecche forth his nekke long and smal.*

This also looks like direct observation and the tiptoes an amusing transfer. There is also Griselda coming home, surprised to find the Marquis there,

> *And she set doun hir water pot anon*
> *Biside the thresshfold.*

Petrarch had "aquam e longinquo fonte convectans" and the French adds "une croche de l'eaue," but *set doun* is Chaucer's and it vivifies the scene. There is, of a different sort, Mars roused from Venus' bed donning his armor and shaking his spear so it almost snaps, but

> *Ful hevy was he to walken over lond.*

This is a factual detail which nineteenth-century illustrators might have borne in mind. There is, also in 'Mars,' the picture of Phebus entering the palace sturdily,

> *With torche in honde, of which the stremes bryghte*
> *On Venus chambre knokkeden ful lyghte.*

The double meanings, with latent impropriety, befit the pervading allegory, but the beams of light knocking lightly on the door is a conceit with realistic backing. Such details abound in Chaucer, from his early work (remember the untrained little dog that fawned on him in the 'Book of the Duchess') to his latest (the mixed metaphor of his muse *That rusteth in my shethe*); and they crowd in among the standbys of Cupid and the seven gods and the omnipresent Fortune and all the other inescapable clichés. The sudden bright contrasts produce an illusion of realism particularly welcome to the modern reader and raise Chaucer in our esteem.

There is another side, however. His fortune with posterity is due so much to a reputation for realistic modes, his concern is so much with concrete reportage (and so little with reflection) that we have to remember what precious hostages he gave to fortune in every poem, except the General Prologue.

The General Prologue is his one finest achievement because along with composition, as structure and as expression, it called for the best qualities of his genius and did not require of him qualities which he possessed in limited measure. His fondness for the dream convention may have been due to artistic instinct as much as to fashion; it allowed him to mingle the real and the unreal to the advantage of both without submitting to the standard checks of accuracy and reality. His flowers white and red may be sublimated (as I have suggested), but they leave us wondering if he was as careful an observer of natural phenomena as of human.

He has his lists of birds and trees, but they are literary, not pictorial. Their attributes are not meant to make us see them. He has his surprising examples of synæsthesia, perhaps borrowed, as in the *statue* of Venus, in the Knight's Tale, floating on the sea, with doves flickering above her head and on it

A rose gerland, fressh and wel smellynge;

and the parallel colored statue of Diana, with little dogs about her feet and under them a waxing moon and before her a woman in childbirth—

> *Ful pitously Lucyna gan she calle . . .*
> *Wel koude he peynten lifly that it wroghte.*

Vivid, certainly, yet not real; not done from nature, though with natural adjuncts. There is the Franklin's beard white as a daisy, with a hint of his ruddy face, and all the daisies of the Prologue to the 'Legend of Good Women,' especially those of Alcestis' crown, whose whiteness was given by Cibella and whose redness by Mars. The flowers are nearly always red and white and the colors are more symbolic or conventional than natural. Here of course he is in the long tradition. A striking example is Dame Pees sitting at the temple door ('Parlement,' 239 ff.) *with a curtyn in hir hond*—you see her holding the curtain aside—and with her Dame Pacience

> *With face pale, upon an hil of sond.*

Away goes the picture in a blur of symbolism. There are the grisly black rocks which terrified Dorigen; you feel them, as she did, but you do not visualize them, you are not meant to, for they are emotional accessories, not pictorial. Chaucer saw the shipping in the Thames and crossed the Channel several times, but you find no impression that ships and the sea made on his mind. He picks up a nautical metaphor from Boccaccio and develops it for literary effect. He frequently mentions music, but for a purpose, not for delight in the sound. Is there any evidence that he listened with pleasure to the motets of Machaut? Is there any sign that he appreciated the beauty of mass, proportion, and decorative elements of Gothic buildings? The castle in Book III of the 'Hous of Fame' is sheer fantasy, and properly so, but without the realistic vividness or the profusion of technical terms that we enjoy in *Sir Gawayne and the Green Knight*. And so on, for there is no need to belabor the point.

It would surprise Chaucer to be told of our modern notions of realism and its poor relation naturalism, the slice-of-life theory—the more disagreeable the better. The idea of reporting contemporary life as a record would surprise him; but so also would the notion that art is a relief from the human situation, a rising from the quotidian to the eternal. The wide spaces between these two, between strict imitation or resemblance and absolute symbol, were his ground. Like all artists he worked from tradition, adding only his own new and different ways of enlarging tradition. As the painter composes but does not reproduce, as his pictures resemble the landscape, not the other way around, so Chaucer gives us not what his eyes saw but what his creative mind selected, and he is most 'realistic' when he chooses from the manifold variety of data the concrete details, necessarily contemporary, which produce the illusion of verisimilitude. It is the quality of his choices and their proportion to the conventional elements which interest us; and it is his constant habit of introducing concrete details, apparently from his own direct observation, though often also from some outlying tradition (proverbs, folk phrases, and such) into the artificial, unnatural settings of his models, his classical borrowings, and the French love visions, which enhances his reputation as a realist.

On the other hand, this habit of using realistic detail tends to disguise the conventionality of his methods in the larger aspects of narrative structure and characterization. That kind of realism which sticks close to the familiar phenomena of normal life, the actual and plausibly probable activities of men, and the situations which display them as we are accustomed to see them, is not his kind. His plots, in a word, his stories seemingly built on probable and natural events, are thoroughly unreal and unrealistic, the fabliau type as much so as the (Physician's) story of Virginia and the (Manciple's) story of the white crow, the 'Palamon and Arcite' as much as the Prioress' miracle or the other nun's St. Cecilia, the tragi-comedy of Troilus as much as the Ovidian martyrology of Cupid's saints. His characters are not psychological constructs or complexly consistent artistic creations, but more or less lively simulacra performing their functions predetermined by the plot.

Moreover, along with his pretensions of ignorance about love and other empirical experience, Chaucer allows himself an almost too positive attitude of æsthetic distance. He will remind us with a wink, an aside, a deprecatory gesture, that this is not a poem, an *œuvre,* but an amusing piece of business which he shares with us as readers or listeners. He will thus insist that it is only a story about people, not a representation of people as they live and move and think and feel. This is all very well, he will say, but we know better than to take it seriously; it may seem painful, but we shall not wince; it may seem wicked, but we shall not pretend to judge: remember, this is a story. Like Thackeray, he will not allow the reader to enjoy for long the illusion of reality; lo! he says, the puppets and the strings—operated by Fortune, Purvei-aunce, Lollius, me (Geoffrey Chaucer). It is an amalgam of the ingenuous and the disingenuous, with corresponding advantages and distractions.

Hence it is worth while to examine some of the ways by which Chaucer deliberately seeks to reduce the improbabilities of his story-matter through realistic levies on the familiar and acceptedly normal or natural matter of ordinary life and the devices which he employs to conceal the palpably implausible while maintaining an air of verisimilitude.

For a very large proportion of Chaucer's poetry the question of realism is irrelevant. 'Realistic' touches, borrowed and original, may appear anywhere. The *Troilus,* always a work apart, abounds in them, though it is a kind of mediæval romance with an antique backdrop. The Knight's Tale has them, thinly and not too felicitously scattered. In the *Canterbury Tales,* however, there are five examples, of varied origin, that illustrate a progres-sion of technical mastery, which may have nothing to do with chronology, in Chaucer's handling of unrealistic materials. There is first the Man of Law's Tale, where he failed, I believe, for want of serious effort; the Clerk's Tale, where he compromised success-fully; the Franklin's Tale, where he failed by virtue of trying too hard; and the Wife of Bath's Tale, where he succeeded eminently by total omission; and lastly, for contrast, the Friar's Tale, where he succeeded by the opposite method. Our criteria now will be purely artistic, divorced of mediæval standards—modern, if you like, or, if there are such criteria, universal.[23]

It used to be held that the Man of law's Tale was early work and so its obvious faults could be accounted for; then Skeat's arguments for revision were strongly opposed by Tatlock; and latterly it has been taken up by those who would praise Chaucer at all costs.[24] Although Chaucer was a man of his time, he was also a poet who has left us pre-eminently successful narrative verse, and like other poets was capable of inferior work. It is therefore proper to look at the literary qualities of the poem and later contrast it with his handling of similar artistic problems. His mediaeval-ism may something extenuate, but it cannot wholly shelter him from all-prevailing standards of literary craftsmanship.

Foremost, then, is the crudity of the story, patterned on or parallel to many and many a saint's legend and with its ultimate origins in märchen tradition, a story preposterously improbable and acceptable to mediæval taste because of its piety. Other stories of Chaucer's are improbable enough, but in the Man of Law's Tale he accepted many of his original's worst elements and when he tried to mitigate them only made them more apparent. That he improved on Trivet's version in many ways is true, and also that in condensing he added some unimprovements. His improvements leave us wondering why he did not go further. The monotony of the repeated motifs—the two wicked mothers-in-law and the two exposures at sea—was probably no deterrent to mediæval readers; but one of each, with a little less violent rhetoric for the mothers-in-law and a little more attention to the trials of an extended solitary voyage would certainly have been more effective in bringing home to us the long-suffering virtues of the heroine. Yet worst of all is what Pollard calls "the unreason-ing prodigality of time" throughout the tale. The sowdanesse appears to have moved swiftly, but the first voyage from Syria to Northumberland lasted for *yeres and dayes* (463); a certain amount of time must have elapsed for the conversion of Hermen-gild and the constable, the murder of Hermengild and the mar-riage to Alla, followed by the birth of Mauricius, and the machi-nations (letters to and from Scotland) of Donegild, though Mauricius is only a crying infant (866) when Custance sets out on the return voyage. This voyage, hardly shorter in miles than the first, lasted more than five years (902), so that it is ten years more or less before the father of Custance learns of the *dishonour* done to his daughter by the Syrians and sends an expedition to wreak vengeance—and also unexpectedly to rescue the derelict Custance, who is unrecognized by her own uncle, somewhere in the eastern Mediterranean. Meanwhile, five years after murdering his mother King Alla is moved to repentance, makes his pilgrimage to Rome to receive penance from the Pope, and when he arrives is welcomed royally (995 ff.) with no mention of guilt or penance. Rather, with some difficulty he and his daughter are brought together and presently, *whan he his tyme say,* he returns to England and dies a year later. Custance goes back to her father. The action has occupied at least a dozen years, most of it spent in the uncharted drifting of the heroine's ships. With reasonable treatment and due allowance for a willing suspension of disbelief, this was material for a good improving story. Chaucer did little enough to give it a proper shape and substance. By the time he had written the Pardoner's Tale, the Wife of Bath's Tale, or even the Clerk's Tale, and above all the Miller's Tale, Chaucer knew enough of narrative technique to have made something first rate of Trivet's story—if he had chosen to try seriously.

Tatlock praised Chaucer for not attempting to rationalize the Tale, especially Custance herself. "To rationalize her would have been to make yet more incongruous than it is a story which is incurably miraculous." But it is just here that Chaucer showed no little concern. He laid it down in the ninth and tenth stanzas that Custance's misfortunes were due in the first instance to the stars; he put into her mouth the piteous lines:

> *Wommen are born to thraldom and penance,*
> *And to been under mannes governance;*

he again blamed the stars *(O Mars, o atazir)* and complained of her father's imprudence; a little later he saw Satan working against her (365 ff.); he alleged divine intervention (471 ff.) to account for her being spared by the wicked Syrians (with the examples of Daniel, Jonah, the Israelites crossing the Red Sea, and Maria Egyptiaca); and again (932 ff.) he cited Biblical precedent for her strength—all of which, amounting to thirteen stanzas, are his additions, that is, have no source in Trivet. Their purpose if not their effect is to lessen our sense of the improbable. Moreover, he took pains to enlist our sympathy with the sufferings of Custance, first in her pathetic leavetaking of her father, later in five really touching stanzas (834 ff.) when she is set adrift for the second time, with her infant now, saying to the constable,

> *So kys hym ones in his fadres name . . .*
> *And evere she preyeth hire child to holde his pees;*

and also in two stanzas emphasizing her piety. These nine stanzas are likewise additions to the source. Further, he borrows from Innocent a stanza (421 ff.) on the suddenness of sorrow after joy, another on the evils of drink (771 ff.), another on the evils of lust (925 ff.), and another on the brevity of happiness (1135 ff.); and nine lines from Boethius on the prosperity of the wicked (811 ff.)—altogether twenty-three stanzas added to Trivet's material, all meant to soften the miraculous elements and to enhance the piety and pathos of Custance, with commonplace moral observations from the *De contemptu mundi* and the *De consolatione philosophiae:* enough to manifest Chaucer's concern with the handicaps of such material; perhaps to offset the horrors of matricide, murder, attempted rape, two more or less judicial deaths, and the multiple slayings of Christians by Syrians and Syrians by Christians.

Still this is not all; there are other additions of a different cast, notably the explosive rhetoric (358 ff.):

> *O sowdanesse, roote of iniquitee!*
> *Virago, thou Semyrame the secounde! . .*

and a matching stanza directed at Donegild (778 ff.). Beginning at l. 631, when Custance is charged with the murder of Hermengild, there is a run of four stanzas of mixed quality. Custance has now no champion to defend her unless Christ (who had bound Satan—who *yet lith ther he lay,* though more than once active in the story) intervenes with a miracle; she prays to God and to the Blessed Virgin for succor; and Chaucer begs queens, duchesses, and other noble ladies to have pity on Custance, who is of royal blood. This leads to the summary line (693),

And thus hath Crist ymaad Custance a queene,

which reminds us of the similarly infelicitous

Now be we duchesses, bothe I and ye,

in the 'Legend of Good Women' (2127). Just preceding this last effort to touch our hearts is the *pale face* stanza, remarkable for its direct realism (645 ff.). A quite gratuitous, less worthy bit of realism is the two stanzas (701 ff.) on the celebration of Alla's marriage: even such good women as Custance must *leye a lite hir holynesse aside* on the wedding night.

So much for the embellishments with which Chaucer adorns the "certain crudity" of the "incurably miraculous" story he found in Trivet's chronicle. The emphasis on pity and piety are to be expected. The explosive rhetoric is explicable but not very effective. At a later date it would be called rant. In the Cock and Fox story he could use it happily for comic purposes. Then there are such exclamatory asides as *God hym see—as God is trewe— almyghty God thee gyde—ther God yeve him meschance—O my Custance—Thus endeth olde Donegild, with meschance.* These and similar ornaments leave an impression of forcing, as though the poet were deliberately raising his voice to conceal an emptiness of feeling.

To say much about the versification is risky, but certainly the verse of the Man of Law's Tale is not so stiff and regular as in the Manciple's Tale, nor so free as in the Canon's Yeoman's Tale; it is not so easy and supple as in the *Troilus,* nor are there so many irregular lines as in the Knight's Tale. But in the style there is along with much smoothness and characteristic competence an unfortunate frequency of such light-hearted insets as *this is the ende* in the very second stanza and repeated at l. 255 and l. 965, *I kan (dar) say yow namoore—Bothe north and south, and also west and est—was blynd and myghte nat see—I kan telle it no bettre.* Moreover, the various massacres and murders are disposed of with remarkably brisk brevity, and there is a notable haste when Alla on his wedding night begot his son and went to Scotland leaving his wife with the constable and a bishop, in three lines.

Palpable humor has been noted by some commentators. A signal instance is the account of the death of that (Spanish) steward who tried to violate Custance on her way home. Trivet says plainly: "Custance, pur sa chastete sawer, priueement luy vient rere au dos e le tresbucha en la mer," but Chaucer has

> *For with hir struglyng wel and myghtily*
> *The theef fil over bord al sodeynly.*

This took place in Spain, as Trivet expressly states, but Chaucer says he could not find the locality in his *text* (905). Another variation, perhaps more significant, concerns the landing place of Custance in Northumberland. Trivet says that it was "pres Humbre" and that Donegild was at "Knaresbourth, entre Engleterre e Escoe"; Chaucer says it was a castle *that nempnen I ne kan* (507). Gower omits altogether the attack on Custance along the Spanish coast, but he twice names "Knaresburgh" (*Confessio* II, 443, 1264). Behind this reticence of Chaucer's has been seen an unwillingness to overpoint the natural association of his heroine with the living Costanza of Castile, John of Gaunt's second wife. The castle of Knaresborough, earlier a refuge for the murderers of Becket and later owned by Isabella, wife of Edward II and mistress of Roger Mortimer, was now the property of Lancaster; he was there during the London riots of the Peasants' Revolt and Costanza fled there after being refused entrance into Pontefract.[25] This almost too obvious contemporary allusion for Chancer's readers, and some parallels which may be coincidental but none the less obvious which Chaucer did not suppress—for instance, the fact that after his marriage Alla left at once for the wars in Scotland, as John of Gaunt had been sent north against Scotland just before the Peasant uprising—were canvassed by Professor Roland M. Smith in a fully documented article.[26] Professor Smith says at the outset that it is "to the credit of students of Chaucer that they have not pressed the identification of the heroine of the *Man of Law's Tale* with John of Gaunt's second Duchess"; and then, having discussed what looks like Chaucer's attempt to disguise the identification by rejecting certain details he found in Trivet, is himself embarrassed to explain why Chau-

cer even wrote the poem. For the name Constance is conspicuous throughout, and from 1371, when she reached England, to
her death in 1394 the duchess was a prominent figure in court
life; and to suppress the words Spain and Knaresborough and
leave the other parallels for curious readers to speculate on is not
much concealment. Would the removal of those two words suc-
ceed in "obliterating any presumptions that he had the Castilian
Constance in mind"? The question is still embarrassing.

Where, one may also ask, was Chaucer's artistic sense when,
having chosen the subject, he was not content to leave it on its
own ground? The margin of credibility varies from age to age;
the miraculous of one day is often the commonplace of the next.
But if Chaucer had not felt himself hampered by the improbabilities of his material, why did he ostentatiously try to cover them up
by appeal to Scripture and resort to rhetoric?

The Clerk's Tale has been almost submerged in arguments
about the Clerk and Petrarch, the Clerk and the Wife of Bath,
and the Envoy whether the Clerk's or Chaucer's. It is interesting
however on other counts: as a study of close translation from
Latin prose to smooth, regular, English stanzas with a minimum
of padding and alteration; and as an example of Chaucer's management of the humanly improbable. Petrarch's moral, which
implies a deprecation of human interest, Chaucer saved for a kind
of surprise ending, as much as to say: If you did not believe in
Griselda's humility, no matter; the real point is the Christian
parable. But throughout the narrative he took precautions against
losing the reader's sympathy. Petrarch had shown the way, Chaucer improved on it. In terms of the story Griselda's submissiveness is one of the data. She is of humble birth and trained to
serve; the marquis, after a preliminary understanding with her
father, makes obedience a part of the marriage contract, which
she accepts freely; her various trials, which Chaucer softens a
little, put him and the reader under considerable strain, and in
compensation he allows her some expressions of feeling which
fall just short of complaints.

> *I have noght had no part of children tweyne*
> *But first siknesse, and after wo and peyne.*
>
> *O goode God! how gentil and how kynde*
> *Ye semed by youre speche and youre visage*
> *The day that maked was oure mariage! . . .*
> *Love is noght oold as when that it is newe.*

This latter exclamation is not in Petrarch. And before the pretended remarriage she pointedly warns the marquis (as he had warned her earlier),

> *That ye ne prikke with no tormentynge*
> *This tendre mayden, as ye han doon mo.*

There is also a small note of the rational in Janicula's premonition—

> *For out of doute this olde poure man*
> *Was evere in suspect of hir mariage.*

The nearest to an improbability in the characterization of Griselda is her sudden access of executive virtues on her marriage.

What is usually regarded as the most improbable element is the marquis's harshness *(sturdinesse),* but even this is both indirectly and directly accounted for. In the very third stanza, into the expected praise of the young lord is injected the hint:

> *Save in somme thynges that he was to blame,*

and when he yields to his people's courteous petition that he marry he firmly insists on making his own choice of a bride. He is called *thoghtful* when he first addresses Griselda and he wears a very serious *(sobre)* look when he presents her to his people. It is his persistence in testing her which troubles most readers and this objection Chaucer faces with a direct admission:

> *But ther been folk of swich condicion*
> *That whan they have a certein purpos take,*
> *They kan nat stynte of hire entencion,*
> *But, right as they were bounden to a stake,*
> *They wol nat of that firste purpos slake.*

This is what we now call an *idée fixe*. Yet in his defense of Walter Chaucer slips into a structural fault. At 460 ff. he adds (for the idea is not in Petrarch):

> *But as for me, I seye that yvele it sit*
> *To assaye a wyf whan that it is no nede,*
> *And putten hire in angwyssh and in drede.*

For this, seen in the light of the concluding moral, has the air of condemning the Most High for suffering us,

> *as for oure exercise,*
> *With sharpe scourges of adversitee*
> *Ful ofte to be bete in sondry wise.*

Some readers profess a low opinion of the Clerk's Tale as a poem, yet the skill with which Chaucer has met the inherent difficulties of the material is remarkable and is favorably comparable with what others who came after him have been able to do with it. His principal failure is in the reconciliation scene at the end. There for five stanzas he enlarges on a few sentences of Petrarch and contrives to make the marquis as unpleasant in explaining himself as he was in action. Chaucer harps on his favorite word *pitous,* but while he cunningly has Griselda think first of her children and then of her husband, he runs a grave risk when she tells them that

> *God, of his mercy,*
> *And youre benygne fader tendrely*
> *Hath doon yow kept;*

whereupon she swoons. His chief merit, however, from the present point of view, is his successful compromise with the irrational. Almost without apology or self-conscious justification he accepts the data, telling the story naturally as though it were natural, and with only a few overt omissions leaving the improbabilities to take care of themselves. This is in significant contrast to his handling of the similarly intractable material in the Man of Law's Tale.

The subject of the Franklin's Tale had many attractions and also certain disadvantages. The critical question would therefore be: Did Chaucer make the most of the former and do everything possible to mitigate the latter?

Assuming, as is now generally done, that the Tale was intended as a conclusion of the Marriage Debate—*an humble, wys accord*—we must agree, though with reservations, that the choice was adequate. The wooing of Arveragus has a Courtly Love coloring and his acceptance by Dorigen with due submission to *swich lordshipe as men han over hir wyves* declares the problem. We may wonder a little at his insistence on *the name of soverayntee . . . for shame of his degree,* but she acquiesces, in the spirit of *gentilesse.* This leads to the homily on mutual forbearance in both love and friendship and finally to the verbal sophistry of

Servant in love and lord in marriage.

The opening lines, moreover, contain many subtle anticipations of the situation to follow. Dorigen hopes there will never be any quarrel between them *As in my gilt* and she promises to be faithful even at the risk of heartbreak—*till that myn herte breste.* And in the *Auctor* comment on the virtue of patience, along with anger, illness, and wine as disturbing causes, are named *constellacioun* and *wo* and *chaungynge of complexioun,* any one of which last might account for her playful but rash promise to Aurelius. She had sworn to her knight

That nevere sholde ther be defaute in here,

and when the fault did appear it had to be accounted for.

There can be little doubt that Chaucer saw clearly and faced resolutely this difficulty, the peculiar action of his heroine. He elaborates on her distress, her almost pathological *hevynesse,* her *rage* in fact, over the prolonged absence of Arveragus—although this is undermined by the flippancy (to which we are accustomed)—

As doon thise noble wyves whan hem liketh.

Her neurotic state is still further emphasized by her obsession with the *grisly feendly rokkes blake* and her excited condemnation of a just God for creating such a maleficent *foul confusion Of werk,* and, at the end of her prayer, the quite feminine (though elsewhere Chaucerian) evasion of this moral issue, by leaving it to the *clerkes*. Even at the picnic arranged by her friends she is inconsolable. The reader is thus psychologically prepared for her rash promise, uttered *in pley,* as it were, when Aurelius has worked himself up to a declaration of his love. Some three hundred lines later, when Aurelius tells her that the haunting rocks have disappeared—Arveragus meanwhile is back from England, so that the irony of her wishing them away *for his sake* is somewhat diminished—and reminds her of her promise, she has nothing to say except, after Aurelius has left her, rather feebly to herself, that she had not supposed such *a monstre or merveille* to be possible. Her two-day-long compleynt (of only a hundred lines, however) may be set aside as a rhetorical convention, or at least taken as intended, to register her despair.[27] But before she resorts to suicide Arveragus returns again and directs her to fulfil her promise; and when she meets Aurelius *right in the quykkest strete* of the town, she answers his question,

> *half as she were mad,*
> *"Unto the gardyn, as myn housbond bad,*
> *My trouthe for to holde, alas! alas!"*

This is perfect. Chaucer has portrayed with complete success a gentle woman and loving wife driven almost to hysterical frenzy by perverse circumstances which she is helpless to escape. She misses being a tragic figure, but misses only narrowly.

Has Chaucer done as well by her husband? Our first hint of the 'character' of Arveragus, after the courtly wooing, is that he stipulated for *the name of soveraynetee . . . for shame of his degree;* he would be technically *Servant in love* but still *lord in marriage.* And it cannot be denied that his treatment of Dorigen at the crisis is masterful, even though he had sworn that he would never assume any *maistrie Agayn hir wyl;* nor can it be denied, either, that he did not consult her wishes when he bade her to keep her promise to Aurelius. Less than two years after the wedding he leaves her for knightly exploits abroad,

> *For al his lust he sette in swich labour,*

and remains away two full years, meanwhile sending her occasional letters that *he wol come hastily agayn*. When he does return he is not suspicious, for he had agreed never to be jealous; and when he hears her story,

> *This housbonde, with glad chiere, in freendly wyse,*
> *Answerde and seyde as I shal yow devyse:*
> *"Is ther oght elles, Dorigen, but this?"*
> *"Nay, nay," quod she, "God helpe me so as wys!*
> *This is to muche, and it were Goddes wille."*

The first words here are ambiguous: their friendly tone implies comfort, but with an undertone of 'Are you keeping anything worse from me?' Dorigen's answer is just right. His next words are surprising: You have made a promise and you must keep it. I love you so much that I had rather be killed than have you false to your oath, for

> *Trouthe is the hyeste thyng that man may kepe.*

Then he bursts into tears and says: Keep this dark and I will bear up as best I can—

> *As I may best, I wol my wo endure—*

with no thought of *her* woe and no recognition that her marriage troth to him should take precedence over such a reckless impulsive promise as that she had given to Aurelius. This looks, on any realistic view, like the ethics of expediency, to say nothing of masculine selfishness and egotism. But realism is out of court here, for our poet finds it necessary to compromise the character of Arveragus in the interests of the story's requirements. It has been claimed that Arveragus had a sure premonition of the Squire's generosity; but that is groundless and even absurd. Arveragus, that is, Chaucer, thought only of one thing, to prove the *gentilesse* of his hero by sacrificing his wife on the altar of an abstract principle. She had made her bed and should sleep on it, whatever the cost to him! Thus *trouthe*, fidelity to one's word, is exalted above every natural feeling; one virtue (which may not even be the highest, in spite of assertion) exalted above all others and all other considerations. The Friar would have called this a *schole-matere*, and so may we. But it is clear that Arveragus is *lord in marriage,* for he gives orders to his wife in the crisis; and the *humble, wys accord* thereby suffers impairment. Everything gives way to a limited concept of *trouthe.* A narrow logic supervenes over common sense and all human decency. As Arveragus sacrifices Dorigen to a principle, so Chaucer sacrifices his Arveragus. *This is th' ende,* which must justify the means.

The case of Aurelius is different. He is the conventional lover, the third side of a triangle, and might have been so left, a mere appurtenance of the plot. He might have been no more than the squire in the Merchant's Tale, though disappointed of his aim. In any event, he does not come off too well; for his conversion is rather sudden and unexpected and his ready adhesion to the *gentilesse* of Arveragus is hardly prepared for. In actual life such flashes of insight may be psychologically valid, but artistically they require careful handling to be made acceptable.

> *And in his herte he caughte of this greet routhe,*
> *Considerynge the beste on every syde,*
> *That fro his lust yet were hym levere abyde*
> *Than doon so heigh a cherlyssh wrecchednesse*
> *Agayns franchise and alle gentillesse.*

He might have thought of this before; or Chaucer should have thought of it before introducing him as *right vertuous, and riche, and wys.* And at the end his release of Dorigen is couched in needlessly legalistic terms:

> *I yow relesse, madame, into youre hond*
> *Quyt every surement and every bond*
> *That ye han maad to me as heerbiforn.*

This is not the language of a lover under emotional strain. It was unfair, moreover, that he should curse the day he was born because he had forfeited *his cost.* In his enthusiastic hopes of getting the lady's favor he might well say to the magician, *Fy on a thousand pound!* but now, even though he realizes that to pay the thousand pounds will beggar him he might be more philosophical about it. Would an hour or so in the garden have compensated for having to sell his *heritage?* But of course all this is

dictated by the requirements of the plot; he must be reduced to a
bleak despair in order to justify his appeal to the magician and
thereby test the magician's nobility.

But in spite of these recessions from art Chaucer has done
something quite special for the young squire: he has given Aurelius a touch of that same madness which makes Dorigen also
such an interesting study. This first appears in the stumbling
incoherence of his declaration of love:

> *"Madame," quod he, "by God that this world made,*
> *So that I wiste it myghte youre herte glade,*
> *I wolde that day that youre Arveragus*
> *Wente over the see, that I, Aurelius,*
> *Hadde went ther nevere I sholde have come agayn. . . .*
> *Heere at youre feet God wolde that I were grave!*
> *I ne have as now no leyser moore to seye."*

It appears even more plainly in the *ravyng* of his prayer to
Apollo—

> *For verray wo out of his wit he breyde.*
> *He nyste what he spak, but thus he seyde: . . .*
> *Lord Phebus, cast thy merciable eighe*
> *On wrecche Aurelius, which that am but lorn. . . .*
> *Wherfore, lord Phebus, this is my requeste—*
> *Do this miracle, or do myn herte breste . . .*
> *Lord Phebus, dooth this miracle for me.*
> *Preye hire she go no faster cours than ye:*
> *I seye, preyeth your suster that she go*
> *No faster cours than ye. . . .*
> *Lord Phebus, se the teeris on my cheke.*

This is the *anguisshous* language of desperation and despair. One
need only recall the conventional stiffness of the prayers of Palamon and Arcite and Emily to feel the difference. Although
Arcite suffered from the Lover's Malady of Hereos, we were only
told about it; we did not suffer with him. But we share the
anguish of Aurelius, unworthy though its cause may have been;
and this does much to offset the treatment of him later.

The two other figures have no particular interest. The brother of Aurelius introduces the magician and thus the rich astrological details which Chaucer lavished on him for the sake of verisimilitude. The brother seems to have been somewhat dilatory or slow-thinking, for he allowed Aurelius to suffer *in languor and in torment furyous Two yeer and moore* before he remembered his old fellow student of Orleans; after that he drops out. There is no question of the magician's competence or of Chaucer's familiarity with the subject; and his special knowledge goes a long way to produce our willing suspension of disbelief, if it was really needed. About the actual accomplishment of the miracle Chaucer is deliberately vague—

> *for a wyke or tweye*
> *It seemed that alle the rokkes were aweye.*

No more: no one goes to see. Aurelius simply *knew* it and Dorigen accepts it sight unseen. Dorigen's incuriosity may be taken as a reflection of her emotional distress: she is by now ready to believe anything. But Chaucer's refusal of what would have made a fine dramatic scene calls for some explanation. Here he differs from the *Filocolo*, which is generally regarded as his source; for there the lady says, "faretelomi vedere domani," and next day a large company enter the miraculous garden and gather flowers and fruits. (So also he differs from Boccaccio later when the husband is more humane than Arveragus in his treatment of Dorigen.) One might surmise that Chaucer was reluctant to admit the full powers of the magician in spite of his elaborate preparations to enforce plausibility. The splendid display before supper in which Aurelius saw himself dancing with his lady was well enough, but an illusion covering nearly the whole coast line of France was something too much. The more probable reason however is simply that Chaucer was less interested in the story as drama and in its noble precept,

> *Trouthe is the hyest thyng that man may kepe,*

than in the final catch question: *Which was the mooste fre?*

The story is told to illustrate and enforce a moral, and so it does; more than one, in fact; and it leads to the bright question: Which was the most generous? Yet this same story, when examined closely, is found to be set up in terms which are questionable. The more Chaucer did to make it humanly interesting and not merely an artificial confection, the more he exposed the underlying fallacies. By making Dorigen a real person and Aurelius (in part) a real person he was obliged, in unfortunate contrast, to reduce Arveragus to a plot-ridden fiction. Or else we must find excuses for the conduct of a husband who obliges his wife to fulfil a promise made in circumstances of unusual strain, which she had no reasonable expectation of fulfilling, and in violation of her prior and predominant marriage vow of fidelity— an impossible situation which could only lead to tragedy, and for which the poet substitutes sophistry. In short, what began, before Chaucer took hold of it, as an intellectually amusing apologue has become, when rationalized and transposed into human values, absurd. Moreover, when to this is added the tricky question, which was the most generous, a fresh set of fallacies emerges. Arveragus tried to give what he had no moral right to give (except his own humiliation, which is hardly considered); Aurelius gave up what he had no right to ask; and little is made of his moral rehabilitation, and that little negatived by his later attitude. Where then is their generosity? But the magician did give up his due reward for services rendered; and if it be objected that his services were evil, it may be urged that Chaucer nowhere indicates a desire to condemn them as black magic. He only says that in *those* days black magic was common, though Holy Church *now* condemns it. For the purposes of his story Chaucer had to allow it; otherwise his story would collapse. But surely it was not Chaucer's purpose to exalt the magician.

The upshot, then, the æsthetic moral, is that nothing artistic can be made of so many complex elements without undue sacrifice of ordinary ethics; and the greater the air of naturalness such a story is given, the greater the risk of exposing its unnaturalness.

Thus the Franklin's Tale, as a treatment of rational and irrational elements, betrays Chaucer's predicament. He was drawn to the subject by its obvious or superficial attractions, which he enhanced by calling it a Breton *lai* with its remote setting in time and place. The remoteness gave him both the picturesque décor of the rocks and the magic element which could go unquestioned. After a fashion the story offered the appearance of a balance between the extremes of sovereignty and subservience in marriage: husband and wife go through a crisis and come out reconciled and happy. Whatever is fortuitous, arbitrary, and artificial in both plot and characters should be accepted with a most willing suspension of everything which makes a plot credible and a character interesting.

Dorigen comes alive; Aurelius comes alive in two or three passages; Arveragus never. Arveragus plays his part as the story requires: he comes and goes, with too obvious manipulation; he asks no questions when no questions are necessary; he is not jealous or even considerate, for if he had been alert he might have known about his neighbor Aurelius; he says what is expected of him; as lord in marriage he plays the selfish, dominant husband, when a word of sympathy to his trapped wife would have given him form and pressure but spoiled the story; he comes out with *Trouthe is the hyeste thing that man may kepe,* a fine *sententia* of limited application, when he should have said: 'My dear, we must find some way to spare you the consequences of this trickery'; he walks into the trap, when he might have said: 'See here, young man, . . .' But that would have been a different Arveragus and a different story, an Arveragus insubservient to the plotted 'moral.' So much for the character of the hero.

These strictures are irrelevant and inconsequent from a certain point of view; but they are necessary to offset the florid enthusiasm of such criticism as that which calls the Franklin's Tale "the last word in the cultivated literature of the fourteenth century" and speaks of "the essential fineness of character, which we would call decency, of Arveragus and Dorigen" and asserts that "the dilemma . . . depends for the credibility of its solution entirely upon the skilful preparation of their characters . . . characters who . . . are so wholly likable."[28]

Finally, these observations are not, and are not meant to be, adverse criticism. They are not inconsistent with a great admiration for the skill and care which Chaucer devoted to the task of making the most of the opportunities offered him by the story.

For the Franklin's Tale has peculiar interests hardly found else-where in his poetry, and one is bound to wonder if the idea of a Breton *lai,* whether real or imagined, did not somehow stir his fancy and spur him to try his powers with something exotic.

If the people of a story are to pass as human beings, the reader's sympathy must be in the right quarter. As a preparation for the final question it is likely that Chaucer meant our sympathies to be equally divided among all four. Are they? He has succeeded with Dorigen, in spite of her rash promise; and with Aurelius, in spite of his attempt to obtain the embraces of a faithful wife by unfair means. But he was not so successful with Arveragus and he all but admitted failure when he wrote:

> *Paraventure an heepe of yow, ywis,*
> *Wol holden hym a lewed man in this,*
> *That he wol putte his wyf in jupartie.*
> *Herkneth the tale, er ye upon hire crie;*
> *She may have bettre fortune than yow semeth.*

The subtle shift of point of view *upon hir crie* instead of *upon him crie* is very cunning; but neither this evasion nor anything the poet can say quite meets the case. At the beginning of the Tale we were well disposed towards Arveragus, but he gradually loses credibility. As for the magician, we admire his skill and accept his performance with indifference to its ethical bearing. We are not much concerned even if he turns out to have been the most generous.

But regardless of modern praise and appreciation, it is Chaucer's own method which is here in question. In his zeal for adding human interest to the apologue, for making the story seem *real,* he contrived to bring two of his main characters alive, while neglecting the third, who had to play the determining role. For what is perhaps most remarkable is this failure (as I see it) with Arveragus, the seeming failure to recognize that if the poem was to illustrate and enforce the edifying lesson of fidelity to one's promise it was necessary that Arveragus, who insists on the virtue of *trouthe* at all costs, should himself have a strong case. His character required not only knightly qualities and the firmness of insisting on his rights as husband, but also something of the strangeness which goes a long way towards explaining the conduct of the Marquis of Saluces, and just that narrowness of the conception of right conduct which would almost necessitate his peculiar attitude towards Dorigen's promise. It may be said that he does exhibit these qualities—but too late. The story as story breaks down just at the crucial point because of his character, that is, because his command to Dorigen is unmotivated and unprepared for. *Lord in mariage* is a mere technical defense: Chaucer does not offer it. We were ready for all the other implausibilities of the plot (or nearly all), but there was no provision for Arveragus' insistence on the great virtue he is supposed to stand for. He should have been the strongest and most redoubtable figure of the poem, with from the outset a marked leaning to literal rectitude or at the least a finical adherence to the minutiae of ethical finesse. This might have made him an unsympathetic figure, but it was inevitable if his attitude and action at the great crisis were to correspond to the dictates of the plot. There is no reason to doubt that Chaucer might have succeeded in this also, or come near succeeding, if he had seen fit to try. At least, one likes to think so.

Thus the Franklin's Tale is not to be taken quite seriously as a representation of actual life; it is more like what the French call *littérature;* and I dare say Chaucer would be the last man in the world to wish it taken seriously. In fact, by turning it all into a game or riddle at end—Which. . . ?—he may have hinted (along with the two not very sly witticisms) that we should regard the Tale as something from the realm of the higher nonsense. This notion could be further developed, remembering Chaucer's great sense of humor, as a specimen of the kind of joke which leads up, by specious logic, to an anticlimax. Arveragus, of whom we expected so much and from whom we get such a beautiful thought, turns out to be a sovereign fool, but he is saved from his folly by an inferior. Aurelius is willing to risk his fortune to satisfy his youthful infatuation, and loses on the very verge of winning. When the question of greatest generosity is posed, the answer is not, as you expected, the Knight or the Squire, but the poor clerk. All of which is, as Euclid would say, absurd.[29]

The Wife of Bath's Tale is a bipartite exemplum to enforce the claims of female sovereignty set forth in her long monologue: the one is *auctoritee* the other *experience,* as she had predicted. There is no doubt that the Tale was written for her, though it comes as a surprise to those who expected from her something as bawdy as her talk. Moreover, not to put too much confidence in certain branches of modern psychology, there may be an unconscious subtlety in her choice of the Loathly Lady as her protagonist, for not only would she fancy herself in that role as a way of renewing her *beautee* and her *pith,* but she could disguise a thoroughly immoral story by laying the scene in the other world of faery. Certainly the outline of events, divorced of their seetting, is improper to the point of cynicism: a young knight evades the penalty of rape and wins a beautiful bride, first through the intercession of King Arthur's queen and then through the help of an ugly hag who has him at her mercy, and all by answering a tricky question. His only merit is to recognize his position and accept its terms. But this is the rational view of the story. It is not Chaucer's. The opening lines give the key and, save for the Wife's little fling at limiters and the overlong sermon on gentilesse, which is dragged in as makeweight, the key is held consistently: we are always in the ancient days of King Arthur, when all the land was *fulfild of fayerye,* and elf-queens danced *in many a grene mede.* Even the inserted incident of Midas, with its covert jest at the end, belongs to the unreal world. (We may suppose that the Wife learned it from her fifth, but she makes it harmonize.) There may be a hinted stricture on courts of love, but it is very slight. There may be a small autobiographical side glance, for Chaucer himself had been up for rape, like the young knight of the Tale, and they both escaped the death penalty—

> *Paraventure swich was the statut tho—*

but this also is a mere passing note. For the rest, everything is in keeping, is irrational, is logical with the logic of its own realm.

What might look like collusion between the queen and the hag and what might look like mere cynical desperation when the knight leaves his option to her judgment are of a piece: they belong to fairyland. There is even a subtle marking of the distinction between the two worlds:

> *To every wight commanded was silence,*
> *And that the knyght sholde telle in audience*
> *What thyng that* worldly *wommen loven best,*

that is, women of the other, the real world.

This is Chaucer's achievement: to manage the supernatural without lapsing into even a pretense that it is anything but what it is, without mixing the molds embarrassingly. This is what he signally failed to do in the Man of Law's Tale, what he almost succeeded in doing in the Clerk's Tale, and all but botched in the Franklin's Tale, and what he succeeded triumphantly in doing with the Wife of Bath's Tale.

Beyond the misapplied or distracting realism of the Franklin's Tale, its amalgam in the Clerk's Tale, and its total absence in the Wife's Tale, there is one further step, and Chaucer took it in the Friar's Tale, which is pure realism *A per se*. The active presence of a devil looks like an invasion, but he is as natural and human a personage as the summoner himself; his simple statement,

> *I am a feend; my dwelling is in helle,*

is accepted by the reader with the same indifference to probability as by the poor summoner. The Tale has more criticism-of-life than more ambitious pieces like the Knight's Tale and is structurally superior to Chaucer's other similar poems. It has no false start like the Nun's Priest's Tale, with its misleading picture of the poor widow, or the Pardoner's, with its long prefatory sermon; it has no padding like the Wife's, with its story of Midas and its lecture on *gentilesse*. It is skilfully integrated into the Pilgrimage by means of the sharp altercation between Friar and Summoner at the beginning and the Friar's mock homily by way of epilogue. It has a steady progress, without interruption or lost motion: the summoner is introduced and described; he meets

the devil; their conversation gradually reveals both characters—
an attractive curiosity in the one and a certain modesty in the
other—and leads naturally to the anecdote, which being only a
third of the whole serves rather as a climax than as the essential
story. The Tale is thus not an anecdote with a long introduction, but a picture of the foolish summoner and the astute devil,
to which the closing anecdote gives point. The little ironies in
the exchanges between the two are delightful, and the latter's
patient explanation of how devils often forward the Almighty's
business adds a kind of weight. The conversation is easy and
natural, like the versification; there is almost no loose syntax or
doubtful meaning; the pronouns, in the absence of proper names,
are readily understood. There is no grossness as in the Reeve's
Tale or the Summoner's Prologue. And the language is both
appropriately colloquial and also adorned with striking words,
phrases, and lines: *ribibe, rebekke, virytrate, smale tytheres, pe-
cunyal peyne, dogge for the bowe, in a chayer rede,*

> *He was, if I shal yeven hyn his laude,*
> *A theef, and eek a somnour, and a baude.*
>
> *As ful of venym been thise waryangles.*

With the kind of poem which this aims to be Chaucer was
never more successful. Elsewhere—apart from the ever exceptional Miller's Tale, which has its own unrealistic indifference to
probability—he takes an amusing incident and builds it up by
accretion of more or less relevant matter, such as the rhetorical
inlays of the Nun's Priest's Tale or the discussion of Justinus and
Placebo in the Merchant's Tale. Here in the Friar's Tale the
incident is a functional part of the whole, which he has imagined
as a setting for it, and which beautifully complements the description of the Friar in the General Prologue. And whereas in the
Wife of Bath's Tale the supernatural presides without any intrusion of the natural, here the natural has fully absorbed its one
element of supernatural and everything is unified on a single
plane.

Note on Chaucer's Clerk: A Study in Ambiguities

There may be a little uncertainty about Chaucer's description of the Clerk. He appears to be a sympathetic figure, wholly admirable in his modest way; and so everyone has taken him. But following a hint from the recognized ambiguities in the description of the Prioress one may cautiously examine the details to see if Chaucer is using a little of the same method for his Clerk.

First of all, the Pilgrim Clerk is in obvious contrast to Hende Nicholas, also a *poure scholer of Oxford* (A 3190), for poor Nicholas did himself very well, with his room *Ful fetisly ydight,* his Almageste and other large and small books, his astrolabe, etc. From John and Aleyn in the Reeve's Tale one gathers that Chaucer had a low opinion of Cambridge men. The other clerk of Oxenford (D 527) was, like the Pilgrim, not *so worldly for to have office;* his unworldliness took a different form.

It is clear from the account of the Pilgrim in the General Prologue that he was poor and unworldly, and at present unambitious—he had not *yet* got himself a benefice or a secular office. The *yet* may refer to the advancement of his studies or more generally to the natural progress of his career; a benefice might follow in due course. About his Oxford studies Chaucer is not at all definite: he had long since got as far as logic—from which we can safely infer only that he had been some time at the university. A glance at Rashdell[1] will show how complex was the system or how irregular the procedure. Perhaps the poet himself was not too familiar with the Oxford curriculum. Ordinarily the first two years, at this period, would be devoted to grammar and logic (*logica utens* or method, a training in dialectic and disputation); in the fourth year would come Responsions, followed by Determination, which would make the student a Bachelor; and after that he could obtain a license from the Chancellor to teach or give "extraordinary" lectures in the afternoons. It would seem, therefore, that *unto logyk hadde long ygo* can only mean that he had entered on his course of studies at the university a long time since. Now "the average age for Determination at Oxford can hardly have been less than 19 or 20";[2] our Clerk would have entered at the age of thirteen to sixteen; and if he was already a Bachelor (which Chaucer does not say) he and the Squire would be the youngest of the Pilgrims.

Was the Clerk in minor orders? an acolyte? *tonsuratus?* Since he prayed for the souls of his friends and benefactors he had presumably received the first tonsure. Chaucer does not say so, however, but emphasizes the Clerk's devotion to study—

> *Of studie took he moost cure and moost heede.*

May we gather that he was more interested in study for its own sake than for what it would lead to? that he was the studious type, content to learn and learn because he liked learning? The nature of his studies may be partly gleaned from his implied wish to own the works of Aristotle—unless this is only a preparation for the pun on *philosophre*.

The *Twenty bookes, clad in blak or reed* is a puzzle which seems not to have bothered the commentators. In the first place, did he have twenty books or did he not? He would rather have had . . . than . . . ; but a few lines later we hear that he spent on books and learning all he could get from his friends. On the other hand, the indicative, *hym was levere,* should be significant, and the sense would be that he preferred to have his twenty books rather than fine clothes and musical instruments (like Hende Nicholas); that is, he did have twenty books. In the second place, twenty books, however clad, would be a considerable library for a poor student to possess. His patrons must have been both wealthy and generous. To be sure, *bookes* may mean works or titles rather than volumes; the Wife's Jankyn, sometime an Oxford student, had six or seven books *bounden in o volume.* Even so, our Clerk would have had a complete Aristotle. For the list of Aristotle's works in Appendix B of Ernest A. Savage's *Old English Libraries* (London, [1911]), contains only fourteen titles recorded for the twelfth, thirteenth, and fourteenth centuries. The concentration on Aristotle is also a little surprising, for one would have expected to hear of a few books on divinity; or perhaps the Clerk had these in addition to his philosophical library. In the third place, his Aristotles (if he had them) were bound in black or red. Most of the manuscript volumes which survive and have not been rebound by collectors are in yellowed skins; the exceptions are the sumptuous bindings for wealthy owners.[3]

Moreover, the Clerk was not only a studious but a silent young man. He spoke only when it was necessary to speak and then only *in forme* (in a formally correct manner, or with a sort of formal stiffness?), and in *reverence* (humility or devoutness?)—seven lines below, the Sergeant of the Law is ironically described as *of greet reverence*—and brief and *quik* (vivid or lively), and full of profound (real, or apparent, for one so young?) wisdom.

The final couplet is likewise curious. The Clerk's speech was *Sownynge in moral vertu* in apparent contrast to the Merchant's, a few lines above, which was *Sownynge alwey th' encrees of his wynnyng. And gladly wolde he lerne*—this by way of repetition for emphasis or perhaps to suggest that he profited by his conversation with other students—*and gladly teche.* This last is so neat and so familiar that we may miss its significance. Does it mean that he looked forward after finishing his university course to a career as teacher? or that he mingled instruction, freely offered, in his conversation with others? The *wolde* implies that he was accustomed both to learn and to teach; but *gladly teche* might also mean that he would be, or was, glad to teach if and when the opportunity offered. *Gladly* may mean habitually as well as willingly.

The account of the Clerk in his own Prologue need not agree at all points with his earlier description, but there is actually no great inconsistency. The Host jocularly accuses him of meditating a sophistry and calls for a merry tale without a display of rhetoric—we should hardly expect it, but the Host could have been wrong or merely teasing—and without preaching; and he obliges with the Griselda story, in fairly simple language, though it is not exactly merry and certainly has a homilectic ending. One is only surprised that the poor Clerk has some time before this made his way to Padua and been on terms of easy familiarity with the great scholar Fraunceys Petrak. One is also a little surprised at the boldness with which he apparently takes up the Wife of Bath's challenge and openly rebuts her views in the final stanza and the *Lenvoy;* but here we face what can only be called a change of plan on Chaucer's part and is not to be reckoned pro or con in the interpretation of the Clerk's 'character.' Or is it perhaps the other way around? that Chaucer knew what he was about all the while? The description of his Clerk in the General Prologue was deceptively mild, and the ambiguities, barely visible at first and therefore easily misunderstood as portraying a gentle, studious fellow, now reveal their true colors. Even the Host was a little taken in by his shy reclusive manner; but he spoke truer than he knew where he suspected him of studying *aboute som sophyme*—for the Marquis, tempting his wife as the Most High tempts and tests us all, for our *exercise,* is himself a figure of sophistry.

But the Clerk's abstraction was only a partial mask. Mixing with the Pilgrims did not so much bring out his hitherto latent tendencies to satire, but rather gave him an opportunity to show the real character which Chaucer had delicately hinted at but cunningly held back. The Clerk was no hypocrite, to be sure: he really enjoyed books and the Oxford life, and all that he could get from his friends he used to keep himself in residence. He was not worldly, neither was he excessively religious. He knew how to suffice unto his own *good* though it was small. He knew also the advantages of travel, yet he was far above the vagabond scholars. He enlarged his scope, modestly of course, by foreign study, stopping probably in Paris and Bologna and elsewhere; and at Padua he met and made himself agreeable to no less than the distinguished and elderly Petrarch and doubtless many other notables, including Lignano. (The pilgrimage took place, supposedly, in 1387. The Clerk would have been, if he went up at the age of thirteen—which is likely, considering his eagerness for learning—at the most twenty; that is, at the most, seven years old when Petrarch died, in 1374.) Petrarch, however, showed him, as they were discussing philosophy and more general topics of human conduct *(moral vertu)*, his Latin prose piece about Griselda; and now years later on the road to Canterbury he remembers it well enough to reproduce it in full detail, with an occasional oblique cut at that Bath Woman (who was likewise deceived at first and thought him harmless). He even speaks with kindly disparagement of Petrarch's opening paragraph. Only Chaucer had appreciated the Clerk's subtleties from the outset, but he was in no hurry to set them forth. The Clerk had got as far as logic, he was continuing his studies, but he preferred the life of a student to a real *office* or the routine of a benefice. He spoke little, but what he did say was lively and properly respectful, and naturally with emphasis on serious subjects; for he was no goliard. We may be sure he was a good talker when occasion arose and when he was with people like Petrarch—from such people he could learn. And now when the Host calls for a story he can make the most of his talents: gladly teach—teach the Wife of Bath that not all clerks are fools and teach the Pilgrims not only how gratifying humility can be in women, but teach them also the larger lessons of Christian patience and fortitude; and finish off with a flourish of transcendant mockery.

It is a highly wrought and shrewdly developed character study which Chaucer here offers us as we now can recognize when all the parts are fitted together, a masterpiece in the Master's best manner. Or so it would seem if we follow the most eminent Chaucerians, of the line and plummet school, in the glorious art of *glosynge*. We recall, for example, Manly's note that if the Prioress was not from the convent of St. Leonard's at Stratford "she might well have been," or that "possibly" the Squire's Tale was a story which his father, the Knight, had heard on one of his campaigns in the Near East. But there is no harm in these embroideries if they are not taken seriously. We recall also Lawrence's statement that "The satirical passage at the end of the *Clerk's Tale* is after all spoken by the Clerk . . . and must be considered as characterizing him. The rubric *Lenvoy de Chaucer* is a scribal blunder."[4] And though the manuscripts have "Lenvoy de Chaucer," we recall also Kittredge's deliverance: "It is not Chaucer who speaks, but the Clerk of Oxenford, and every word is in perfect character."[5] These are but a few of the many such critical dicta, well meant, but tainted with an air of priestly guardianship which no one would resent sooner than Chaucer.

Note on the History of the Clerk's Tale

The variations in the manuscript tradition of the end of the Clerk's Tale and the conflicting views of scholars as to the appropriateness of the Envoy to the Clerk leave us with still another unsolved problem. The following hypotheses, so far as they can be justified by what evidence we have, may throw a little light on Chaucer's methods and supplement the brilliant work of Mrs. Dempster.[1]

The initial assumption is that Chaucer's rendering of Petrarch's Latin into stanzas, the 'original' Clerk's Tale, was an independent poem written either before the so-called *Canterbury Tales* period or at least not written for the Clerk, and certainly before the conception of a Marriage Group. This poem would comprise the present ll. 57-1162, or perhaps through l. 1169.

The next stage is the assignment of the Tale to the Clerk for its eventual position in the *Canterbury Tales.*[2] For this Chaucer would have written the Prologue, or a draft of it, and the Host stanza (ll. 1212a-g) to follow either l. 1162 or l. 1169.[3] Thus far there is no overt mention of the Wife of Bath, although there are latent connections which seem now to have more or less direct reference to her or her Tale.[4] Moreover, at this stage, including Petrarch's moral, the Tale is an illustrative parable of Christian fortitude and forbearance in the face of God's way to man. Whatever emphasis on the husband's sovreignty the story might seem to carry is removed or at least greatly reduced by the Petrarchan moral.

When the "Lenvoy de Chaucer" was written and added to the Tale can only be conjectured. It must have been, in the first instance—or why the title—just what it says: the poet's own envoy. It could even have been part of the earlier version; and if so the *lat no clerk* (l. 1185) would be a general statement without reference to the Pilgrim. It would be an effective afterpiece for Chaucer's own oral delivery of the poem, a fine rhetorical flourish and climax, satirically disposing of the whole story—Griselda and Petrarch both.

The fourth state is Chaucer's deliberate use of the Clerk and the Clerk's Tale to answer the Wife's argument for the submission of husbands. Certainly the Griselda story *seems* to illustrate the husband's ascendancy, though its theme is the wife's submissiveness, and Petrarch's moral gives it a different turn. It does well enough, however, in its new function; well enough, at any rate, to satisfy Chaucer, and so we may leave it. The hitherto latent connections now take on noticeable emphasis and the addition of ll. 1170-1176 signals the direct attack. This stanza, which contains the only specific reference to the Wife, is lacking in the twenty-four manuscripts of Manly's group *d**, and "those having the Envoy arrange the last three stanzas so as to end with l. 1200."[5]   Hence it would seem that this group of manuscripts represents a stage of the whole process before the final arrangement, i.e., before the Clerk's Tale became a reply to the Wife of Bath.   That they are all later manuscripts than El-*a*,[6] which contains the final arrangement, only signifies that their common ancestor did not have access to the revision which we have in El-*a*.

This stage, with its addition of ll. 1170-1176, introduces the problem of the Envoy, for it makes the Envoy appear as a deliverance from the Clerk himself, or seems to do so.   Critical opinion has been sharply divided on this point.   Tatlock, for example, said flatly: "The *Envoy* is egregiously out of character for the Clerk"; on the other hand, Kittredge and Lawrence accept it enthusiastically as *in* character for the Clerk, in spite of the manuscript evidence, *Lenvoy de Chaucer,* followed by all the editors, and in the face of Chaucer's description of the Clerk in the General Prologue and in the Prologue to his Tale as a quiet young man—*Noght o word spak he moore than was neede,*— and *that* was spoken in *reverence* and *Sowning in moral vertu.*   There are ways of resolving this contradiction, to be sure, but they really amount to admitting that Chaucer for his own reasons altered the character of the Clerk to suit the new situation.

But another possibility is worth considering, which, while it has its own weakness, is quite as reasonable as assigning the Envoy to the Clerk, and which has the advantage of conforming to the manuscripts' *de Chaucer.*[7]   Either the Envoy belongs to a pre-*Canterbury Tales* version (as suggested above), or it was added to the Clerk's pre-Marriage Group version and marked as Chaucer's, not the Clerk's, in an early manuscript and the heading retained in all its descendants. A corollary to this would be the possibility that the new stanza, ll. 1170-1176, is also the poet's rather than the Clerk's.   That is to say, after the Clerk has ended his Tale the poet steps forward, addressing both the listeners and the Wife herself—*Ne lat no clerk*— and delivers his palinode to the Griselda story.   The ambiguity of allowing the Envoy thus to seem like the Clerk's, though plainly marked as his own, would accord well with Chaucer's often extravagant humor.

This possibility has of course the drawback of being what Tatlock called, apropos of Justinus' reference to the Wife of Bath in the Merchant's Tale (E 1685), a *dramatic impropriety,* an intrusion by the poet into the dramatic scheme of the *Canterbury Tales* framework. Other examples of this impropriety are the Summoner's *My prologe* (D 1708) and the punning use of *poynt* at the end of the Canon's Yeoman's Tale (G 1480).   And the dual meaning of *I* in the General

Prologue, Chaucer the Pilgrim and Chaucer the poet, may well persist through the subsequent links.

The fifth and last stage of this history is simple and clear: the cancellation of the Host stanza, with its unimpressive hint of the Host as abused husband, the transposition (if necessary now) of ll. 1207-1212 of the Envoy to the end, the writing of the Merchant's Prologue, with its echo *Wepying and waylyng,* and the transfer of the motif of abused husband from the Host to the Merchant, to be used by the Host with more effect in the Merchant's Epilogue and again in the Monk's Prologue. This transfer is an obvious device to launch the Merchant's Tale, but it must have been an afterthought. It provides a kind of reason for the Merchant's pilgrimage, but principally it forges the links of the discussion of marriage, though not quite on the Wife's theme of sovereignty.

THERE have been divergent views of the so-called Epilogue to Chaucer's *Troilus,* ranging all the way from full acceptance to total denial of its appropriateness or consistency with the poem. Probably no wholly satisfying answer to the questions it raises will ever be found, partly because it involves other questions, equally difficult, concerning the general interpretation of the poem, and partly also because Chaucer himself has opened the way to conflicting opinions.

I

As the story ends, Pandarus has the last word, and it is very effective: *I hate, ywis, Cryseyde.* But he at once adds what is thoroughly characteristic of him, though otherwise anticlimatic: What I have done I have done in your interests, Troilus, regardless of my own honor or rest; this treason of hers is a grief to me; *I kan namore seye.* When Pandarus is speechless we may be sure he is deeply moved. Then the poet adds: Fortune continued her way, leaving Troilus to weep—

> *Swich is this world, whoso it kan byholde:*
> *In ech estat is litel hertes reste.*
> *God leve us for to take it for the beste!*

The poem continues, however, for seventeen more stanzas, which show, says Tatlock, Chaucer's "lingering unwillingness to make an end."[1] Lingering, certainly, and highly miscellaneous. Two stanzas, largely from Benoit, tell us that Troilus often met Diomed in battle. Then come three stanzas, in perhaps too light a tone: the first refers us to Dares for the martial details; the second urges all women readers to absolve the poet for the infidelity of his heroine; and in the third the poet says he would rather write of faithful Penelope and Alcestis—

> *N'y sey nat this al oonly for thise men,*
> *But moost for wommen that betraised be*

> *Thorugh false folk. God yeve hem sorwe, amen! ...*
> *Beth war of men, and herkneth what I seye!*

Then follows a stanza of farewell to his book, *litel myn tragedye;* then a stanza with the prayer that his poem will be faithfully copied and rightly understood; then a stanza (from Boccaccio) describing the death of Troilus at the hands of Achilles. Now follow three stanzas, not in the first draft of the poem, borrowed from Boccaccio's *Teseida,* describing the translation of Arcita; then a stanza taken from the *Filostrato:*

> *Swich fyn hath, lo, this Troilus for love!*
> *Swiche fyn hath lo his grete worthynesse!*
> *Swiche fyn hath his estat real above,*
> *Swich fyn his lust, swich fyn hath his noblesse!*
> *And thus bigan his lovyng of Criseyde,*
> *As I have told, and in this wise he deyde.*

The emphasis is properly on Troilus, and significantly Chaucer omits Boccaccio's epithet "vilana" for Criseyde. Next come the two troublesome stanzas exhorting all young people to turn from worldly vanity and love only Him who died on the cross to save our souls. Then a stanza in the very vein of Pandarus, echoing, almost mocking, the anaphoristic *Swich fyn...*:

> *Lo here of payens corsed olde rites....*

This is the way Jove, Apollo, Mars, and *swich rascaille* reward their followers, this is the end of the wretched world's *appetites,* this is the poetry of *olde clerkis*—but not a word against the god of Love. Finally, the dedication of the poem to moral Gower and philosophical Strode and the impressive prayer to the Holy Trinity, from Dante. A medley of seventeen stanzas, with twelve different subjects, shifting back and forth from grave to gay, this Epilogue may well seem puzzling and leave us wondering what Chaucer meant by it.

II

The first answer is literary tradition: a pious ending to a worldly poem is conventional. There is abundant mediæval precedent, and parallels to the *Lo here* stanza may be found in Guido and Benoit: they may have contributed something indirectly. But we shall agree with Tatlock that here "Chaucer was in no sense following a mere convention," and perhaps even agree "That Chaucer was sincere in this quasi-retraction of his great love poem goes without saying." Chaucer's sincerity is not in question, or rather it is not *the* question. No doubt there is something here of "the age-long dispute as to the right attitude for a Christian man toward pagan poetry"; the whole poem shows a conflict of pagan and Christian loyalties which was inevitable in the mediæval treatment of such a story with such a background. More than this, the poem comprises a whole series of dualisms which have been skilfully held in solution until the very end. One solvent was of course the Comic Spirit strongly supported by Pandarus. Another is the poet's announced detachment in the proem to Book 1 and his frequent assertion of his own irresponsibility for everything: the story comes from old books and after all, and in all, he is merely following his author Lollius. There is a great deal, he frequently insists, which is out of harmony with his contemporary standards of conduct; and when he comes to the climactic scene on that rainy night at the palace of Pandarus he issues an express apology:

> *I kan namore, but of thise ilke tweye,—*
> *To whom this tale sucre be or soot,—*
> *Though that I tarie a yer, somtyme I moot,*
> *After myn auctour, tellen hire gladnesse.*

Here he is thinking not so much of the conflict of past and present, of pagan and Christian feeling, as of the difference between conventional ethics and the conventions of *amour courtois* which he has taken over from Boccaccio and adopted as a literary convenience and which he has felt obliged to follow, for the purposes of his narrative, in spite of their conflict with his own ethic and that probably of most of his readers. The religion of Love and the religion of the Church, each orthodox in its place and each heterodox to the other, are continually blended all through the poem, until the Epilogue. The poet serves the servants of the God of Love but abides himself in outer darkness; he prays to *God so dere* both for those who are in despair and for those who are *at ese* in Zion; and over and over again the language of one religion is transposed into that of the other without any sense of incongruity or blasphemy. Examples are hardly needed, but it will be recalled that when Pandarus first finds Troilus overcome with love he charges him with *som remors of conscience or attricioun;* in Troilus' song at the end of Book III, Love is a fine fusion of both Gods; and so on. How far Chaucer will go when it suits his purpose may be seen in the exclamation of Pandarus—

> *"Immortal god," quod he, "that mayst nought deyen,*
> *Cupid I mene, . . ."*—

and more seriously in the prayer of Troilus when he believes Criseyde is dead—

> *And Atropos, make redy thow my beere.*
> *And thow, Criseyde, o swete herte deere,*
> *Receyve now my spirit!*

How boldly he can risk outright blasphemy is revealed in his paraphrase of St. Bernard's supplication to the Blessed Virgin, at the beginning of *Paradiso* XXXIII:

> *Donna, sei tanto grande e tanto vali*
> *Che qual vuol grazia ed a te non ricorre,*
> *Sua disianza vuol volar senz' ali,*[*]

in Troilus' 'prayer' while he first lies with Criseyde in his arms:

> *Benigne Love, thow holy bond of thynges,*
> *Whoso wol grace, and list the noght honouren,*
> *Lo, his desir wol fle withouten wynges.*

So much for the mingling of heavenly and earthly love: it is rich in comic overtones.

Another dualism which Chaucer accepted with great readiness is the treatment of love according to the code and love as a natu-

---

[*] So mighty art thou, Lady, and so powerful that one who desires grace and comes not to thee—his desire would fly without wings.

ral human experience, that is, literary convention and simple realism. Chaucer had his English readers to think of. It was well enough for Boccaccio to follow the code: his readers were familiar with many of its practices if not with its formal theories. The Prologue to the 'Legend of Good Women' tells us something of how English readers took it, but within the poem itself there are evidences that Chaucer was not at all times comfortable with it. The principal actions of the poem conform and both Troilus and Criseyde subscribe: they nowhere reveal any sense of what ordinary ethics (and the Victorian critics) would regard as immorality; they are guilty of no sin. The emphasis on secrecy is merely part of the code. With Pandarus, however, who is the mainspring of the action as well as the immediate representative of the Comic Spirit, it is different. He looks both ways. He follows the code, he lectures Troilus on it; but he is conscious both of his own cunning, not altogether innocent of downright deception, in stage-managing the two lovers, and of his own ambiguous position: he is a loyal, devoted friend of Troilus but he has also cast himself in the unseemly role of go-between. He seems at times too indecently eager to bring his two lovers to bed. Chaucer recognizes this. The morning after his success there is a brief serio-comic meeting between Pandarus and Criseyde. He rallies her about the storm's interfering with her sleep and asks her how she feels.

> *Criseyde answerde, "Nevere the bet for yow,*
> *Fox that ye ben! God yeve youre herte kare!*
> *God help me so, ye caused al this fare*
> *Trowe I," quod she, "for al youre wordes white.*
> *O, whoso seeth yow, knoweth yow ful lite."*

Not that she has any regrets for what has just taken place, but that she wants him to know that she sees through his machinations; and she has always been slightly resentful of his continual pushing her about. Then comes the remarkable line:

> *And Pandarus hath fully his entente.*

This is in a way the real climax of the poem. After this there is no more laughter. But Troilus is exalted and sings his glorious

song to Love: he has felt *a newe qualitee* within him and Love
has *altered his spirit so withinne*. He has found salvation, according to his religion.

A third dualism, akin to the first, but more troublesome because so much has been attached to it, is the opposition of Fate,
or Fortune, and the Divine Foresight and man's free-will—what
has been called Chaucer's determinism.[2] It is a subject which appears in various places, some appropriate and some not, through
Chaucer's poetry; and usually he is inclined to turn it off with a
cheerful "this I leave to the professional theologians." His long-
est treatment of it (based directly on Boethius) is in the middle
of Book IV of the *Troilus:* eighteen stanzas which he added both
to Boccaccio's and to his own version of the story. Here, on a
generous accounting, it may be said to have a little the effect of a
prayer, and to represent Troilus' desperate attempt to find comfort in his misfortune; but artistically it is a blemish, and the
parenthetic *nowe herkne, for I wol not tarie* betrays that Chaucer
was thinking more of the reader than of Troilus. In truth, the
last stanza of it reveals the function of the whole inserted passage.

> *And over al this, yet sey I more herto,*
> *That right as whan I wot ther is a thyng,*
> *Iwys, that thyng moot nedfully be so;*
> *Ek right so, whan I woot a thyng comyng,*
> *So mot it come; and thus the bifallyng*
> *Of thynges that ben wist bifore the tyde,*
> *They mowe nat ben eschued on no syde.*

This is hardly Chaucer notifying us of the deterministic basis of
his poem, least of all Geoffrey Chaucer wrestling with his own
soul over a private problem. It is not so much Troilus trying to
wring comfort from despair, as the poet facing his artistic difficulty. What with the fascinations of his heroine and the exaltation of his hero, transfigured by the beneficent power of Love,
he approached the end of his poem with misgiving. Although he
announced at the very outset that Criseyde would forsake Troilus
and both by subtle hints and open declaration frequently reminded us of her eventual infidelity, somehow the story kept

moving in a different direction. This is not a matter of the inconsistent characterization of Criseyde or even of Criseyde portrayed as a developing character. Chaucer could say, as we can, that with all her good qualities Criseyde was *weak*—

> *Tendre-herted, slydynge of corage,*

and no match for the frontal attacks of sudden swift-moving Diomed. Many a woman before and since has been deeply in love and afterwards faithless. He could also say, in his own defense, if we should urge against him that his Criseyde of Book v is positively not the Criseyde of Book ii and Book iii—he could reply that we misjudged her before we had all the evidence; we saw how she would act at home in Troy with Troilus in love with her, we could not yet see how she would act in the Greek camp in utterly different circumstances. But these are shifty arguments. The point is that as the story developed before our eyes we were not, in spite of the warnings, prepared for Criseyde's treachery, her *treason* as Pandarus finally called it. And Chaucer saw this and was unhappy about it; hence, *inter alia,* his eagerness to defend his heroine. Boccaccio had his reasons, personal and other, for giving us a faithless Criseida; Chaucer had accepted from Boccaccio the data of his story, but he altered and improved so much that his end would not quite fit his beginning. He therefore, somewhat in desperation, turned back for Book v to his other sources and superimposed their Criseyde upon his own, without trying very hard to smooth out the differences, even in such a trifling detail as her height. He was, as one might say, caught in a snare. When he saw it before him he lightly called in predestination:

> *Ek right so, whan I woot a thyng comyng,*

and so on. The change in Criseyde was in her stars; he could appeal to

> *Almyghty Jove in trone*
> *That woost of al this thyng the sothfastnesse,*

and so absolve himself.

It would be absurd to dismiss the problem of Fate and predestination as a mere literary convenience, as it would also be idle to raise the question of Chaucer's personal orthodoxy. But the sense of an over-ruling power pervades the poem, sometimes called *the fatal destyne* or more poetically *Fortune, executrice of wyrdes,* or more lightly

> *Fortune .*
> *That semeth trewest whan she wol bygyle,*

and sometimes, as in the soliloquy of Troilus in the temple,

> *That forsight of divine purveyaunce,*

and is summed up in the couplet:

> *For al that comth, comth by necessitee:*
> *Thus to ben lorn, it is my destinee.*

It may be expressed in Christian terms or in pagan: Troilus uses the word *God* eight times in his seventeen stanzas of argument and ends by appeal to *Almyghty Jove.* It hovers above the doom of Troy, it dictates the exchange of Antenor and the separation of the lovers, it determines the character of Criseyde and that of Diomed also, the *ineluctabile fatum.* For a moment Troilus considers the possibility of free will but is soon lost in the complexities of Boethian logic; and elsewhere in the poem Chaucer is silent. It will not do therefore to say (as some have done) that Troilus and Criseyde decide their own fate, that Troilus chose to fall in love with Criseyde and she chose to return his love, or that later she was free to reject the overtures of Diomed. Such is not the sense of the poem, nor is it the philosophy of Boethius, Chaucer's authority. Almost the last words of Philosophy to her philosopher are: "whiderward that thou torne it, thou ne maist nat eschuen the devyne prescience . . . althogh that thou torne thiself by thi wil into diverse acciouns." Her admission "thanne is ther fredom of arbitrie, that dwelleth hool and unwemmed to mortal men" is only a subtle evasion: it does not go beyond the paradox as Tennyson put it: "Our wills are ours to make them thine"; the old subterfuge, which Chaucer understood, of conditional necessity. But the question is really of no importance in the *Troilus*. What must be kept in mind is that the poem, its actors and their actions, are under the sway of fate, fortune, destiny, and in some sense the divine will, all intermingled as a general over-ruling power, as elsewhere in this poem the terms of pagan mythology are intermingled with the terms of Christian theology.

III

If one inquires what is the *moral* of the poem, assuming that the question is at all a proper one, the answer is not obvious. Chaucer has provided one just before the Epilogue which fits well enough the background of fatalism: philosophical resignation—

> *Swich is this world, whoso it kan byholde:*
> *In ech estat is litel hertes reste.*
> *God leve us for to take it for the beste!*

The wheel of fortune stands before us. We had heard this a little before:

> *Thus goth the world. God shilde us fro meschaunce,*
> *And every wight that meneth trouthe avaunce!*

and earlier still, in Book IV, from Pandarus:

> *Swich is this world! forthi I thus diffyne,*
> *Ne trust no wight to fynden in Fortune*
> *Ay propretee.*

But this is hardly enough. Boccaccio also had offered a simple moral drawn not so much from his poem as from his experience with Fiammetta: a warning to young men to take example from Troilo and avoid the "appetito rio," for "Giovana donna è mobile"; but there is also the "Perfetta donna" who desires to be loved and delights in loving: "queste son da seguire"; let her pray for Troilo:

> *Ch' el posi in pace in quella regïone*
> *Dov' el dimora, ed a voi dolcemente*
> *Conceda grazia sì d'amare accorti,*
> *Che per ria donna alfin non siate morti.**

*. . . that he may rest in peace where Love dwells, and that Love may kindly grant you the grace so to love that you shall not die in the end for an evil woman.

The emphasis is on Maria's failure—"Criseida vilana"—but the hope of a better and wiser love is not excluded. Chaucer gave no heed to this. He borrowed the appeal "O giovanetti," but altered the rest.

Reconsider now the story. Troilus, at first a proud scorner of Love, sees Criseyde at the spring festival, is converted, and becomes an ardent worshiper; through the energetic aid of Pandarus and his own merits he wins her love; they are happy together for more than a year; then through the fortunes of the Trojan war they are separated, and while he, faithful always, mourns her loss she falls prey to the wiles of Diomed. Throughout the poem Troilus has but one religion, that of Love. He is neither pagan nor Christian but always a devout follower of *amour courtois,* an embodiment of the best elements of the code. He has no thought, commits no act, which is not in perfect harmony with the tenets of his religion. He is loyal even unto death. Love rewards him first with the possession of his beloved and also by the spiritual ennoblement of his whole being. The sensual is not minimized, neither is it exaggerated (except by Pandarus), and the spiritual exaltation of Love's worship is dwelt upon over and over. The beneficent power of Love is announced early in Book I:

> *evere it shal byfalle,*
> *That love is he that alle thing may bynde,*
> *For may no man fordon the lawe of kynde....*
> *Now sith it may not goodly ben withstonde,*
> *And is a thing so vertuous in kynde,*
> *Refuseth nat to Love for to ben bonde.*

It is celebrated at the end of Book I, it is hymned in the proem to Book III, it is glorified in the great Song at the end of Book III— in these places and elsewhere—but always with reference to Troilus. We are not permitted to feel the ennobling influence of love in Criseyde, for the simple reason that she is destined to prove false, and also because the story is his story and her role is the subordinate one of being the object of his love.

Yet the God of Love is not omnipotent. Above him stands Destiny, guiding his affairs now for good, now for ill, and most visible in the greater affairs of Troy. A small incident, the capture of Antenor, sets everything wrong. We are brought back to the philosophy of fatalism, with this difference, however, that passive acceptance—*God leve us for to take it for the beste*—opens the way to tragic protest. In the Epilogue Chaucer called his book a tragedy and added *litel* only in a mock-modest tone. The central theme now appears to be Fate's disastrous interference with the course of true love: Fate, fickle Fortune, the Divine Will, the Something-not-ourselves, all combine to overthrow love. But no; this will hardly do. The tragic answer is either abject, crushed submission or proud, unsubmissive defeat, and neither is the proper issue of a romantic love story half of which is told in the spirit of a comedy of manners. It will not do to charge Chaucer with a failure to fuse potentially tragic material and a serio-comic tale of Courtly Love.

The tragic aspects of the *Troilus* deserves a further word, and even if the critic now exceeds his commission the risk is worth taking. The chosen components of the poem have been so elaborately mingled that perhaps no completely harmonious solution was possible; Chaucer may not have foreseen the total complexity of his problem or may even have dismissed it too lightly; but the critic, who has not the same responsibility, can fairly submit his *ex post facto* analysis as a trial both of method and of ultimate estimate of Chaucer's success, which is brilliant in so many ways, and of his failure, which is disheartening in comparison.

Enough has been said of the Courtly Love element; it pervades the poem both as story and as treatment. It is the framework and without it the story would not exist. But it cannot be blamed for the catastrophe. (See Note on the Code, below.) Troilus is its ideal lover and illustrates the code at its best. Criseyde, when she is false to Troilus, is also false to the code. She is the one to cry

> *All mine, all mine the sin. The love*
> *I bore him was not deep enough.*

Pandarus teeters on its edge. He betrays it when he becomes unpleasantly aware of the other ethic, he supports it when in his function as go-between he exerts himself to satisfy the lovers. His genuine friendship for Troilus and his blood relationship to Criseyde render his functional duties difficult, but Chaucer has done what could be done to keep him in line—not however without allowing his own awareness of the double standard to show through. It is only the modern moralists who, not accepting the code even as a literary device, fall into confusion between the two modes and impute sin to Troilus for loyalty to his own religion and hence his downfall to his having accepted a code which they regard as immoral. But nearly all the great love stories end unhappily and the moral we draw from them is the uncertainty of human happiness.[3] We do not repudiate earthly love; nor did Boccaccio. What he said is that not all women are to be trusted, for some of them are "volubil sempre come foglia al vento." What Chaucer could well say is that although the loves of Troilus and Criseyde came to grief there is a love which never betrays. What he seems to say is that young people should turn their hearts from earthly vanity to the love of God; but he cannot mean that they should all forsake the love of kind and substitute for it the divine love. Is it possible that he did not express himself clearly? or that in saying the conventionally expected he gave way to a little too much enthusiasm? Life *is* a vanity fair, but not altogether. Criseyde did her poet a greater wrong than she did her lover if she betrayed him into generalizing her weakness into a pattern of all women. That this is what some of his readers did is apparent from the Prologue of the 'Legend of Good Women,'—if we can take more seriously the charges of the God of Love than we can take the defense by Alceste.

Recently the problem has been attacked on a different front.[4] Chaucer's poem on the twin sorrows of Troilus is but the *De consolatione philosophiae* writ new. The Chaucerian catharsis is not *vanitas vanitatum,* but the folly of submitting to Fortune; nay, more, Troilus is not the victim of chance or the victim of inevitable destiny. Like the speaker in the *De consolatione,* he is the victim of his own failure. He forsook reason; for "in alle thingis that resoun is, in hem also is liberte of willynge and nillynge" (Bo. 5, p. 2). Troilus is "a man who has allowed himself to be

elevated spiritually by 'good' fortune. Having achieved this emi-
nence, he is beset by 'evil' fortune or adversity, before which he
falls." He "turns from the way and seeks false worldly satisfac-
tions, abandons reason and becomes subject to Fortune." In
other words, Troilus sinned in willing to love; he is a replica of
Adam, who subjected himself to Eve; he followed Adam's "tropol-
ogical fall": "the temptation of the senses [Criseyde], the corruption of the lower reason in pleasurable thought [the worldly wisdom of Pandarus], and the final corruption of the higher reason,"
all lead to "confusion, despair, and death." But what evidence
is there that Chaucer saw his subject in the light of Boethius'
attempt to reconcile free will and divine foresight? Chaucer
over and over in the poem emphasized the power of Fortune
along with the controlling power of God: Troilus was destined
to love and lose. Even in the inserted Boethian passage in Book
IV he got no farther than balancing predestination and free will
and concluding that what will be will be. A better question
would be: From the poem of *Troilus* what can we infer to have
been Chaucer's concept of tragedy? The simple mediæval concept, to be sure, of a fall from happiness to unhappiness. What
more? Is the *Troilus* a tragedy in any other sense?

In the Greek and the modern sense tragedy springs from a flaw
in the hero's character, a flaw of which he may be unaware, or
from some conflict of forces outside himself which he cannot be
expected to control. If Troilus and Criseyde were the helpless
victims of the combined powers of fortune and divine guidance,
or if they sinned in yielding to the power of human affection, the
poem has high tragic implications. Chaucer's adherence throughout the poem was plainly with the former alternative, but he
never represents them as victims. Only in the last-minute conversion of Troilus and his contrast of heavenly felicity with the uncertainty of earthly pleasure did Chaucer assert that since Troilus
had loved and lost it would have been better not to have loved
at all, and dismiss his poem as the work of ancient poets and the
damnable pagan gods.

Is this dualism of pagan and Christian theology, so cheerfully
accepted by Chaucer and up to the finale so well blended, the

double moral of the two religions (the religion of Love which exalts the hero and betrays him because one woman was weak, and the religion of Christ which repudiates the world as a vanity fair) conducive to true tragedy? Or does it so confuse the mind that in the outcome neither element preponderates and each one loses cogency? The answer, it seems to me, must be that Chaucer was an incomparable storyteller, not a tragic poet, that he did not conceive his subject in terms of tragedy in any Aristotelian or Hegelian sense. It cannot be too often repeated that his use of Courtly Love was a literary convenience enabling him to handle a situation sometimes salacious and fundamentally immoral to the common view as though it were genuinely moral and even ennobling to the hero. But this brought with it a series of data inimical to human or tragic interest, a hero who as lover is not heroic, a heroine whose role is to return the love and then betray it, a go-between whose persistent gaiety offsets the sorrows of Troilus in winning his lady.

"I could think so little," said Henry James, "of any situation that didn't depend for its interest upon the nature of the persons situated, and thereby on their way of taking it." Troilus has in the poem no character to meet this test; he responds to love but not to suffering. Criseyde has two characters, one given by Chaucer and one by the inherited story—however reconciled or reconcilable—but neither quite of natural growth. In truth, the *double sorwe of Troilus* and the double character of Criseyde yield two different subjects: one (half of the poem) immensely alive with comedy, the other merely pathetic. The happiness of love

> *That altered his spirit so withinne,*

at the end of Book III, has made a new Troilus, but when faced with the suffering of Criseyde's desertion he returns to the ineffectual pathos with which he was introduced. Troilus is what Pandarus and Criseyde made him; without them he is uninteresting.

True, Boccaccio and Chaucer gave him one fine moment, when he cries

> *O Criseida mia, dov' è la fede?*

and Chaucer following closely but with more moving words—

> *"O lady myn, Criseyde,*
> *Where is youre feith, and where is youre biheste?*
> *Where is youre love? where is youre trouthe?" he seyde....*
>
> *"Who shal now trowe on any othes mo?*
> *Allas! I nevere wolde han wend, er this,*
> *That ye, Criseyde, koude han chaunged so; ...*
>   *Allas, youre name of trouthe*
> *Is now fordon, and that is al my routhe....*
>
> *"Thorough which I se that clene out of youre mynde*
> *Ye han me cast; and I ne kan nor may,*
> *For al this world, withinne myn herte fynde*
> *To unloven yow a quarter of a day!"*

The simplicity, dignity, and moderation of Troilus here are very fine. We feel sympathy for his suffering, but he remains only a pathetic figure. The real tragedy, which was Criseyde's, Chaucer did not touch. To have developed the latent tragedy of her situation, her brightness and beauty dwindling as soon as she leaves Troy, her moment of self-realization in the presence of the crude Diomed, when she acknowledges her weakness, her feeble efforts to recover as she slides backward, would have made a different poem, which was not what Chaucer set out to write and which— one says this hesitantly—he was incapable of writing. He had sowed the seeds of it when at the beginning he emphasized her timidity—

> *Criseyde, which that wel neigh starf for feere,*
> *So as she was the ferfulleste wight*
> *That myghte be.*

For a time this seemed to be untrue, but when she was alone, among the Greeks, it returned for her undoing. The seeds of treachery were also in her father's treason and her uncle's shifti- ness; but Chaucer neglected the opportunities of showing her moral disintegration because his subject was still the double sorrow of Troilus.

It will not do, on the other hand, to excuse Chaucer for missing the tragic import and possibilities of his tale by saying that he came too late to grasp the significance of Courtly Love as tragic material; for we have Malory, a full century later, as witness against him. It is rather that Chaucer's mind and artistic gifts were not tempered towards the tragic conception of human experience. Pity he understood. But terror or fear in the Aristotelian sense was not in his reading of life—not as we know him from his works, and therefore it may be a critical error to charge him with failure in this field. His gifts were for comedy, for a close observation and portrayal of human frailty and a cheerful, smiling condonement of such frailty. We may feel here perhaps, as Matthew Arnold felt, without alleging the right reasons, a want of high seriousness, or of high artistic integrity, which is perhaps much the same. It is something of course to recognize his improvements over the *Filostrato*. But when he took over so much of Boccaccio's fable and Boccaccio's code of love, it is to be feared that he did not thoroughly explore the consequences of the alterations and improvements which he added. By making Pandarus so different and Criseyde so different he assumed responsibilities for the outcome which he may be thought to have shirked. In Book v he faced a dilemma, looked about for other helps, fell into contradictions and almost seems to have lost interest. He certainly subjected the Book to no careful revision. If we can trust the text (iv, 26-28) he expected to finish the poem in four books, but instead prolonged the story with Troilus' sentimental excesses of pity and pathos as though he could not bring himself to face the final disaster. And at the end he quite threw up his hands crying 'All is vanity'—which is *not* the moral of his fable.

Another solution was possible, but it was not Chaucer's, and may appear here as a gratuitous grace-note. Since Chaucer was not bound by Boccaccio's purpose in writing for his Fiammetta, he was really free to alter the ending; but, as he of course felt, a Criseyde who was not false would make quite a different story. He might have found, however, in Dante a hint for replacing the laughter of Troilus in heaven with a vision of the Criseyde who had failed as a beatified image of the true Criseyde. There he would have had a conclusion both logical and consistent—the final glorification of Love—and, if such seemed necessary, a conclusion pious and uplifting in the terms of the essential story. As Dante's poetry began with romantic love and moved, after the death of Beatrice, to the great vision of the *Divina Commedia,* so, after the death to Troilus of his Criseyde, she might have become for him the symbol, purified of its human dross, of that merging of earthly and heavenly love which transcends our limited experience and ennobles by the imagination both mind and spirit. For Troilus the love which betrays here below would become an approach, a guide, to the divine love; Criseyde forgiven and transfigured would become "la gloriosa donna della mia mente." This would have been the rightful climax and just reward of Troilus' devotion to his God.

IV

Instead, we have the laughter of Troilus in heaven—"a peal of celestial laughter," Root calls it—his scorn of this wretched world and its earthly pleasures. (It is a wonder that no one has cited the Psalmist: "He that sitteth in the heavens shall laugh.") Here is the supreme difficulty. It is only intensified by the appeal: *O yonge, fresshe folkes. . . .* It has been condemned as a contradiction and defended as a proper moral "implicit in the whole poem."

In Chaucer's first version there was no celestial laughter. The death of Troilus was immediately followed by Boccaccio's rhetorical but natural

Swich fyn hath, lo, this Troilus for love!

then the address to all young people, suggested no doubt by Boccaccio's "O Giovanetti" but going far beyond Boccaccio's limited warning; and this is followed in turn by the condemnation (rather mockingly expressed) of the paganism of the poem. Here we recognize the rightness of Tatlock's stricture: "The feeling in the Epilogue is in no way foreshadowed at the beginning or elsewhere; it does not illumine or modify; it contradicts. . . . He tells the whole story in one mood and ends in another." But remembering that Chaucer was a mediæval, we might find ample extenuation in literary convention and in the mediæval principle that a good story deserves a good moral, more or less fitting—a Christian, even a Catharist, moral.

Chaucer was not content, however, to leave it so. He inserted three stanzas meant, as Tatlock charitably suggests, "to avoid too abrupt a shift from sympathy to detachment." That is, "piety with a pagan touch forms a transition from pagan worldliness to Christian devoutness." This may well be. Boccaccio set the trap with the closing prayer for Troilo:

> *Ch' el posi in pace in quella regïone*
> *Dov' el dimora—*

in that region where Love dwells. The trap was sprung by Chaucer's recalling Boccaccio's own three stanzas in the *Teseida* on the translation of Arcita. We do not know why he rejected these stanzas in the Knight's Tale (assuming that the 'Palamon and Arcite' came first); we can only guess why he introduced them into the *Troilus*. But here they now are.

In rendering these stanzas from the *Teseida* Chaucer takes a few liberties. There is some uncertainty about which sphere Arcita attains: Boccaccio is, as often, not too clear in his language and the *Troilus* manuscripts are at variance.[5] Chaucer adds pictoral vividness by his apparent mistranslation of

> *a cui intorno il mare*
> *girava e l'aere e di sopra il foco.*

But the interesting difference is between the laughter of Arcita:

> *e seco rise de' pianti dolenti*
> *della turba lernea, la vanitate*
> *forte dannando dell' umane genti,*
> *li quai, da tenebrosa cechitate*
> *mattamente oscurati nelle menti,*
> *seguon del mondo la falsa biltate,*
> *lasciando il cielo;**

* and then he laughed at the sorrowful complaints of the delicate crowd, greatly condemning the vanity of mankind, who, foolishly darkened in their minds, follow, from shadowy blindness, the false beauty, abandoning heaven.

and the laughter of Troilus:

> *And in hymself he lough right at the wo*
> *Of hem that wepten for his deth so faste;*
> *And dampned al oure werk that foloweth so*
> *The blynde lust, the which that may nat laste,*
> *And sholden al our herte on heven caste.*

Chaucer's *lough* repeats Boccaccio's *risi* (and more remotely Lucan's "risitque," *Pharsalia,* IX, 14); but compare Dante's gentler "sorrisi" in a similar situation (*Par.* XXII, 135). Boccaccio's *la falsa biltate,* however, has become *the blynde lust,* just as in the preceding stanza

> *e ogni cosa nulla stimare*
> *a rispetto del ciel**

has become

> *and fully gan despise*
> *This wrecched world, and held al vanite*
> *To respect of the pleyn felicite*
> *That is in hevene above.*

Chaucer has not only expanded, he has strengthened, intensified the language to match the heightened vigorous language of his appeal to the *yonge fresshe folkes.*

The surprise, however, is that Troilus is translated to a Chrisian heaven and at once made fully acquainted with its *pleyn felicite.* We were accustomed throughout the poem to a mingling of pagan and Christian terms and the modernization of pagan ideas into mediæval ideas, always with the solvent of Chaucer's humor and a pervading sense of the oneness of humanity. Troilus we knew was a devout worshiper of his God and his recompense was naturally to be transported to the heaven of Love; but from the heaven of Love he could never look down with contempt on this wretched world as a vanity fair. This runs counter to every tenet of his religion and every meaning of the poem. By substituting *the blinde lust* for "la falsa biltate," says one scholar, Chaucer has "emphasized Troilus's confession of his

---

* and everything of no value in respect to heaven.

own folly." What folly? Troilus has been guilty of no folly. He has loved not wisely but too well (if you like), but it is not folly to love a woman with Troilus' devotion, and it is no derogation to human love such as his that his beloved forsakes him. The same scholar seems to regard the loves of Troilus and Criseyde as "a temporary affair": that *is* folly, for it is not true to Chaucer's text. There is no sign in the poem that Criseyde would have been unfaithful if there had been no separation, no exchange of prisoners, no exposure of her to the desolation of absence and to the masterly seduction by Diomed. She was weak, she was false to love as Troilus was true, she deserves perhaps less excuse than Chaucer, and we, are willing to offer. But while they were together they were bound by the same pledges, the same oaths, in the terms of the ethic to which they subscribed and by which they lived as though their union had the ecclesiastical sanction of

> *the bond*
> *That highte matrimoigne or mariage.*

G. K. Chesterton (to leave the scholars for a moment) contributes in picturesque language his own twist to this confusion. "In a series of verses of great beauty and power," he says, Chaucer "gives his ultimate decision that happiness is not to be found by dancing after any heathen god of love; but by looking up . . . to where a more terrible but a more tender god of love hangs, not on Olympus but on Calvary." That is to say, Troilus, son of the King of Troy, should have delayed a few centuries, until after the Crucifixion: he should simply not have been a pagan, for no pagan can find happiness.

It may be suspected, moreover, that the reason—or part of it— why many readers have welcomed the about-face of Troilus (his "realization of his folly"), and probably Chaucer's for providing it, is their uncomfortable feeling that there has been something shady and illicit about the whole love affair. They cannot reconcile themselves to the cardinal principle of secrecy in Courtly Love and so cannot accept Courtly Love as a literary convention. This is of course to their credit as moralists but reveals a certain want of detachment as critics. As one scholar exclaims: "Mar-

riage is so obviously impossible that neither of them suggests it,"
neither Troilus nor Criseyde. But if Troilus had gone straight
to Priam and said: "Father, I love Criseyde and wish to marry
her," the exchange could have been avoided and everybody made
glad. There might have been a small crisis in the government,
but no tragedy. The city would still have a valiant defender, a
happy warrior, and Love would be doubly triumphant because
sanctified by marriage. But no: the lovers insisted on remaining
secretive; when the exchange was proposed they were obliged to
hide their shame and take the tragic consequences. Yet when
Troilus gets to heaven he recognizes his folly; he *should* have gone
to his father, or to a Priest of Holy Church, or better still, he
should not have allowed himself to fall in love. Now he repents
and condemns his old ways, and all the pleasures of this our
transitory life as well. Thus the standards of modern morality
are preserved and loose living punished by loss of love and loss
of life—at some sacrifice of artistic probity.

And finally, Chaucer's hesitation, not to say confusion, is betrayed by the different tones manifest in this patchwork Epilogue:
the offhand reference to Dares for martial details; the apology for
Criseyde; the leavetaking of his poem; the translation of Troilus
to the Fixed Stars (or perhaps the Moon) and his sudden awareness of Christian *felicite* in Heaven, followed immediately by his
being turned over to Mercury; the exhortation to all young people
to love only Jesus; the sarcastic dismissal of the whole story as
ancient paganism; the half-serious dedication to Gower and Strode
(let them *correcte* whatever is amiss); and the wholly serious
prayer to Christ and the Trinity. He has finished a romantic tale
of simple, sensuous, and passionate love, with an ideal lover betrayed by a weak faithless heroine. The mixed elements remained
soluble until now, when he looks back and is not too confident.
It is too late to admit embarrassment, but he can at least end
with a smiling deprecatory gesture to the benighted heathen and
with a genuflection to the High Altar:

And loveth hym, the which that right for love. . . .

Love may have two meanings. Here it becomes almost a pun: heavenly and earthly love.

One word more, beyond all the sophistications of argument: it is the word of a man who was a lesser poet but a greater humanist than Chaucer, a poet whose understanding sympathy found the true solution, which (as Sir Herbert Read has told us) produces "a real"—one must even say *the* real—"*catharsis*." For Henryson had the last and the right word.

> *O fair Cresseid! the flour and* A-per-se
> *Of Troy and Grece, how was thou fortunait, . . .*
> *I have pity thee suld fall sic mischance!*
>
> *Yit nevertheles, quhat-ever men deme or say*
> *In scornful langage of thy brukilness,*
> *I sall excuse, als far-furth as I may,*
> *Thy woman heid, thy wisdom, and fairnes,*
> *The quilk Fortoun hes put to sic distres.*

Instead of an address to all young people to forsake this world, there is Cresseid's heart-wrung appeal—

> *O ladyis fair of Troy and Grece, attend*
> *My misery, quhilk nane may comprehend,*
>   *My frivoll fortoun, my infelicitie,*
> *My greit mischief, quhilk na man can amend.*

Instead of Troilus's laughter in heaven there is his epitaph for her:

> '*Lo! fair ladyis, Cresseid of Troyis toun,*
> *Sumtyme countit the flour of womanheid,*
> *Under this stane, late lipper, lyis deid!*

Troilus' love is once more ennobled by this, and Criseyde's self-punishment, of which leprosy is but a symbol, is the realization of her own failure. What precluded Chaucer from seeing and saying this is not for us to know; we can only guess; but we are reminded by it that nowhere (certainly not in his story of Custance or his story of Virginia) does he sound the note of true pity for the men and women who must suffer the strokes of fortune.

Note on the Code

The poem ends properly at v. 1750: Criseyde now loves Diomed, great is the sorrow of Troilus, Fortune has had her way, and such (heaven help us) is life. This was enough. But somehow it did not satisfy Chaucer; and so his rescission in the Epilogue and his Retraction at the end of the Parson's Tale (if the list there is genuine) have given birth to a special heresy. This critical heresy, that the Epilogue is Chaucer's repudiation of Courtly Love, is advanced with great confidence by two eminent Chaucerians and is echoed by an impressive list of still others. (See Robinson's note, 2nd edition, p. 837.) Says Lawrence (*Shakespeare's Problem Comedies,* New York, 1931, pp. 148-49):

To Chaucer, on the other hand, the tale reveals ultimately only the hollowness of the service of Love. Troilus dies in profound disillusion; Criseyde lets passion lead her into breaking both the natural and the conventional laws of true love. What is the answer? Well, Love is not the deity for men to serve; they should put their trust in God, who will treat no man falsely. . . . In short, the story is, in the hands of Chaucer, an attempt to analyze the validity of the conventions of love by a minute examination of a specific instance, which leads to the decision that those conventions break down as a rule of life.

Says Kittredge (*Chaucer and His Poetry,* Cambridge, 1915, pp. 143-44): "Yet we come more and more to suspect that Troilus was right in his first opinion of lovers:

> *O veray fooles, nyce and blynde be ye!*
> *Ther nys nat oon kan war by other be.*

We come to suspect

that the principles of the code are somehow unsound; that the god of love is not a master whom his servants can trust. And then, suddenly at the end of the poem, when the death of Troilus had been chronicled, . . . the great ironist drops his mask, and we find . . . that he has no solution except to repudiate the unmoral and unsocial system which he has pretended to uphold. . . .

This manifestly involves an utter abandonment of the attitude so long sustained, and therein lies its irresistible appeal.

One questions how far the appeal of the *Troilus* lies in the poet's adoption of the chivalric code, for the purposes of his story, through eight thousand lines and his repudiation of it in an Epilogue. It implies a miracle of genius. Or does it imply that the poem is to be read as a tract?

To show that Chaucer meant to repudiate Courtly Love at the end of the poem it would be necessary to prove that the tragedy is consequent on his choice of the code as a basis of his fiction, that the unhappy outcome is due to the acceptance by Troilus and Criseyde of the social and ethical conventions of the code. But this is impossible. Both lovers recognize the statutes of secrecy and honor, but neither of them regards their love as illicit in any moral sense. (Only Pandarus is out of line, when he permits his practical realism to intrude, but even then he follows the rules in his function as go-between.) It is true that the requirement of humility renders Troilus less active as a lover than we should prefer in a hero, but Chaucer offsets this by his martial vigor; and while this may weaken the story for modern readers it in no way precipitates the catastrophe. The catastrophe springs from Criseyde's weakness, which does not invalidate the code, and even more from the controlling power of Destiny, which separates the lovers and exposes her weakness. Both of these tragic elements are outside the code.

Even the death of Troilus is curiously detached, almost an afterthought picked up from *thise olde bokes* and following the grand dismissal of the story, *Swich is this world.* . . . The city has lost one of its stoutest warriors, second only to Hector, but nothing is said of this, or of any general lamentation as at the death of Arcite. And, what is more significant, his death is not presented as a tragic culmination, as his punishment for having lived and loved according to a false code, as it would have to be presented if Chaucer meant to repudiate Courtly Love.

It is a narrow interpretation, therefore, which would explain the hero's translation and apparent denial of the faith by which he has lived as a sudden revelation of heavenly felicity and thus the poet's acknowledgement that one of the important elements of his story was all wrong. It is merely perverse to reason that his God has betrayed him and therefore his was a false god and to be repudiated. Nor does Chaucer hold this: he says that as soon as Troilus reaches heaven he despises all the changes and chances of this wretched world and condemns all our pursuit of transitory pleasures. Neither Troilus in heaven nor the poet in his appeal to young people actually forbids the love of mortals, although Troilus seems to include human love in the *blynde lust, the which that may nat laste.* It is true that worldly life is *al vanite* compared with the felicity of heaven. It is not true that therefore men should forsake the love of kind.

Just before the Epilogue, says Tatlock, Chaucer "draws a worldly conclusion; then after dismissing his book and rounding off the story, he ends in a loftier vein . . . a devout transcending of all earthly love." And finally, "on the whole, the ending is a return from the Renascence to the Middle Ages." Perhaps so. He went back to Boccaccio and transposed Boccaccio's exciting, heady tale into something unattempted yet in English prose or rhyme; and when it was framed in the sophisticated assumptions of *amour courtois* it became almost impossibly complex. But he gave it all he had. He ran full sail before the wind, pennons flying—and then found himself on a lee shore. He had, for a time, the best of both worlds, sacred and profane; he kept them weaving and unweaving with a dazzling success. What wonder then if having poured his libation to Venus he saw fit to light a candle to the Holy Trinity. But this is far from being a repudiation of the ethics of Courtly Love. It is more like a way of saying that "ancient Troy and modern England are different and you must not think that I advocate Trojan mores for young people nowadays." It is more like a last minute repetition of what he said at the beginning of Book II—

> *if it happe in any wise,*
> *That here be any lovere in this place*
> *That herkneth, as the story wol devise,*
> *How Troilus com to his lady grace,*
> *And thenketh, 'so nold I that love purchace,'*
> *I noot; but it is me no wonderynge.*

As people say, *ecch contree hath his lawes.*

CHAPTER V. OBSERVATIONS ON THE ART OF CHAUCER

THESE observations, starting with the Chaucerian laughter, inquire first by what means and to what ends Chaucer
applies his gift of humor to the criticism of life, and then
turn to a more general view of his style, its felicities and its way-
wardness. After this follow a note on the important but still
unsettled subject of his audience and a few illustrative notes on
his textual borrowings.

I

The laughter of Pandarus is usually pointed with malice or
innuendo, but Criseyde's is nearly always genuine. With it she
parries his efforts to maneuver her and when he *gan his beste
japes forth to caste* he

> *made hire so to laughe at his folye,*
> *That she for laughter wende for to dye.*

But when the separation is determined we are told that

> *The pleye, the laughter, men was wont to fynde*
> *In hire*

were all fled. Most remarkable is Troilus' memory of her laughing. When in Book v he rides past her empty palace he cries:

> *And yonder have I herd ful lustyly*
> *My dere herte laugh.*

It is one of his most poignant memories of her. And when she
left Troy she left laughter behind: Diomed noticed it—

> *nevere, sythen he hire thennes broughte,*
> *Ne koude he sen hire laugh or maken joie.*

Elsewhere the Chaucerian laughter is touched with scorn, or
has something unpleasant behind it. The examples range from
lat us laughe and pleye as spoken by the merchant's wife to her

husband, at the end of the Shipman's Tale, to *Woodnesse, laugh-ynge in his rage* in the Temple of Mars. There are only half a dozen exceptions. The Host laughs when the Knight's Tale is ended and things have started well, and the Pilgrims laugh, or most of them do, when the Miller has finished his Tale. The Host laughs when the Manciple has pacified the drunken Cook. The Wife of Bath had a hearty laugh—

> *In felaweship wel koud she laughe and carpe—*

and her fifth husband laughed when he read his *Valerie and Theofraste*. It is notably part of the praise of the Duchess that she could

> *Laughe and pleye so womanly.*

But this is about all. For most of the laughter is colored with mockery.

Smiles are not very common. There is the peculiar smile of the Prioress, the sarcastic smile of the miller in the Reeve's Tale, and the Devil's smile in the Friar's Tale, and the old hag's in the Wife's Tale, and the God of Love's in the Prologue to the 'Legende,' and Ariadne's smile at the *stedefastnesse* (itself a weighted word) of Theseus; and the wicked smile of the assassin,

> *The smylere with the knyfe under the cloke.*

In the *Troilus* there is this same obliquity of meaning. Troilus smiles at the folly of lovers and at Pandarus' quip when Criseyde is brought to his bed of sickness. Pandarus smiles at Criseyde when she betrays her interest in Troilus and she smiles when Pandarus thrusts the letter into her bosom and Cassandra smiles as she expounds Troilus' dream. Evidently for Chaucer a smile was not a politely unfinished laugh but a signal of malicious pleasure, of something withheld out of contempt or scepticism. Thus, reading backwards, it would seem that the Prioress' smile was professional rather than sincere; it was simple and coy like her Tale.

Chaucer does not often invite laughter in the modern reader; both in language and in situation he favors the shared smile. When the situation is gross the temptation to laugh outright is tempered by other considerations; for as a recent editor of *Punch* has told us, "Good taste is the enemy of humor." And so the element of incongruity which most analysts find at the root of humor shows also in the *tendre croppes* of the reader's appreciation. Emily at her prayers, Pandarus with his cushion, demoiselle Pertelote with her laxatives, the Host with his *rude speche and boold,* the Shipman with his closing puns, the Wife of Bath with her *experience,* even Alceste with her gracious but illogical apologies, make us smile. Laughter is inhibited by decorum.

On the other hand, there is wit, which is never quite harmless. It can be coarse and cheap; it can also aspire to the levels of art, when the mutual satisfaction of maker and recipient become æsthetic pleasure. For wit is a miniature drama—usually comedy, sometimes melodrama—a situation of meanings, a period of suspense while the mind reviews the possibilities, and a pleasing dénouement—sometimes a catharsis—when the purpose and the effect are recognized. But because its essence is swiftness the pleasure is likely to be ephemeral. Only the finest specimens are cherished in memory.

II

The pervasive humor of Chaucer's poetry sometimes opens him to the charge of not taking serious things seriously. It breaks out in the most incongruent places.

A catalogue of these misplaced levities would be tedious, but a certain number must be gathered up. Two of the most notorious occur in the Knight's Tale and have already been noted—

> *Fare wel phisik! go ber the man to chirche!*

and

> *His spirit chaunged hous . . .*
> *Arcite is coold, ther Mars his soule gye!*

(Fancy the gentle Knight talking like this.) In the Franklin's Tale, after Aurelius' desperate prayer, the Franklin says:

> *Despeyred in this torment and this thoght*
> *Lete I this woful creature lye;*
> *Chese he, for me, wheither he wol lyve or dye.*

On a larger scale is the brilliant tag to the Clerk's Tale, the
"Lenvoy de Chaucer," often fathered on the Clerk himself. Then
there is the gratuitous impropriety on the wedding night of Custance. After the delicate lightness of the introductory stanzas
of the *Troilus* the serious description of Criseyde is polished off
with Chaucer's

> *But wheither that she children hadde or noon,*
> *I rede it naught, therfore I late it goon,*

though he had just read in Boccaccio that she had neither son nor
daughter. Nor could he resist the same kind of Byronic flippancy
when he summed up her character in Book v,

> *Tendre-herted, slydynge of corage;*
> *But trewely, I kan nat telle hir age.*

In a spirit of music-hall levity he introduces the very serious first
Canticus Troili with

> *loo! every word right thus,*
> *As I shal seyn; and whoso list it here,*
> *Loo, next this vers he may it fynden here;*

and similarly, though in a more suitable context, the birds'
roundel is introduced:

> *The wordes were swiche as ye may heer fynde,*
> *The nexte vers, as I now have in mynde.*

The closing line of his 'elegy' on the Duchess of Lancaster is

> *This was my sweven; now hit ys doon.*

Near the end of the Man of Law's Tale, he says of Custance:

> *I may nat telle hir wo until to-morwe,*
> *I am so wery for to speke of sorwe.*

In the 'Hous of Fame' gaiety is in order, but

> *And nere hyt to long to endyte,*
> *Be God, I wolde hyt here write*

is rather strong. The 'Legend of Good Women' has its own
uneven balance between *game* and *ernest*, but was it necessary to
end the story of Cleopatra with

> *Now, or I fynde a man thus trewe and stable,*
> *And wol for love his deth so frely take,*
> *I preye to God let oure hedes nevere ake!*
> > *Amen.—?*

The burlesque description of the festivities before the grand tournament for Emily's hand has elsewhere been noted; there is also the salacious hint about the maiden rites of Emily in Diana's temple:

> *But hou she dide hir ryte I dar nat telle, . . .*
> *And yet it were a game to heeren al.*

Some of these errancies are explicable as a humorous reaction to formal rhetoric. The emphasis on ingenuity and palpable artifice was bound to produce its own antidote in a mind like Chaucer's. Hence he could write in the Tale of his Franklin, who explicitly denied knowledge of any flowers save those of a meadow:

> *For th' orisonte hath reft the sonne his lyght,—*
> *This is as muche to seye as it was nyght.*

And so of Troilus:

> *By day, he was in Martes heigh servyse,*
> *This is to seyn, in armes as a knyght.*

Of the same cast, but more amusing because less facetious, is the little footnote he adds to the poetic flourish (from Dante) in the Proem to Book II:

> *Out of thise blake wawes for to saylle,*
> *O wynd, o wynd, the weder gynneth clere;*
> *For in this see the boot hath swych travaylle,*
> *Of my connyng, that unneth I it steere.*
> *This see clepe I the tempestous matere*
> *Of disespeir that Troilus was inne; . . .*

In the speech of the falcon the annotation or gloss is curious, as though a good phrase could not stand on its merits:

> *That my wyl was his willes instrument;*
> *This is to seyn, my wyl obeyed his wyl.*

The deliberate parody is obvious in the Merchant's Tale:

> *Now wol I speke of woful Damyan, . . .*
> *Therfore I speke to hym in this manere:*
> *I seye, "O sely Damyan, allas! . . .*

Somewhat different is the familiar formulaic playfulness (explained, if not always justified, on grounds of real or pretended oral delivery) of *ye get namoore of me—of me namoore—I sey namoore—I kan sey yow namoore—I wol namoore endite—ther is namoore to telle—ther is namoore to seye.* Elsewhere when a convenient phrase comes in naturally he does not hesitate to repeat it, as in the Cassandra scene of *Troilus,* Book v: *er he stente—er he wolde stente—er she stente* within thirty-odd lines. The number of lines beginning *And namely—Nameliche—But nathelees* is striking if one's memory is set to note them. The word *joie* occurs eighty-two times in the *Troilus,* thirty-five of them at the end of a line—a ready rime for *Troie.* It is by such repetitions that he achieves that ease and flow of narrative which we admire—by avoiding an anxious effort for variety, by accepting convenient shortcuts.

III

The collocation of *ernest* and *game* which one thinks of as characteristically Chaucerian occurs actually only seven times, but the juxtaposition of the two moods is pervasive. The phrase occurs first in the 'Hous of Fame,' 822; the Eagle explains to Geffrey how all earthly sounds are carried to Fame's house, believe it or not:

> *Take yt in ernest or in game.*

In the Legend of Hypermnestra it represents something doubtfully credible:

> *Be as be may, for ernest or for game.*

In the Merchant's Tale it stands for a divided point of view: *bitwixe ernest and game* January decided on a particular girl for his wife. Similarly, but negatively and in a different context,

Griselda never mentions her daughter's name *in ernest nor in game,* and a bit later the Marquis *for ernest ne for game* would not leave off testing his wife. These five examples turn chiefly on a verbal contrast. The significant use, significant for Chaucer's almost habitual blend of grave and gay, the serious and the not-so-serious, is found at the end of the Manciple's Prologue, where the Host, gratified by the reconciliation of the Cook and the Manciple, says with a laugh:

> *O thou Bacus, yblessed be thy name,*
> *That so kanst turnen ernest into game!*

And best of all, in the Miller's Prologue, when Chaucer in person submits his apology for the *harlotrye* of his Miller and Reeve, he warns that *men shal nat maken ernest of game.* Life is filled with a certain gaiety, even foolish gaiety, if we will only take it so and not always look on the serious side. This attitude colors all the bawdy Tales of the Canterbury Pilgrims, *thilke that sownen into synne* and also no doubt the *translacions and enditynges of worldly vanitees* which he felt it proper to *revoke.* There could be no better introduction to Chaucer's comic view of life as he has it in his poetry. "Ah, take the *game* and let the *ernest* go."

That the comic view of life has limitations one can agree; but there is so much to be said for it and we have the worthy Knight's word for it (though he took the words from the plebeian Host, and neither of them was quite up to the playful use of *litel* and *muche*) that

> *litel hevinesse*
> *Is right ynough to muche folke, I gesse.*

But how much of it was natural and how much a mask? All that persistent cheerfulness, was it a native gift, a spontaneous overflow of high spirits? a loving sympathy for suffering humanity which points up the ridiculous to ease the pain? a half cynical detachment or withdrawal amounting sometimes to studied indifference? a shield to cover his own hurt heart? We cannot know, of course. The apparent self-revelations are probably literary convention. Certainly the occasional remarks on his feeble wittedness and on his decrepitude in matters of love are not evidence. The frequent emphasis on domestic unhappiness is probably but a reliance on the universal jest. We cannot help seeing him in the lineaments of Pandarus, with his *joly wo, a lusty sorwe,* but we cannot be too confident. The advice to Bukton against re-marriage is hedged by *as seyne these wise* and the authority of the Wife of Bath. The fancy picture of the poet on a May morning—

> *Adoun ful softely I gan to synke,*
> *And lenynge on myn elbowe and my syde,*
> *The longe day I shoop me for t'abide . . .*

until nightfall, when

> *in a litel herber that I have . . .*
> *I bad men sholde me my couche make;*
> *For deyntee of the newe someres sake,*
> *I bad hem strawen floures on my bed*

with all its Pre-Raphaelite exactitude is not to be trusted. And the one passage which we accept as veridical, the Eagle's charge that, his reckonings finished at the Customs, he goes straight home in stony silence to sit

> *at another book*
> *Tyl fully daswed ys thy look,*

is topped with a witticism,

> *And lyvest thus as an heremyte,*
> *Although thyn abstynence ys lyte.*

This, if read literally, does not make for domestic felicity at the one period of his life when he is supposed to have had a home of his own; but all we are entitled to infer is that like Pandarus he would have his little jest at himself. Is this a literary affectation, like his boasted indifference to love, or a natural trait? No doubt he found love amusing—others have—both for himself and for his friends; but it is a fact (also) that nowhere did he attempt a story of true love as a thing of beauty—nothing like *Aucassin et Nicolete* or even like *Floris and Blanchefleur*—not in the 'Book of the Duchess,' where the terms are those of Courtly Love; nor in the Knight's Tale, where love is only the basis for a situation; nor in the Clerk's Tale, where it really does not enter; nor in the Franklin's Tale, where the interest is in a disturbance of married happiness; hardly even in the *Troilus,* where Pandarus is always intruding his comic sense. Whatever else, this is Chaucer's way when he writes.

There is scarcely an interruption to the sustained pathos of the last two Books of the *Troilus.* After Pandarus has brought his lovers to bed and *hath fully his entente* there is no laughter in the poem, not even a smile, except Cassandra's ironic smile. The reader may be permitted to smile when Troilus disdains to hunt the *smale bestes* and when his anguish leads to extremes in the *Hercules furens* tradition and when he plans his funeral. Chaucer is serious in condemning astrology, though he may use it for literary decoration; in the 'Astrolabe' II, 4 he says *these ben observ-aunces of judicial matere and rytes of payens, in whiche my spirit hath no feith.* He is serious in condemning alchemy—

> *Thanne conclude I thus, sith that God of hevene*
> *Ne will nat that the philosophres nevene*
> *How that a man shal come unto this stoon,*
> *I rede, as for the beste, lete it goon.*
> *For whoso maketh God his adversarie,*
> *As for to werken any thyng in contrarie*
> *Of his wil, certes, never shal he thryve,*
> *Thogh that he multiplie term of his lyve.*

His seriousness in condemning other follies and wickedness of mortals is another matter.

The paradox of laughter and tears is pointed up in three places which are not Chaucer's own: in the 'Complaint of Venus,' which is a paraphrase, where love is characterized as

> *Wepynge to laughe, and sing in compleynyng;*

in the doubtful 'Complaynt d'Amours':

> *Your plesaunce is to laughen whan I syke, . . .*
> *It is hir pley to laughen whan men syketh;*

and in the translation of the *Roman* (4741):

A laughter it is, wepyng ay.

Fortune, who, in the 'Book of the Duchess,' is

*ever laughing
With oon eye, and that other weping*

is from Machaut. Something better than mere oxymoron is in Criseyde's feeling when she sees through her uncle's vicarious wooing and *with sobre chere hire herte lough.* There is a mixture of pathos and humor when Troilus finds in bed beside him only a pillow to embrace and when he rides mournfully through Troy, passing Criseyde's closed palace—a ring without its ruby— whose cold doors he would stop and kiss if there weren't so many people watching. But the comedy is too deep for laughter. Has Chaucer touched that anywhere else than here, with Boccaccio as guide? or its obverse? "I thought my problem," said Yeats to Lady Dorothy Wellesley, "was to face death with gaiety, now I have learned that it is to face life." This Chaucer knew. But he was hardly one of those who

*know that Hamlet and Lear are gay;
Gaiety transforming all that dread.*

His laughter is too quick and spontaneous for such a transfiguration.

IV

Chaucer's comedy is bright; it does not penetrate the depths. Enough has been said by others about Chaucer's irony; on his satire there are still contradictory judgments. Satire is usually understood as indignation tempered with humor, or, better, with wit; for humor and indignation are incompatible. It combines the notions of ridicule and reproof. When it deals with human follies it shares the properties of comedy and when with human vices the properties of tragedy. It ranges from the simple pleasure of exposing to the bitter determination to castigate; and the proportions are variously mixed according to the author's intention, his temperament, and his subject. "Your satirist is mostly a robust fellow, laying about him lustily, for the purpose of hurting, of injuring people, who, in his opinion, ought to be hurt and injured"—this from Sir Max Beerbohm.

Chaucer has a quick eye for faults; hence among all the people in his poetry there are very few without some carefully noted blemish. The Knight has his *Al bismotered* tunic, the Squire his lavish costume, the Prioress her unprofessional affectations, the Monk his indifference to monastic regulations, the Merchant and the Man of Law their sharp and shady methods, the Franklin his indulgence in high living, and so on. These are not quite damning faults; they are registered without deprecatory comment, without approval or disapproval. The Friar is exposed in elaborate detail, yet with no sign of condemnation: the last we are told of him is the excellence of his singing and the story assigned to him is one of the best. The Shipman was frankly a pirate, but also a skilful mariner. The Doctor was learned and capable, but also much interested in his fees; perhaps he worked too closely with the apothecaries. The Manciple was a cheat, the Miller a vulgar cheat, the Reeve a highly accomplished cheat; their good and bad qualities are displayed impartially. Lastly, the arch villains on the Pilgrimage: they are a good test. Without changing the previous tone of the descriptive analysis, without raising his voice, without sign of indignation or reproof Chaucer expounds their viciousness—save for two couplets, which are unique in the whole Prologue and which have been overlooked or strangely misinterpreted. The Summoner is quoted as saying *Purs is the ercedekenes helle* and the poet enters a prompt and pointed denial. The *I* can only be the poet, whether as fictive Pilgrim or as Geoffrey Chaucer himself.

> *But well I woot he lyed right in dede;*
> *Of cursyng oghte ech gilty man him drede,*
> *For curs wol slee right as assoillyng savith,*
> *And also war hym of a Significavit.*

The last line is a little weak, to say nothing of the rime, but the rest is unmistakable. When the Summoner said that, he lied outright. *'I tell you that every guilty man should fear excommunica-tion.'* Otherwise the two compeers are self-condemned: no more was needed. The Summoner, repulsive as he appears at first, is recompensed with the lively exposure of wheedling friars, itself a satire evenly tempered by comedy, and with the Summoner's own grossness at the end. The Pardoner, who escapes now, has his turn later. The Wife of Bath represses him firmly in her Prologue and in his own Prologue he unmasks his evilness so brazenly and so exhaustively that the poet could add nothing— except reward him with a superior Tale. His villainy is counter-balanced with his successful energy; he is so honest in his self-denigration that one is more amused by his forthrightness than revolted by his vices. Thus the ambivalence holds. Chaucer does not suspend judgment on his villains. One cannot say that he tolerates them, or that he deplores them. *There they are.* If this is satire, it is satire with a difference; perhaps *implied satire* will do. We do not know what Chaucer thought of them, only that he saw them plain and whole. In satire there may be an element of distortion to sharpen the effect, and the nearest Chaucer comes to it is in the Pardoner's Prologue. Yet even there he spits out no venom. It is only part of the portrait that the Pardoner can be so self-crucifying.

In the picture of the Prioress the 'satire' is subdued to a suav-ity which hints at irony, the kind of irony which rests on superior knowledge and the pleasure of withholding some of it. Chaucer sees her more clearly than she sees herself or than the reader is likely to see her. He shares part of his understanding and leaves the rest to our intelligence. He passes without pointing. And this dilute satire is common elsewhere. It takes the form of innuendo and occasionally is so potent as to resemble sarcasm with a concealed weapon, depending on the degree of malice we are prepared to recognize. It may be ever so restrained, as with the repetitively *worthy* Knight (not to mention Arveragus and January, who were also worthy knights), followed by the worthy *limitour* and the twice worthy Merchant; or with the *conscience* of the Prioress, which turns out to be a love of little dogs; or the fine casuistry of the Friar; or the Merchant's costume:

> *He rood but hoomly in a medlee cote,*
> *Girt with a ceint of silk;*

or the lurking, almost invisible suggestion that the Clerk would rather stay at Oxford as a student than get on with his work in the world; and even the Host's double-edged

> *The blisful martyr quite yow youre meede!*

(one reward for the Parson and another for the Pardoner). Then there is the full-scale compound irony of the Wife of Bath falsely accusing her drunken husbands of accusing women of all their frailties known to man, and herself validating the accusations in her confessional monologue; and the Wife's own innuendo that nowadays the only incubi are the Friars and they are too enfeebled to do more than *dishonour* a poor girl; and the repeated flings at the Wife in the Merchant's Tale, by means of echoing phrases as well as overt allusions, including the so-called Epilogue to his Tale.

Chaucer's pretended denials of the experience of love—

> *For al be that I knowe nat Love in dede,*
> *Ne wot how that he quiteth folk here hyre.*

> *Ne dar to Love, for myn unliklynesse,*
> *Preyen for speed, al sholde I therfore sterve,*
> *So fer am I from his help in derknesse—*

are eloquent of innuendo, even if the Cecilia Chaumpaigne story is not invoked. Scipio Africanus is permitted such a side-slap introducing the poet to the Garden of Love:

> *Yit that thow canst not do, yit mayst thow se.*

There is obvious innuendo a little later in the poet's suggestive withholding of three names—actually, in Boccaccio, "il folle Ardire Con Lusinghe e Ruffiani"—as though they might be offensive; and his addition of the *sceptre* of Priapus; and his satisfaction, *my pay,* in seeing Venus clad in a transparent *coverchef* from the waist down. And many more. If more examples are wanted, Pandarus offers a rich collection as he treads uncertainly the line between grave impropriety and frank salaciousness.

As 'satire' slants into irony and harmless innuendo while humor keeps the upper hand, it can by indirection at least descend to coarseness implying a judgment.

> *The Miller is a cherl, ye knowe wel this;*
> *So was the Reve, and the othere manye mo,*
> *And harlotrie they tolden bothe two.*

The Cook rejoiced in that *jape of malice in the derk* and enrolled himself with the other churls, but Chaucer cut him short: we leave him with his *compeer of his owene sort* and his compeer's wife and her dual profession. How much malice shall we see in their vulgar Tales? The fabliaux deal in practical jokes with a strong element of *Schadenfreude*. But does Chaucer lead our sympathies to the sufferer, or does he side with the perpetrator? A great measure of the fun is in his exhibition of low caste humor to the *gentils* of his courtly readers, and it would be difficult to prove *Tendenz*. Churls will be churls; such is this world,

> *God leve us for to take it for the beste.*

So the circle turns and the pointer comes to rest at tolerance. The laughter is light, without bitterness—what Lowell called heat-lightning, without audible thunder, that is, without satire in the ordinary sense. "You have a knife," says one of Yeats's characters, "but have you sharpened it?" Chaucer had not. It shines sometimes with only a faint glimmer; it does not cut. He used it as a pointer, not an edged tool. In apologizing for the Miller and Reve he was only explaining his plan, to report what he saw and heard; and note that next to the Knight's their Tales have pride of place.

> *He was to synful men nat despitous, . . .*
> *Ne maked him a spiced conscience.*

He saw, and let it be seen; and so the more Chaucer he. If this is aloofness, detachment, it is still not complacency.

V

The notion of a poem as an artifact, something newly created in space and time, came into England with the Renaissance, too late for Chaucer. For him a poem seems to have been what he wrote out of a desire to write and enjoyed writing. He knew the mediæval rhetoricians and adopted some of their devices or used them spontaneously. But mediæval rhetoric was more concerned with ornamentation than with formal structure, and neither perfection of form nor perfection of language seems to have lain within the scope of his thinking. Yet he frequently surprises us with the happiest felicities of expression and the "excellentest artificialities" of form. On the same page he can be slovenly and curiously expert. He will pad his lines impenitently —*thus, in this wise—perchaunce—par aventure—atte laste—for the nones—as I gesse*—or dilute them: *in that seson on a day . . . At nyght.* Pandarus is known for his *Diffusioun of speche.* Chaucer will play tricks—

> *How may of the in me swich quantite.*

> *He took his hoost, and hoom he rood anon.*

He will pile up fillers—

> *And here on warde, ryght now, as blyve.*

> *And further over now ayenward yit.*

Even in the carefully written General Prologue he will put *For sothe* and *sooth to seyn* in consecutive lines; and end two lines, with only three intervening, *hadde he be,* and include *hadde he been* in the following line.

He will also write such perfect verses as

> *And hope is lasse and lasse, alway, Pandare.*

> *And clepe ayeyn the beaute of your face.*

> *Unto the gardyn, as myn housbonde bad,*
> *My trouthe for to holde, alas! alas!*

He will contrive the metrical bravura of Anelida's compleynt and set before us such metrical delicacies as the imitation of Anglo-Saxon versification in the Knight's Tale and in the Legend of Cleopatra; or the three consecutive all-trochaic lines in the prologue to the Wife of Bath's Tale; or the fusion of two different movements (5-stress iambic and 4-stress trisyllabic) in

> *Whoso that buyldeth his hous al of salwes,*
> *And priketh his blynde hors over the falwes,*
> *And suffreth his wyf to go seken halwes,*

(as the Wife herself is then doing)

> *Is worthy to been hanged on the galwes.*

He will also allow himself such 'irregular' lines as

> *Th'eschewing is only the remedye.*

> *Noght wiste this preest with whom that he delte.*

> *Consumed and wasted han my reednesse.*

> *And by eterne word writen and confermed.*

He will turn out such a masterpiece of sarcasm as the Envoy to the Clerk's Tale, but leave us in doubt whether the Clerk spoke it or the poet inserted it. He will compose a *tour de force* of grace and sprightly humor, the 'Parlement,' and yet leave us puzzled about its total meaning or intention. He will give us in the 'Hous of Fame' the gaiety and liveliness of Book II and also the dull résumé of the *Aeneid* in Book I and the tiresome list of petitioners for fame in Book III.

In large and in small he mingles and juxtaposes both grave and gay, both good and bad, both high and low, to our confusion when we wish to judge him as an artist or even as a skilled craftsman. He seems not to have a style, or a variety of styles, but only a fortuitous mixture of what happened to come from his pen. At one moment he is astonishingly subtle and cunning and careful; at the next alarmingly indifferent, lax, negligent. Are we to understand these contrasts as a superior kind of art-cum-artlessness, or are the felicities happy accidents only? (His occasional success with the aureate manner proves that he could and would try, but those examples are not to our taste, nor very much to his.) Can we avoid the conclusion that his artistic conscience was wanting in rigor, that he satisfied himself too easily, and too often simply refused to make the last effort?

A twofold extenuation must be allowed. The language of English poetry has been worked upon for several centuries now. Standards of high and low, of tense and easy have been cumulatively set. But for Chaucer the language was immature, fluid, experimental. If he achieved brilliant results, it is only to be expected that he would sometimes fail. He had not our standards to hamper him or to aid him; he is therefore exempted from them. Moreover, poetical composition was for him, as Tatlock and others have emphasized, an avocation. He wrote when he could find time to write amid the pressures of an active life in other endeavors. He was, in the best sense, an amateur, and honestly humble, even at times apologetic. He knew his own limitations better than most of his critics, and if he did not devote himself strenuously to Art, he at least achieved a sweet disorder like that of Nature. *And with this swerd,* he could say, *shal I sleen envie,* envy and overexigent stricture.

Nonetheless, some illustrations are in order.

VI

Landor praised Chaucer for "the broad and negligent facility, of a great master." It is a fine phrase but leaves unset the limits of safe negligence.

Syntax he regarded with tolerance. He can produce, for humorous effect, an encyclopedic sentence of fifty-one lines on dreams at the beginning of the 'Hous of Fame,' or, without humorous intention, one of forty-four lines on Arcite's pyre interweaving two formulas based on 'how . . .' and 'what . . .' and a shorter one of similar weaving based on 'is turned to . . .' and 'is . . .' in the 'Book of the Duchess,' and another in the *Troilus* v, 1373-79. In the 'Book of the Duchess' also he has a brave sentence of twenty-one lines which seems to get lost in a series of comparisons and a six-line parenthesis, but is caught up neatly by the repetition of *I wolde* (1054 ff.). Just before this however is a sentence, or perhaps two sentences, which no editorial punctuation can straighten out. He can develop a passage of Boethius on love and a song of Troilo's based on it into five and a half stanzas for a Proem to Book III and then into four masterly stanzas as a song of Troilus for a climax to Book III, in which *that* is repeated six times in the first and fourth stanzas and seven times in the second and third—twenty-six in all—while preserving the constructions clearly. (In *Troilus* IV, 1632 ff. the stanza has *that* eight times, without the excuse of musical effect in the Song.) At the very end of Book III there is a stanza which requires careful reading (Robinson's punctuation is wrong): he addresses Venus, Cupid, and the Muses—

> *That ye thus fer han deyned me to gyde,*
> *I kan namore but, syn that ye wol wende,*
> *Ye heried ben for ay withouten ende.*

That is: 'Since you now will leave me I can only say, "Praised be ye who have thus far deigned to guide me." This is the end of Troilus' joy and henceforth I can expect no help from the Muses or from Venus and Cupid, since it is the end also of love.' After this the Daughters of Night must be his guide.

He can manage without serious sacrifice such an intricate periodic sentence as

> *Than sey I thus,*
> *That stondyng in concord and in quiete,*
> *Thise ilke two, Criseyde and Troilus,*
> *As I have told, and in this tyme swete,—*
> *Save only often myghte they nought mete,*
> *Ne leiser have hire speches to fulfelle,—*
> *That it bifel right as I shal yow telle,*
>
> *That Pandarus, that evere dide his myght*
> *Right for the fyn that I shal speke of here,*
> *As for to bryngen to his hows som nyght*
> *His faire nece and Troilus yfere,*
> *Whereas at leiser al this heighe matere,*
> *Touchyng here love, were at the fulle upbounde,*
> *Hadde out of doute a tyme to it founde.*

When he is consciously trying for the formal style, as in the Prologue to the Second Nun's Tale, he cleverly puts the main verb in the sixth line and its dependent infinitive two lines above, and in the second stanza builds up a parallel climax on the formula *because . . . therefore. . . .*

> *The ministre and the norice unto vices,*
> *Which that men clepe in Englissh ydelnesse,*
> *That porter of the gate is of delices,*
> *To eschue, and by hire contrarie hire oppresse,*
> *That is to seyn, by leveful bisynesse,*
> *Wel oghten we to doon al oure entente,*
> *Leste that the feend thurgh ydelnesse us hente.*

> *For he that with his thousand cordes slye*
> *Continuelly us waiteth to biclappe,*
> *Whan he may man in ydelnesse espye,—*
> *He kan so lightly cacche hym in his trappe,*
> *Til that a man be hent right by the lappe*
> *He nys nat war the feend hath hym in honde,—*
> *Wel oghte us werche, and ydlenesse withstonde.*

(Because he lies in wait to snare idlers—he can so easily catch one that a man doesn't know until he is fairly caught—therefore we ought to exert ourselves. . . .)

Another example on the good side occurs in the lively exchanges between the Devil and the stupid but eager summoner of the archdeacon. Why, asks this summoner, do you assume different shapes? Because, replies the Devil, we choose the form most suitable for our prey.—Why do you go to all this trouble? asks the summoner.

> *"Ful many a cause, leeve sire somonour,"*
> *Seyde this feend.*

But, the Devil continues, time is passing and I have accomplished nothing so far to-day.

> *I wol entende to wynnyng, if I may,*
> *And nat entende oure wittes to declare.*

> *For, brother myn, thy wit is al to bare*
> *To understonde, althogh I told hem thee;*

(*hem* goes back to *Ful many a cause* seven lines before)

> *But, for thou axest why labouren we—*

(the summoner had asked this nine lines above), it is

> *For somtyme we been Goddes instrumentz, . . .*

The two *for's* are neatly balanced.

On the other hand, Chaucer will write such a straggling sentence as

> *This passeth yeer by yeer and day by day,*
> *Til it fil ones, in a morwe of May,*
> *That Emelye, that fairer was to sene*
> *Than is the lylie upon his stalke grene,*
> *And fressher than the May with floures newe—*
> *For with the rose colour stroof hire hewe,*
> *I noot which was the fyner of hem two—*
> *Er it were day, as was hir wone to do,*
> *She was arisen and al redy dight;*
> *For May wole have no slogardie a-nyght.*

Probably the worst specimen is in Book III of the *Troilus*, which Chaucer is said to have revised more carefully than the other Books.

> *But right so as thise holtes and thise hayis,*
> *That han in wynter dede ben and dreye,*
> *Revesten hem in grene, when that May is,*
> *Whan every lusty liketh best to pleye;*
> *Right in that selve wise, soth to seye,*
> *Wax sodeynliche his herte ful of joie,*
> *That gladder was ther nevere man in Troie;*
>
> *And gan his look on Pandarus up caste*
> *Ful sobrely, and frendly for to se,*
> *And seyde, "Frend, in Aperil the laste,—*
> *As wel thow woost, if it remembre the,—*

How neigh the deth for wo thow fownde me,
And how thow dedest al thi bisynesse
To knowe of me the cause of my destresse.

"Thow woost how longe ich it forbar to seye
To the, that art the man that I best triste;
And peril non was it to the bywreye,
That wist I wel, but telle me, if the liste,
Sith I so loth was that thiself it wiste,
How dorst I mo tellen of this matere,
That quake now, and no wight may us here?

"But natheles, by that God I the swere,
That, as hym list, may al this world governe,—
And, if I lye, Achilles with his spere
Myn herte cleve, al were my lif eterne,
As I am mortal, if I late or yerne
Wolde it bewreye, or dorst, or sholde konne,
For al the good that God made under sonne—

"That rather deye I wolde, and determyne,
As thynketh me, now stokked in prisoun,
In wrecchidnesse, in filthe, and in vermyne,
Caytif to cruel kyng Agamenoun;
And this in all the temples of this town
Upon the goddes alle, I wol the swere
To-morwe day, if that it like the here."

Here all begins well with the simile; then *herte* has to serve for
the omitted subject of *gan;* then the direct discourse begins with
the clause *as wel thow woost,* which seems to be repeated in the
following stanza but turns out differently, for the second *woost* is
the main verb; and the sentence comes to a kind of end with
That wist I wel (in false parallelism with the repeated *woost*).
The next stanza is hopelessly confused with interlocking parentheses. Of course Chaucer is here translating, but Boccaccio is
reasonably clear and direct until the end of this passage and even
then is not difficult:

> *Ma nondimen per quello Dio ti giuro,*
> *Che 'l cielo e modo egualmente governa,*
> *E s' io non venga nelle man del duro*
> *Agamemnon, che se mia vita eterna*
> *Fosse, come è mortal, tu puoi sicuro*
> *Viver, che a mio poter sarà interna*
> *Questa credenza, e in ogni atto servato*
> *L' onor di quella che m' ha 'l cor piagato.**

Surely this is rough and ready work, still awaiting revision. Another example may serve to show Chaucer more successful in a similar case, though he asks us to turn without warning a nominative into a dative.

> *Lord, trowe ye a coveytous or a wrecche,*
> *That blameth love, and halt of it despit,*
> *That of tho pens that he kan mokre and krecche*
> *Was evere yit yyeven hym swich delit*
> *As is in love, in o poynt, in som plit?*
> *Nay, douteles, for also God me save,*
> *So perfit joie may no nygard have.*
>
> *They wol seyn "yis," but Lord! so that they lye,*
> *Tho besy wrecches, ful of wo and drede!*
> *They callen love a woodnesse or folie,*
> *But it shal falle hem as I shal yow rede;*
> *They shal forgon the white and ek the rede,*
> *And lyve in wo, ther God yeve hem meschaunce,*
> *And every lovere in his trouthe avaunce!*

Compare Boccaccio:

> *Deh pensin qui gli dolorosi avari,*
> *Che biasiman che è innamorato,*
> *E chi, come fan essi, a far denari*

* But nevertheless I swear to you by that God who governs equally heaven and earth—and if I wish not to fall into the hands of strong Agamemnon—that, if my life were eternal as it is mortal, you can be certain that so far as is in my power this secret will remain within me, and in every act of mine the honor of her who has wounded my heart will be safe.

> *In alcun modo non s' è tutto dato,*
> *E guardin se tenedoli ben cari*
> *Tanto piacer fu mai da lor prestato,*
> *Quanto ne presta amore in un sol punto,*
> *A cui egli è con ventura congiunto.*
>
> *Ei diranno di sì, ma mentiranno;*
> *E questo amor, dolorosa pazzia*
> *Con risa e con ischerzi chiameranno;*
> *Senza veder, che sola un' ora fia*
> *Quella che sè e' denari perderanno,*
> *Senza aver gioia saputo che sia*
> *Nella lor vita: Iddio gli faccia tristi,*
> *Ed agli amanti doni i loro acquisti.**

Besides the shift from nominative to dative, there is also the change from singular to plural. Chaucer both omits and supplies: "in un sol punto" becomes *in o poynt, in som plit;* his *wo and drede* is padding; his *white* and *rede* is decoration out of the common stock; and he missed Boccaccio's final point.

When Troilus returned to his own chamber after being smitten by Criseyde in the temple he daydreamed of her beauty:

> *Thus gan he make a mirour of his mynde,*
> *In which he saugh al holly hire figure;*
> *And that he wel koude in his herte fynde,*
> *It was to hym a right good aventure*
> *To love swich oon.*

Boccaccio cannot be blamed here. Does this mean: He could find this in his heart, namely, that he was fortunate in loving such a

---

* Now let these unhappy misers who blame those who have fallen in love and who, as they do, have devoted themselves wholly to making money (and) reflect whether, holding it precious, as they do, so much pleasure was ever granted to them as love gives in a single point to one who has this good fortune.

They will say, Yes. But they will lie. And this love they will with laughter and jesting call wretched folly; without seeing that in a single hour they will lose both themselves and their money without having known in all their life what joy is. May God make them sad and give their gains to lovers.

one; or, It was fortunate for him that he could find it in his heart, etc.? There is a similar uncertainty in the lines describing Arcite's last moments:

> *Oonly the intellect, withouten more,*
> *That dwelled in his herte syk and soore,*
> *Gan faillen whan the herte felte deeth.*

Does this mean: Only the intellect failed when . . . , or, the intellect failed only when. . . ? Neither alternative is satisfactory. Or can *only* be loosely used as a conjunction? The answer is in Boccaccio.

> *sol nello 'ntelletto*
> *e nel cuore era ancora sostenuta*
> *la poca vita; ma già sì ristretto*
> *gli era il tristo cuor dal mortal gielo,*
> *ch'agli occhi fe subitamente velo.**

This is different, and clear; but Chaucer atoned by his *Dusked.*

It could hardly be expected that Theseus would be quite lucid in his brief account of the chain of being; he lacked the Eagle's leisurely professional manner; but he ends majestically, with a slight air of apology

> *This maystow understonde and seen at ye.*

Some of the incoherence of the Wife of Bath's speech may be intentional; there is a kind of madness in Aurelius' declaration of love; and elsewhere the confusion of syntax matches a mental confusion in the speaker; but often it is Chaucer who fails us. When the guests assemble for the Marquis' supposed wedding, Griselda welcomes them handsomely,

> *And worthily they preisen hire prudence.*

Then she commends the two children

> *So wel that no man koude hir pris amende.*

Does this mean: so well that no one could improve on her praise

---

* The little (remnant of) life was sustained only in his intellect and in his heart; but already his sad heart was so constricted by the chill of death that a sudden veil came over his eyes.

of them? or, it was impossible to increase the esteem due to her, to praise her too highly for her treatment of the children?

Sometimes he will violate an expected parallelism without compunction, as in *The hunte strangled . . . The sowe freten . . . The cook yscalded;* or reverse a construction without notice:

> *If cow, or calf, or sheep, or oxe swelle*
> *That any worm hath ete, or worm ystonge;*

or he will vary the expected parallelism by three different formulas, as in *be ye redy . . . and that I frely may . . . And nevere ye to grucche it* when the Marquis puts the prenuptial contract to Griselda.

The reference of *he* in a A 101 is a familiar ambiguity; it ought to be to the Squire but is regularly understood as to the Knight. At the end of the great tournament the pronouns have to be separated by inference (A 2638-42). In the G text of the Prologue to the 'Legend of Good Women,' supposed to be a revision, both pronouns and syntax are careless:

> *To hem have I so gret affeccioun,*
> *As I seyde erst, whan comen is the May,*
> *That in my bed ther daweth me no day*
> *That I n' am up and walkynge in the mede,*
> *To sen these floures agen the sonne sprede,*
> *Whan it up ryseth by the morwe shene,*
> *The longe day thus walkynge in the grene.*
> *And whan the sonne gynneth for to weste,*
> *Thanne closeth it, and draweth it to reste, . . .*

The F text is a little fuller and clearer but has an additional confusion in the feminine pronoun for the daisy. At the beginning of the Friar's Tale there is the archdeacon's summoner and the Pilgrim Summoner: which is meant by *this somonour* of D 1327, and by *his* in the following line?—But English pronouns have always been troublesome, from the days of Cyneheard down.

VII

There are other ways in which Chaucer did not feel himself bound by strict logic. There is an amusing example, doubtless deliberate, in the 'Book of the Duchess,' 434 ff.: the forest was so full of various animals that not even Argus could compute the marvels in my dream. In describing the temple of Venus which was part of the amphitheater erected by Theseus, and which was first announced as *an auter and an oratorie,* Chaucer lists eight instances showing that no power can successfully compete with Venus, and concludes

> *Suffiseth heere ensamples oon or two,*
> *And though I koude rekene a thousand mo.*

In the corresponding temple of Mars the deaths of Caesar, Nero, and Antony are depicted as lovers slain by the influence of Mars:

> *Suffiseth oon ensample in stories olde;*
> *I may nat rekene hem alle though I wolde.*

(Robinson comments here: "The reference is inexact.") In the temple of Diana there were representations of *Calistopee* (i.e., Callisto), *Dane* (i.e., Daphne) not to be confused with Diana, and Acteon and Meleager—

> *Ther saugh I many another wonder storie,*
> *The which me list nat drawen to memorie.*

(Thus Chaucer avoids the risk of inexactitude.)

Meanwhile, the decorations on the wall of Theseus' temple of Mars contain *First* a wild forest in which stood a temple of Mars, which is described; and then one is surprised to read: *Ther saugh I first* followed by *Yet saugh I* twice, and finally, more than fifty lines later: *Depeynted was.* Even the loyal editors have noticed this blending of the Knight and the omniscient poet narrator. Not comparable is the situation in the 'Hous of Fame' where the same formula, *First sawgh I,* etc. occurs in profusion, with its mixture of possible still pictures and frank narrative as a device to summarize the Dido and Aeneas episode; for all this was a dream. And, *a fortiori,* the glorious confusion of details in the account of Fame's castle carved from a single beryl is part of the dream technique, like the strange comings and going in the 'Book of the Duchess.' But in the Knight's Tale no such explanation is proper. The inference that the Knight, or Chaucer himself, had seen those temples still intact, or the ruins of them, and so describes them at first hand is merely bizarre. It is true, as Manly says, that the method of first-person direct observation adds vividness, but it would be truer to admit that Chaucer was indifferent to this inconsistency, as he was to others in the Knight's Tale.

The numberless loose ends in the unfinished *Canterbury Tales* hardly call for extenuation or explanation, but diligent critics frequently devote themselves to saving the Master. They have spaced out the Tales from day to day along the Pilgrims' road. They have divined that the Host called on the Cook towards the end because Chaucer meant to throw out the earlier Cook's Prologue and incomplete Tale, or that he never meant the Tale to be more than a fragment, or that this was part of the projected return journey. All which and all such vaticinatory efforts are works of supererogation. The inconsistencies in the *Troilus* are a different matter. They may not seem important, and the rapid reader—or especially the auditor if the poem was read aloud to him—may not even catch them; but they stand as evidence against the poet in his most careful and elaborate masterpiece. In Book I Criseyde is a widow

> *and allone*
> *Of any frend to whom she dorste hir mone.*

But a few lines later she appeals to Hector, who seems to know her, and later Helen and Deiphebus seem to know her well; Deiphebus says clearly *Criseyda, my frend*. To say nothing of her uncle Pandarus, who stood very high at court. At the end of Book II Pandarus maneuvers Helen and Deiphebus up to the sick bed of Troilus and then to get them out of the way Troilus happens to find

> *at his beddes hed*
> *The copie of a tretys and a lettre*

from Hector. Helen and Deiphebus obligingly go down to the garden for an hour to consider it, and when they return Troilus passes *ful lightly* over it, groans, and says he must sleep. This is perhaps good comedy. A little later, when Criseyde has already gone, Helen and Deiphebus have taken their leave, *hom went every wight* (III, 226),

> *And Pandarus, as faste as he may drive*
> *To Troilus tho com,*

and the two spend the night talking together and next morning go about their separate affairs. Well, Helen goes home, Deiphebus was home. But has Troilus so speedily recovered from his *accesse* that he hurries home, with Pandarus in pursuit? On the great night Pandarus has invited Criseyde to supper *whan it was eve;* after which she says she must go home, but the heavens open and the *huge rayn* prevents. Meanwhile Troilus has been in that little room *bishet syn mydnyght* of the preceding day—that is, eighteen to twenty hours. We are not told when that rain ceased, but by dawn the morning star

> *Gan for to rise, and out hire bemes throwe.*

When Troilus returns to his palace there is no mention of a storm; only Pandarus says jokingly that the rain had kept him awake all night. In Book III the lovers met at the house of Pandarus; afterwards, without any indication of change, they meet at Criseyde's (IV, 914 f., IV, 1125) as had been the custom from the start according to the *Filostrato*. In Book V Troilus rides past her closed empty house, with no mention of Antigone and all the attendants (*meyne*, I, 127-30). At the beginning of Book V, why should her heart bleed, why should Criseyde feel so downcast, when she has every intention of returning in ten days? Why should Troilus escort her from the city, at the grave risk of betraying his special interest in her? Where was Pandarus, her uncle? Where her other friends, Hector, Helen, Deiphebus? It will not do to say simply that Boccaccio is to blame. Chaucer, when he chose, made happy changes in his source; he could have grasped his nettle here also.

A few lapses elsewhere are worth mention. That Theseus at the age of twenty-three has a marriageable son ('Legende' 2075, 2099 f.) has provoked frequent comment. That Canace *heeld hir lappe abrood* to catch the desperate falcon, yet it *fil to grounde* (F 441, 473) and had to be picked up later can hardly be misplaced humor. In the Wife's Tale the hag acknowledges three handicaps: *thogh that I be foul, and oold, and poure* (D 1063) and in reply the young knight accuses her of being *so loothly, and so oold . . .* [and] *of so logh a kynde.* Then the hag begins her discourse:

> *But, for ye speken of swich gentillesse*
> *As is descended out of old richesse,*

although he has said nothing about such gentillesse, and continues for nearly seventy lines on the subject. Then she takes a fresh start:

> *And ther as ye of poverte me repreeve,*

although all he had said was *of so lough a kynde.* Then she devotes a few lines to his accusation of being old and a few more on *foul and old,* and she is done. Her lecture of 110 lines in rebuttal of his threefold charge that she was ugly, old, and low-born is devoted chiefly to one of Chaucer's favorite topics, true nobility —"a commonplace of Christian literature" (Robinson) which he picked up from Boethius and perhaps Dante.

Hot and cold, fire and ice afford such a ready contrast that it is easy to be careless with them. Troilus ends his Canticus, from Petrarch, with

> *For hete of cold, for cold of hete, I dye.*

This gives the pitch. *The fyre of love* (1, 436; *Fil.* 1, 40, "L'ardenti fiamme amorose") did not spare him; he was so burned that he went pale sixty times a day; he sought eagerly to look upon her,

> *And ay the ner he was, the more he brende;*

and this was apparently only in his imagination. Then the fire image lapses for a few lines, till 1, 488, where he feigns another sickness lest *the hote fir of love* should be noticed in him. In his following compleynt he supposes that

>   *also cold in love towardes the*
> *Thi lady is, as frost in wynter moone,*
> *And thow fordon, as snow in fire is soone.*

Said Boccaccio,

> *Fredda come al sereno interza il ghiaccio,*
> *Ed io qual neve al fuoco mi disfaccio.*＊

Chaucer has added the winter moon but followed Boccaccio in confusing the roles: first Troilus is fire and Criseyde is ice, then he is ice and she is fire. In Book II, when Criseyde debates *What shal I doon?* she becomes *Now hoot, now cold,* and Troilus when Pandarus has brought hopeful news lifts up his eyes to Venus

> *right as floures, thorugh the cold of nyght*
> *Iclosed, stoupen on hire stalke lowe,*
> *Redressen hem ayein the sonne bright.*

The simile is from Boccaccio out of Dante, but Troilus is again on the cold side and the warmth is by inference from Criseyde. Later, in Book IV, when Pandarus comes to comfort Troilus after the exchange has been settled, Troilus

> *Gan as the snow ayeyn the sonne melte.*

He is again snow, but the warmth is Pandarus.

Some of Chaucer's mistranslations may be due to manuscripts which differ from ours, others to haste or indifference, others to imperfect knowledge, and some to real inspiration. In the first Canticus Troili he renders Petrarch's "S' amor non è" (if this be not love) and "Ma s' egli è amor" (if it be love) by *If no love is . . . And if love is. . . .* This looks like undue literalness but it exactly expresses what he wants Troilus to say. For Petrarch's "a mal mio grado" (in spite of myself) he has *If harm agree me,* which is certainly a mistranslation, but it carries on the paradoxical opposites and may well be the judicious use of a hint rather than a blunder.[1] In a later Canticus he transforms Boccaccio's "disii porto di morte" (I bear, feel, desires of death) as though he mistook "porto" for port or harbor, into *with wynd in steere I saille;* but this may be only a continuation of the nautical metaphors he had already gleaned from Boccaccio, and so rather invention than error.[2] Less can be said for *Smokynge the temple*

＊ (She remains) as cold as ice which hardens under a clear sky, and I like snow before a fire waste away.

(A 2281) for Boccaccio's "Fu mondo il tempio" (*Teseida* VII, 72), since a smoking temple hardly makes sense; or for *Shippes hoppesteres* (A 2017) for Boccaccio's "navi bellatrici" (*Teseida* VII, 37), since dancing ships are hardly suitable in context. But these two from the Knight's Tale may serve as contributory evidence of an early date for the 'Palamon and Arcite.' More amusing, whether a blunder or a picturesque invention, is the *Partriches wynges* on Fame's feet ('Hous of Fame' 1393), where Vergil (*Aeneid* IV, 180) has "pernicibus alis."

Anyone can extend the list for himself; some may deplore or even censure the undertaking. They are content to leave an impression of unrelieved excellence, but the attentive reader will catch up with them and wonder at the contrast of Chaucer's undoubted skill in expression and every so often its opposite. Some poets, of a later time, produce their effects with a conjuror's air: there it is, but how did I do it? Chaucer has none of this. He is eminently natural. When he does a fine thing we know he did it naturally, just as when he missed we feel sure that the failure was natural. Sometimes we feel sure that he did not care enough, but at his best there is a transparent skill which came of practice more perhaps than from painstaking. So much for generalization, although exceptions are obvious. So much also in spite of Kittredge's emphatic dictum that "Chaucer always knew what he was about."

Thus he disappoints us often enough. He could leave *This litel laste book* for Book III of the 'Hous of Fame,' which though unfinished has 1068 lines and Books I and II together have only 1090. He could introduce Book IV of the *Troilus* as though it was the last—

> *So that the losse of lyf and love yfeere*
> *Of Troilus be fully shewed heere.*

He would not go back to make sure there were *wel nyne and twenty* at the Tabard Inn. Even in larger matters he will not make sure beforehand whither he was going and foresee the outcome; he will move in two directions at once. But no sooner has he disappointed us than he pushes on to a triumph.

Such notes on Chaucer's negligent facility are set down for the
record, lest they be overlooked or minimized, not for derogation.
They are counterbalanced by numberless felicities. The 'Parlement' is thickly sown with them. The blend of Dante and the
Roman de la Rose in the inscription over the gate to the Garden is
perfect and worthy to stand at the head of all Chaucer's works—
Lowell wrote it out on the flyleaf of his copy.

> *Thorgh me men gon into that blysful place*
> *Of hertes hele and dedly woundes cure;*
> *Thorgh me men gon unto the welle of grace,*
> *There grene and lusty May shal evere endure.*
> *This is the wey to al good aventure.*
> *Be glad, thow redere, and thy sorwe ofcaste;*
> *Al open am I—passe in, and sped thee faste!*

The garden itself has more colors than Chaucer usually puts
together:

> *A gardyn saw I ful of blosmy bowes*
> *Upon a ryver, in a grene mede,*
> *There as swetnesse everemore inow is,*
> *With floures white, blewe, yelwe, and rede,*
> *And colde welle-stremes, nothyng dede,*
> *That swymmen ful of smale fishes lighte,*
> *With fynnes rede and skales sylver bryghte.*

Venus lay in a dim corner of her temple on a golden bed—

> *Hyre gilte heres with a golden thred*
> *Ibounden were, untressed as she lay,*
> *And naked from the brest unto the hed*
> *Men myghte hire sen; . . .*

And so on, with wit and laughter, to the roundel performed by
a select choir of birds. Even in unlikely places one meets a
startling line: in the third stanza of 'Anelida and Arcite' (dis-
tilled perhaps from Dante and Boccaccio)—

> *Singest with vois memorial in the shade*
> *Under the laurer which that may not fade.*

Chanticleer, just before his fall,

> *Soong murier than the mermayde in the see.*

Mermaids have always sung, like the sirens; Chaucer had read about them in the *Roman* and translated

> *But it was wonder lyk to be*
> *Song of meremaydens of the see.*

But the magic is in Chanticleer's singing. So with

> *The soleyn fenix of Arabye.*

The idea is familiar, but *soleyn* makes all the difference. *For craft is al* sometimes, or as the Wife put it, in another connection:

> *Divers praktik, in many sondry werkes,*
> *Maketh the werkman parfit sekirly;*

and sometimes the word rises from the deep well.

The question was how Chaucer's pervasive humor in its various manifestations and the eccentricities as well as the felicities of his style combine to give his poetry its fundamental character. The answer, implied here and there, will wait on a review of other qualities which determine the whole.

VIII

It is often recognized and often forgotten that Chaucer wrote for an 'audience,' but just what that audience was and how far it affected his choice of subject and manner of writing are matters of speculation. The mediæval poet was not a professional, like say Tennyson and Browning; he had no general public, he addressed his work "to a very definite and restricted circle . . . to his patron, and his patron's family, friends and neighbours."[3] Sometimes he records his patron in a kind of dedication, but from Chaucer the most we have is

> *And whan this book is maad, yive hit the quene*

in the Prologue to the 'Legend of Good Women,' with the implication (but no more) that she had requested something to correct the seeming slander of women in the *Troilus*. There is no record of how the queen received it, and since there are signs of humor in the Prologue and in some of the legends we can only infer that Chaucer took the request somewhat lightly. Shirley gave it as a fact that Chaucer wrote the 'Mars' "at the comandement" of John of Gaunt. The case of the 'Book of the Duchess' is different: John and Blanche are not named; the poem is more than an elegy, it is a celebration of the duke as a courtly lover; and we are left to wonder if Chaucer wrote it in the courtierly spirit of engaging the duke's favor, or out of feeling for his wife's attachment to the late duchess, or possibly on a hint from the duke himself, after his return to England, that such a tribute would be acceptable. It seems to be agreed that Edward III was not a literary patron of Chaucer; that John of Gaunt and Richard were his literary patrons remains a case not proven. Various claims, usually in the search for dates of composition, have been put forward, and opposed, that the 'Hous of Fame' and the 'Parlement of Foules' were intended for royal marriages. For the rest, it is taken for granted that Chaucer because of his connections with the Court wrote for the purpose of entertaining the members of the Court, however vague such an entity might be. There are abundant signs that many of his poems were meant for oral delivery,[4] and doubtless were so delivered by Chaucer himself: the frontispiece of the early fifteenth-century *Troilus* manuscript, C.C.C.C. 61,[5] is presumptive evidence of other similar occasions. Often we can imagine we see and hear Geoffrey Chaucer reading his poems to a real audience; and this may help to explain the little winks and impertinences which look rather stark on the page but could be very effective as oral asides with a change of voice or an appropriate gesture.

On the other hand, it is hard to suppose that a man of his poetic temperament did not sometimes write to please himself. He would have felt sometimes a motion of the spirit and composed because there was something which had to 'come out.' His *rifacimento* of the *Teseida* and of the *Filostrato,* for example, would spring from a desire to retell those stories in his own way, not for particular occasion or a special group. He could rightly assume that the 'Palamon and Arcite' would entertain any sophisticated or educated audience, and the *Troilus* would provide a series of (five) readings very acceptable to his friends;[6] but this need not be his reason for writing. Other poems, the 'Hous of Fame' and the 'Parlement of Foules,' for example, seem better adapted to silent reading, from a manuscript copy lent by the author. So also the Clerk's Tale, with its formal division into Parts, looks like a poem written perhaps as an exercise in close paraphrase, but mainly to be just what it is, a verse narrative with a moral. The Man of Law's Tale may be an early experiment in metrical composition. The St. Cecilia poem and the Manciple's Tale have likewise the air of being literary exercises. A few poems, moreover, contain some slight evidence of having been meant for a particular audience, for example, the address to *goode men* (twice) and *ye lordes* (twice), and the phrase *as seith my lord* at the end of the Cock and Fox poem; though these may be mere rhetoric. The beginning of the Canon's Yeoman's Tale (now called Pars Secunda):

> *Ther is a chanoun of religioun*
> *Amonges us,*

followed by the direct address to *worshipful chanons religious,* suggests another special audience. The Wife of Bath's *Ye wise wyves* (D 275) is only a rhetorical apostrophe and is offset by *Lordynges* (D 379), who are presumably the Pilgrims; but her Prologue, omitting its interruption by the Pardoner, would with a suitable introduction and an altered last line give vast pleasure to a carefully selected audience.

But the *Canterbury Tales* as a whole and as an artistic conception is certainly a work to be read, not recited, and assumes a reading and not a listening audience. Where did Chaucer expect to find it, when he had finished the work? How would the Court, which took offense at the *Troilus* (or so Chaucer pretends) receive the Miller's and the Merchant's Tales? Some portions of the *Canterbury Tales* could have been written with an eye to amusing the aristocrats by exposing the follies of their inferiors; and the twenty-odd tales which we have (including those which are not tales at all) afford something for every taste. Yet Chaucer must have expected *readers,* and the history of the manuscripts, although all that we now have were written after his death, justifies that expectation. To put the matter another way, he had not an audience but audiences.

The *Canterbury Tales* in fact mingles rather than combines the moulds. There is an odd compound of both points of view in the Miller's Prologue which shows that such indications are not to be understood too literally:

> *And therfore, whoso list it nat yheere,*
> *Turne over the leef.*

It would be trying for an audience to listen to those brilliant but short analytical descriptions of the thirty Pilgrims, yet Chaucer assumes a kind of address—*whil I have tyme and space ... Now have I toold you,*—and it would be difficult to imagine even a series of readings while they listened to the whole nineteen thousand odd lines, with so much more to come. The "I" both is and is not the poet with pen in hand. But the fiction of oral narrative along the Canterbury road requires that the Tales themselves, as distinct from the links, be understood as spoken. And here also there are two voices: the Knight, the Miller, the Reeve, and the rest are speaking, but they speak with the voice of Geoffrey Chaucer, with his skill in language and meter. One does not suppose that the Man of Law could talk in rime royal.

In sum, two conclusions may be drawn. Certain poems of Chaucer were composed expressly to be read aloud, in the first instance by the poet himself and later by others if so inclined; and this manner of oral delivery he employed as a convention or fiction in other poems or parts of poems which were not intended primarily for recitation. It is not always possible or important to make the distinction; but to this manner may reasonably be attributed certain peculiarities of his style which seem calculated to get a quick response or which would not be expected in more sober writing but would be easily pardonable by immediate listeners less exigent than modern readers. Second, Chaucer wrote, like all poets, with the hope of being heard and read, that is, with a real or a vaguely imagined 'audience.' This audience would be first of all his personal friends and their friends, who would naturally be his literary friends—Gower, Clanvowe, Scogan, across the channel Deschamps, and of course many others whom we cannot call by name. After these would be his business associates, including the lesser nobility and the politicians who might enjoy a good story well told in verse; and then in the more restricted sense the royal family, with whom he had both business and personal relations; a few short poems, 'Stedfastnesse,' 'Purse,' 'Compleynt of Venus,' 'Fortune,' 'Rosamounde,' are clearly addressed to these. But to connect any part of his important work with any part of this audience would be hazardous and unfructuous, although a few generalizations might be made; and in every case the poet's own temperament, his *experience,* his artistic impulses would have to be considered. The permutations are hardly worth facing. And after all the Court of Richard, the Gowers and Clanvowes and Scogans, are now no more. Posterity is the audience now, and what counts is his ability to amuse, instruct, regale, entertain, enlighten the successive centuries of readers. Geoffrey Chaucer reading aloud to certain groups in the late fourteenth century is for us a fiction; what remains is Geoffrey Chaucer addressing us from the printed page. It is the same, with a very great difference.

IX

It is clear that Chaucer had read Dante attentively; many parallel passages have been noted and tested; but as Mario Praz has said, the *Commedia* "was to Chaucer primarily a mine of learned information," as well as a quarry for local borrowings. "Nowhere can the difference of stature between Dante and Chaucer be better gauged" than in their treatment of the Ugolino story, where he courts comparison by declaring his source.[7] But his mind was not saturated with Dante as it was with the *Roman de la Rose*. A single example will illustrate this.

The Friar and the Summoner, separated in the General Prologue, are brought together in the Friar's Prologue. The Friar and the Summoner's compeer, the Pardoner, share a common

inheritance from Faux-Semblant in the *Roman*.[8] Says Faux-
Semblant (Michel 12489 ff.):

> *Car, ains que soit vuis mes trésors,*
> *Deniers me vienent à resours.*
> *Ne fais-ge bien tumber mes hours?*
> *En aquerre est toute m' entente,*
> *Miex vaut mes porchas que ma rente. . . .*
> *Par tout vois les ames curer,*
> *Nus ne peut mès sans moi durer*
> *Et préeschier et conseillier,*
> *Sans jamès de mains traveillier;*
> *De l' apostle en ai le bule. . . .*

This is rendered in the Middle English (6834 ff.):

> *For whanne the grete bagge is go,*
> *It cometh right with my japes.*
> *Make I not wel tumble myn apes?*
> *To wynnen is alwey myn entente;*
> *My purchace is bettir than my rente. . . .*
> *Of al the world [the] cure have I*
> *In brede and lengthe; boldely*
> *I wole bothe preche and eke counceilen;*
> *With hondis wille I not traveilen;*
> *For of the Pope I have the bulle.*

These ten lines of the *Roman* are curiously distributed. First
note that the English rime in 6836 called for a different animal,
which turns up in the description of the Pardoner (A 705 f.):

> *And thus, with feyned flaterye and japes,*
> *He made the person and the peple his apes.*

The next two lines are divided between the Pardoner and the
Friar. The Pardoner says in his Prologue (C 403):

> *For myn entente is nat but for to wynne,*[9]

and in his description of the Friar Chaucer says (A 256):

> *His purchas was wel bettre than his rente;*

and this is echoed in the Friar's Tale, the Devil speaking (D 1451):

> *My purchas is th' effect of al my rente.*

Later in his Prologue the Pardoner says (C 443 f.):

> *For I wol preche and begge in sondry landes;*
> *I wol nat do no labour with myne handes.*

Such parallels are a tribute to Chaucer's memory and his creative use of it by combining. What he could do by expanding and developing may be seen in the whole passage, C 439 ff.

When to this richness are added the direct borrowings from Boccaccio and the direct observations of the daily realities about him, the material for his poetic miscellany is complete. His varied uses of it are controlled by humor, his management of it by the art which comes from practice and that "broad and negligent facility" which often astonishes and often disturbs the modern reader and which seems to have disturbed Chaucer not at all.

CONCLUSION

IN the first chapter there was some attempt to discover the
kind of person he was whom we learn about in the *Life-
Records* and who composed the poetry we now enjoy—the
pattern of his mind, *la qualité de son âme,* as well as the pattern
of his daily life. They both elude us; the results are fragmentary
and approximate.

Now in this last chapter 'Chaucer' has been only a convenient
term for the poet: not the man who wrote the poetry but the me-
dium through whom the the poetry came into being. The two are
inseparable, but they are different. Just as the man who audited
the Customs accounts was not the man whom Africanus introduced into the Garden of Love, even so the man who sat for Kent
in the Parliament of 1386 was very different from the man who
had just written the *Troilus*. It is too simple to relate the external
events of his public life and try after a fashion to fit them into the
writing of his poems; they do not mesh. We can only see that his
education at Court led naturally to his writing at first in the
fashionable aristocratic manner; that his brief acquaintance with
Italy as the King's agent brought him fresh inspiration; that during the twelve years of his residence at Aldgate and his work at
the Customs he became gradually less involved with the intimacies of the Court and more familiar with the life of the lower
classes, and so wrote less in the fashionable mold and more for the
amusement of his audience as they would view the lower classes;
that when he lost his position at the Customs and retired (if that
is the word) to Kent he had more leisure for writing; and that
when he became Clerk of the King's Works he was brought still
closer to the common people and wrote more about the rogues
and roguery which we hear about on the road to Canterbury. But
these are rough approximations.

It is even more futile to select passages from his poetry which
seem to reveal something of his thought and feeling as a *persona;*
it is tempting, but futile. A start was made long ago by Louns-

bury, but it has not been followed up, perhaps because the conclusions indicated were negative. There are few places in Chaucer's whole work where we can securely trust that he is speaking for himself; he was not a 'subjective' poet; and even where we may think we have found something revealing we face the alternative possibly that the views were second-hand, or we recognize an undertone of irony. For the rest, he speaks for his characters as their attitudes or situations require. Dreams are safe to believe or not according as Chanticleer or Pertelote, Troilus or Pandarus, is speaking, and in the 'Hous of Fame' Chaucer refuses to commit himself because the hesitation is pertinent there. On the subject of Fortune he follows tradition. On the subject of gentilesse he echoes Boethius, Dante, or the *Roman*. On the subject of freedom and necessity, in which he might seem to be especially interested, he borrows from Boethius direct and has Troilus decide for necessity, as the poem demands, but nowhere does he present the 'solution' for which Boethius argued in his Book v; and in the Nun's Priest's Tale he succinctly reviews the three possibilities, with citation of authorities, only to brush the question aside as unsuitable for the story of a cock. His whole attitude on such doctrinal and philosophical questions is to let the *clerkes* worry—which is also the attitude recommended to Adam by the Archangel—and this may be mere humorous evasion or a personal conviction that it is useless to discuss the unknowable. It may mean that he has no fundamental principles of his own, or that the artistic situation of any context was best served by not taking sides or airing his private views. Thus he lays himself open to the charge of wanting high seriousness, that seriousness which "comes from a keen vision of life and a deep feeling about it," and which is "the vital quality of enduring literature." But Chaucer has a vital quality the springs of which lie elsewhere. He may never have attained to a synthesis which without paradox or oversubtlety comprehends in a unity the multitudinousness of life; he was not greatly concerned with spiritual values or the mysteries of the soul; he was not one of those "whose creative work proceeds from an achieved center of being, and whose continual creativeness is the expression of the constant extension of their grasp upon and penetration into reality." So far forth he was an unfinished man, just as so much of his literary work betrays an unfinished artist. He never cried, with Blake, "O that men would seek immortal moments," or experienced that moment "où le dernier trait de lumière pénètre dans l'âme et rattache à un centre commun les vérités qui y sont éparsés." Ecstasy and exaltation and inward illumination he seems not to have known, and does not give. His was no casement opening on the seas of perilous thought. His gaze was on this world, such as it is. It is his praise that he saw so much of it and reported it so faithfully, its changes and chances, the curiosities of human behavior, while he stood back from its painful anxieties and tragic suffering, with no desire to penetrate their dark recesses. Instead of *Le monde, c'est terrible* he said *Swich is this world.* When he came near to tragedy at the end of the *Troilus,* he turned aside with a pious platitude. It may be, it may well be, that his tolerance, his Laodiceanism reflects his personal unrest, his unwillingness to accept the violence and viciousness he could not help seeing, his protection against the climate in which he had to live. His gift was not for tragedy but for comedy, and one notes that he rarely handles subjects which are distressing or painful. This may be a matter of temperament or may be due to that 'audience' for which he wrote.

Thus to admit his limitations, the limitations of his art, of his vision, is not to condemn him for what he was not but to see him more clearly. It in no way diminishes the clearness of his eye, the brightness of his smile, the genuineness of his sympathy. His specialty is worldly wisdom, and that is without a trace of contempt.

There are some critics however who are not satisfied with poetry unless it exhibits moral values, and when these values are not obvious they peer between the lines and bring up from their own ingenious depths the profundities they desiderate. The favored term now is moral imagination; its opposite is a moral vacuum. Chaucer was too mediæval to admit such a vacuum. He attached a string of morals to the Cock and Fox poem, all of them very practical. He was not content to leave the Griselda story as a parable of wifely patience, although he did everything possible to make her actions plausible; he made it a lesson in Christian fortitude, after Petrarch. He solved Dorigen's dilemma not in terms of the story but by insistence on a *sententia* of dubious fitness. He was not content to end his 'Palamon and Arcite' as a simple love story, but forgetting that Arcite had recommended the marriage and that Palamon's long patience deserved its reward, he injected the political motive—an element of practical wisdom with perhaps a topical allusion. He quite lost sight of the underlying theme of friendship and sworn brotherhood. This is not vacuum but confusing plenitude. Again, the basic situation of the Merchant's Tale is itself moral: the folly of a nasty old knight marrying a young virgin; it is developed through arguments pro and con and resolved through a kind of poetic justice when January is cuckolded. But by the frivolous *dei ex machina* the justice is reversed, cuckoldry is justified, and immorality palliated by a hearty laugh. The joke is still on January, but the two young people have had their struggle—albeit in some discomfort —and Chaucer's last word is

God blesse us and his moder Seinte Marie.

If this is not blasphemous flippancy, it is sarcastic self-criticism of a high order.

What we learn from Chaucer is that men and women in his day had much the same foibles and follies as now, and within the range of fourteenth-century opportunity the same vices; whereby we can perhaps see ourselves more clearly. Whether they had any confidence or serenity, faith or aspiration, or any sense of the dignity of man must be gleaned from inference, without much certainty. He might have said with Sir John Davies:

And to conclude I know myself a Man,
Which is a proud, and yet a wretched thing:

or with King Lear, "Is man no more than this?" His pride took the form of unconquerable cheerfulness and sympathetic tolerance; but if this was founded on or accompanied by hope he gave little sign. His world was too much with him and against him.

> *Trouthe is put doun, resoun is holden fable;*
> *Vertu hath now no dominacioun;*
> *Pitee exyled, no man is merciable;*
> *Through covetyse is blent discrecioun.*
> *The world hath mad a permutacioun*
> *Fro right to wrong, fro trouthe to fikelnesse,*
> *That al is lost for lak of stedfastnesse.*

So to himself; and to Sir Philip he said finally,

> *Suffyce unto thy good, though it be smal, . . .*
> *looke up, thank God of al;*

and, with a wry smile, *trouthe thee shal delivere, it is no drede.*

There is a twofold corollary. The detachment which comes of amused observation is not the detachment of the artist, who fills his work with his own enthusiasm for the subject while he controls as from a distance the active creation. Chaucer writes from his own fulness and when the subject moves him he takes us with him; he not only shares with us his enjoyment of it, he cannot help joining in the fun—though at a sacrifice of aesthetic perspective—and his high spirits become contagious. But when he is bored he is indifferent to craft and he all but tells us so. Not only does he lack the artist's arrogance, self-confidence, and sense of vocation, he lacks also the passion for form, for composition, which, as Henry James said, "alone is positive beauty." What came easily, naturally—which is a great deal because his natural gift was great and was strengthened by the 'second nature' of much practice—he communicated with gusto; the rest he left to chance, which often happily supported him and often left him stumbling. Discipline seems not to have interested him.

And the desire to amuse helped to determine the form of his poetry. It led him in his work as a narrative artist to the short narrative, the anecdotal—often worked up with rich observation of human nature as well as with obvious fillers—instead of sustained narrative; and to the use, almost a habit, of ready devices for the quick response, a diversion of interest, even a substitution of irrelevant interest, the opposite, in a word, of strictly unified composition. This may be well tested in the Wife of Bath's Tale, for example, and the Franklin's Tale. Only in the Canon's Yeoman's Tale was he wholly serious, illustrating two varieties of the malpractice of alchemy, with a severe condemnation at the end; but the long introduction, lively as it is, makes against unity of effect. His one sustained work falls apart both in the double character of the heroine and in the double focus of Troilus as the titular hero and Pandarus as master of the action. In short analytical description of persons he is at his best, as in the General Prologue and the specimens scattered through the Tales themselves. Dr. Empson can speak of "The poignant and in time cloying simplicity of most of the characters of the *Canterbury Tales,*" and though this is an off-hand judgment based on Chaucer's vague use of the word *honest,* it has a substantiating value when one looks closely at the other repetitions which rely on immediate effects suitable for a listening audience which must be kept attentive.

When to these reservations is added the apparent want of a serious—serious as the Comic Muse can be serious—criticism of life: the general attitude of tolerance even for what cannot be approved and ought not to be allowed; the absence of a philosophical foundation, whether secure or insecure; and the failure to ask the questions which wait for no answer; then it would seem that a 'case' may be made out against "our incomparable poet."

Chaucer has a great deal of "auxiliary brightness"—in the spirit of the Gothic builders who experimented in reducing masonry to accommodate more glass and then to glass added painting which gave color but diminished the light. He has a pervasive ambiguity which might be an ironical position deliberately taken—both *What do I know?* and *Why should I care?*—or a token of the divided mind unreconciled to uncertainty. He teases us with evidences of system without symmetry, design without logic, a plan offered and withdrawn to please that part of the mind which revolts against formalism and to titillate by thwarting expectancy. He creates people who seem real "for the moment," but are not part of a surrounding atmosphere which holds them in place; who live and move but cast no shadows. He has an astonishing gift for dispelling the need of illusion. He leaves us with a series of paradoxes and contradictions, such as inhere in mankind. He is devoid of spirituality and filled with a kindly humanity. His is an undisciplined natural genius capable of skill, craft, and telling passages and likely at any moment to disappoint us. It could be taken as an index that his best success in presenting character is with Pandarus and the Wife of Bath. There is then no need to exalt his work as a civil servant to match his genius in another sphere, nor any need to deplore his failings as a genius. His imperfections "should be regarded as qualities rather than faults." He will not suffer from the free recognition of them as much as he has suffered from mistaken eulogy.

NOTES

CHAPTER I

OBSERVATIONS ON THE LIFE OF CHAUCER

1. The actual date is of small importance, but the lease on 24 December 1399 of a tenement in Westminster for fifty-three years, or until death, for an annual rent of 53*s* 4*d,* looks like a witty corroboration of the two statements at the Scrope Grosvenor trial, and would place the birth in 1346. See Hazel Allison Stevenson, "A Possible Relation between Chaucer's Long Lease and the Date of his Birth," *MLN* L (1935), 318-22.

2. Elizabeth was first cousin of John of Gaunt's first wife Blanche. The only daughter of Elizabeth and Prince Lionel married in 1368 Edmund Mortimer, third Earl of March, who later took the side of the Black Prince and the clergy against John of Gaunt and the barons. The political complications for Chaucer are obvious.

3. Cf. O. F. Emerson, "Chaucer's First Military Service—a Study of Edward Third's Invasion of France in 1359-60," *Romanic Rev.* III (1912), 321-61 (repr. in *Chaucer Essays and Studies,* Cleveland, 1929, pp. 182-246) for additional details.

4. The relationship cannot be proved but is generally accepted as fact. She may have been the Philippa Pau' mentioned in the Countess of Ulster's records and therefore a kind of boyhood sweetheart; cf. Haldeen Braddy, "Chaucer's Philippa, Daughter of Panneto," *MLN* LXIV (1949), 342-43.

5. The rime scheme of the Envoy is different from that of the balade; hence the Envoy may have been added to an earlier poem.

6. Emile Legouis, *Geoffrey Chaucer,* Paris, 1910, p. 27.

7. Roger S. Loomis, "Was Chaucer a Laodicean?" in *Essays and Studies in Honor of Carleton Brown,* New York, 1940, pp. 129-48.

8. In "Chaucer and the Parliament of 1386," *Speculum* XVIII (1943), 80-86, Florence R. Scott, approving Loomis, supplements his essay by emphasizing the actions of the Parliament and the dangers of alluding to them. His failure to do so showed his "high sense of reality." Which is true, a part of the truth. For further exceptions to Loomis, see Gardiner

Stillwell and Henry J. Webb, "Chaucer's Knight and the Hundred Years' War," *MLN* LIX (1944), 45-47.

9. Obvious are Chaucer's references to his friends Gower, Bukton, Scogan, and to *lyte Lowys my sone,* and the punning reference to Sir Philip de la Vache; to Petrarch and Bradwardine by name; indirectly to John of Gaunt and his first wife in the 'Book of the Duchess'; and the Knight's campaigns and his son's *chyvachie.* Accepted and of real significance are the Envoy to 'Stedfastnesse,' addressed to Richard, and the Envoy to 'Purse,' addressed to Henry IV; and the modern instances in the Monk's Tale (cf. *tiraunts of Lumbardye* in the Prologue to the 'Legende,' F 374). Almost equally definite is the mention of Jack Straw and hence an allusion to the Peasants' Revolt (but note the context) in the Nun's Priest's Tale, B 4584; and cf. *blase of straw* (*Troilus* IV, 184), *cherles rebellyng,* A 2459, and Jankin, B 1172: and also *O stormy peple,* E 995ff. Likewise accepted is the so-called dedication of the Prologue of the 'Legende' to Queen Anne, which brings with it other possible parallels to Richard and Anne, and to which may be added the possible reference to Anne in *oure first lettre* (*Troilus* I, 172). Similarly, allusions to the marriage of Richard and Anne have been seen in the tempest at the homecoming of Theseus and Hippolyta and in the intercession of Hippolyta and Emily for Palamon and Arcite in the Knight's Tale (A 883-84, 1748-59); and possibly also, though indirect, in A 1018, 1545-51, 2967-74, 3084; to say nothing of the 'Hous of Fame.' Uncertain but probable is the identification of Richard as the *beste frende* in 'Fortune' (though John of Gaunt has also been proposed). Gloucester has been seen as Nimrod in 'The Former Age.' The affair of John Holland and Elizabeth of Lancaster has been seen in the Physician's Tale (C 72 ff.), and either this or Holland and Isabel of York in 'Mars.' Finally, there are the attempts to find contemporary parallels in 'Anelida and Arcite' and the 'Parlement of Foules'; to say nothing of Hotson's hypotheses regarding the Melibeus and the Nun's Priest's Tale. A few of these are discussed below.

10. "Chaucer's Doctrine of Kings and Tyrants," *Speculum,* XX (1945), 133-56.

11. J. M. Murry, *Pencillings,* New York, 1925, p. 161.

12. Robert A. Pratt, "Chaucer and the Visconti Libraries," *ELH* VI (1939), 191-99; "nothing definitely militates against" it, says Professor Pratt.

13. "The Route of Chaucer's First Journey to Italy," *ELH* XVI (1949), 174-89; *The English Traveller to Italy, I. The Middle Ages,* Roma, 1954, pp. 511 ff.

14. Albert S. Cook, "The Last Months of Chaucer's Earliest Patron," *Trans. Connecticut Academy* XXI (1916), 1-144.

15. Edith Rickert, *Chaucer's World,* New York, 1948, pp. 272-73.

16. A variant of this is the route of Adam of Usk a year or two after Chaucer's death (*Chaucer's World,* p. 278; Parks, p. 522). Adam sailed first to Bergen-op-Zoom, thence went overland to Aachen, Cologne, up the Rhine to Basel, thence to Berne, to Lucerne, over the St. Gothard to

Bellinzona, Milan—and on to Rome. He left London 19 February 1401[2], reached Milan 18 March and Rome 5 April. His words for the pass are: "in caruca per bovem tractus, nivis frigoribus, oculis velatis, ne loci discrimina conspiceret."—*Chronicon Adæ de Usk,* ed. E. Maunde Thompson, London, 1876, p. 72.

17. Robert A. Pratt, "Geoffrey Chaucer Esq., and Sir John Hawkwood," *ELH* XVI (1949), 188-193, with references in n. 1. In the Exchequer Accounts Chaucer's name is not given as one of the members of the commission; cf. Haldeen Braddy, "New Documentary Evidence concerning Chaucer's Mission to Lombardy," *MLN* XLVIII (1933), 507-11.

18. Parks, pp. 523 ff. In 1379 Michael de la Pole and John de Burley were sent to Rome by Richard; they were imprisoned in Germany on their return journey (*Chaucer's World,* p. 276).

19. *Chaucer's World,* p. 278.

20. To the long vexed controversy Professor Parks adds a nice point (p. 515). Petrarch's Latin version of the Griselda story, which Chaucer followed very closely, says that the Po flows eastward to "Emiliam, atque Flaminiam Veneciamque." Chaucer renders this (which has no equivalent in the French version) *To Emelward, to Ferrare, and Venyse* (E 51). Ferrara is on the road from Bologna to Padua. Had Chaucer been there or did he learn its classical name from some literary source?

21. Mario Praz, "Chaucer and the Great Italian Writers of the Trecento," *The Monthly Criterion* VI (1927), 18-39, 131-57, 238-42; 156-57.

22. This balade names sixteen ladies (Penelope, Marcia Catoun, Helen, Lavinia, Lucretia, Polyxena, Cleopatra, Thisbe, Hero, Dido, Laodamia, Phyllis, Canace, Hypsyphile, Hypermnestra, Ariadne) of classical extraction, along with Alcestis. Iseult is from the North and Esther from the Bible.

Note on Cecilia Chaumpaigne

1. This William Chaumpeneys was a wealthy London baker who died 1360-61. Cf. Samuel Moore, *Angl.* XXXVII (1913), 13 f. On her brother Robert, see Kirk, *Life-Records,* p. xxx.

2. On Morel, see Kuhl, *PMLA* XXIX (1914), 270 ff.

3. The case of Chaucer's father, usually mentioned in this connection, is irrelevant. John was kidnaped when he was less than twelve years old by two Staces and his aunt, Agnes de Westhale, to marry him to her daughter Joan. The offenders paid a fine of £250. Some years later, 1387, Chaucer was himself on a commission to investigate the abduction of Isabella, daughter and heir of William atte Halle, out of the custody of Thomas Kershill, at Chislehurst, Kent.

4. See P. R. Watts, "The Strange Case of Geoffrey Chaucer and Cecilia Chaumpaigne," *The Law Quarterly Review* LXIII (1947), 491-515; and T. F. T. Plucknett, "Chaucer's Escapade," *ibid.* LXIV (1948), 33-36.

CHAPTER II

CHAUCER AND THE SCHOLARS: THE PARDONER

1. Cf. Walter Clyde Curry, *Chaucer and the Mediaeval Sciences,* New York, 1926. Exactly half of the Pardoner's lines are given to his character and half to his professional skills. Carleton Brown (cited below) says incautiously that the Pardoner "receives unusually extended treatment in the General Prologue"; but the Friar, the Parson, and the Prioress outrank him in number of lines, and the Summoner equals him.

2. As the manuscripts are interpreted, the appearance of the Pardoner now was an afterthought. Cf. J. Burke Severs, "Author's Revision in Block C of the Canterbury Tales," *Speculum* XXIX (1954), 512-30, with references to Manly and Rickert.

3. Inconsistencies have been noted between the Pardoner of the Prologue and the Pardoner on the road. For example, in A 688, 691 he has a *smale* voice like a goat's, but in C 331 he says he can *rynge it out as round as gooth a belle.*

4. This alone might warn those who like to interpret overdelicately. From the modern point of view it is a violation of verisimilitude for either the Parson or the Pardoner to indulge in this bit of learning. But Chaucer, who was after all a mediæval, could be above such demands of consistency as we now cherish. He followed a convention, added his spot of color, and thought no more about it.

5. One possibility is that the Pardoner altered his tone, with a wink at the Pilgrims, for just those six words, *And lo, sires, thus I preche,* and resumed his suave address to the imaginary listeners: *And Jhesu Crist, that is oure soules leche . . .* —"I have shown you the dangers of avarice, now buy my pardon, for I would not deceive you." The *And* favors this reading, rather than the alternative, that the Pardoner means: "This is the way I fool the ignorant, *but* I will not try to deceive you, fellow Pilgrims." The pronouns are ambiguous: *ye* and *yow* for both audiences. Why should the Pardoner think it in place to offer any pardon to the Pilgrims—until later, when he is carried away by his enthusiasm? On the other hand, will anyone deny that the poet must share the onus of our uncertainty? In one of his exuberant moods, he saw and seized the opportunity for a brisk ending, even at some sacrifice of verisimilitude, as he did with the Envoy after the Clerk's Tale. The dramatic moment was too tempting; and it is all plausible enough if no sharp questions are asked. The similar situation at the end of the Friar's Tale should not be overlooked; the narrator addresses the Pilgrims with an ironic or hypocritical prayer.

6. A convenient summary, up to its date, with fresh contributions, may be found in G. G. Sedgewick, "The Progress of Chaucer's Pardoner 1880-1940," *MLQ* I (1940), 431-58.

7. A. L. Kellogg and L. A. Haselmayer, "Chaucer's Satire of the Pardoner," *PMLA* LXVI (1951), 251-77, suggest (p. 276) that the satire is directed not so much at the pilgrim Pardoner as at "those who made the Pardoner possible."

8. *The Prologue and Four Canterbury Tales,* ed. by Gordon Hall Gerould, New York, 1935 (a school edition), and *Chaucerian Essays,* Princeton, 1952, "The Vicious Pardoner."

9. 1935, p. 331. In 1952, pp. 55-57, the picture is not withdrawn, nor is it so precise; but doubts are met by way of comparative dates: perhaps Chaucer added the ale-stake passage to the General Prologue to prepare for its reappearing in the Words of the Host.

10. "The Pardoner's Tavern," *JEGP* XIII (1914), 553-65. The last line of the end-link is enough to exclude any tavern interior. The quarrel of Host and Pardoner has halted the cavalcade for a moment; then *Anon they kiste, and ryden forth hir weye.*

11. Carleton Brown, ed., *The Pardoner's Tale,* Oxford, 1935. "Professor Tupper is right. . . . And during the Prologue it is clear, the Pardoner continued to sip his ale—a procedure hardly consistent with the view that the Prologue formed part of the structure of a sermon." Then he adds: "Only when he has concluded his Prologue does the Pardoner, pushing back his tankard, . . ." But that tankard was Jusserand's.

12. *Geoffrey Chaucer,* Paris, 1910, p. 185.

13. Dorothy M. Norris, "Chaucer's 'Pardoner's Tale' and Flanders," *PMLA* XLVIII (1933), 636-41.

14. Gerould, *Chaucerian Essays,* p. 69, makes this clear—if it was not sufficiently obvious. But Brown had said (p. XVI): "The reader will search in vain for any previous mention of the three rioters."

15. Cf. Manly, *Canterbury Tales,* New York, [1928], p. 614; and especially Morton Donner, "Pulpit Rhetoric in Three Canterbury Tales," *MLN* LXXX (1955), 235-245.

16. Gerould, 1935, p. 331.

17. Sedgewick insists that the Pardoner preached for money, not for logic. He quotes the peroration, *O cursed synne. . . ,* and says: "This is something more than 'logic'—it is demagogic genius" (p. 440). Moreover, if incoherence is a sign of inebriation, one would have to believe that Chaucer was himself abroad when he wrote the Words of the Host before MLT.

18. *Some New Light on Chaucer,* New York, 1926, p. 130.

19. Gerould was doubtful about "mare." Perhaps, he says, Chaucer did not distinguish between gelding and *eunuchus ex nativitate.* "The alternative surmise that the Pardoner might be 'a mare' has escaped comment, as far as I know. Does it mean that he might be suspected of being homosexual?" Likely enough, but the ground for such a surmise would be his association with the Summoner.

20. Like Curry's expansion of C 395-97 (the Pardoner stretches his neck, when he preaches, like a dove sitting on a barn) to mean "his neck is long and scrawny" (p. 55). There are hundreds of such gratuitous embroideries in Chaucer criticism.

21. *Chaucer and His Poetry,* Cambridge, 1915, pp. 213-18.

22. Professor Patch's comment is a variant of this. The self-portrait "is all defense. He is insecure at many points" and his bravado is a kind of

compensation; "outwardly he is a hypocrite; but inwardly he runs a risk of being a cheat with himself when he is trying to be 'honest' with the pilgrims" (*On Re-reading Chaucer,* Cambridge, 1939, p. 164).

23. *Geoffrey Chaucer,* Boston, 1934, p. 230.

24. Similar is Legouis, p. 187.

25. "Conjecture concerning Chaucer's Pardoner," *Tulane Studies in English* 1, New Orleans, 1949, pp. 1-49.

CHAPTER III

THE CANTERBURY TALES

1. Cf. A. S. Cook, "Chaucerian Papers—I," *Trans. Connecticut Academy* xxiii (1919), 1-27; and also John H. Fisher, "Chaucer's Use of *swete* and *swote,*" *JEGP* l (1951), 326-31.

2. Of course the general statement about all pilgrims need not carry over to Chaucer's special selection. Their motives were certainly mixed. But the line is from any point of view an anticlimax—unless there lurks an irrecoverable (personal) allusion. It can only signify that the chief reason for visiting the Becket shrine was gratitude for past cures, and this does not harmonize either with the situations which follow or with the tradition of St. Thomas' miracles. But Chaucer was not much concerned with St. Thomas. He never uses the name Becket; he uses St. Thomas of Kent, or merely St. Thomas, five times in oaths.

3. The authorial "I" has always confused simple minds. Most readers are aware of the risk of taking Chaucer's text literally when he uses the first personal pronoun, but here the warning is clearly sounded by Manly's assumption that Geoffrey Chaucer the poet was going on the pilgrimage: "Chaucer does not tell us what was the cause of his devotion. He may have received the help of St. Thomas, and have been fulfilling a vow. It is also possible. . ." (*Canterbury Tales,* New York, 1928, p. 497). At the opposite extreme is the postulation of a fictional *character* assumed or created by the poet. Cf. E. Talbot Donaldson, "Chaucer the Pilgrim," *PMLA* lxix (1954), 928-36.

4. He does not, for example, quite match Froissart's tribute to Sir Guichard d'Angle, Earl of Huntingdon: "in his time he had all the noble virtues that a knight ought to have. He was merry, true, amorous, sage, secret, large, hardy, adventurous, and chivalrous." Cf. further Gervase Mathew, "Ideals of Knighthood in Late-Fourteenth-Century England," *Studies in Medieval History Presented to Frederick Maurice Powicke,* Oxford, 1948, pp. 354-62.

5. Cf. J. R. Hulbert, "Chaucer's Pilgrims," *PMLA* lxiv (1949), 823-28.

6. The notion that the Parson's Seven Deadly Sins were meant to provide each and every Pilgrim with matter for reflection in the cathedral is surely gratuitous.

7. For recent commentary on the Prologue, see W. H. Clawson, "The Framework of *The Canterbury Tales,*" *University of Toronto Quarterly*

xx (1951), 137-54; J. V. Cunningham, "The Literary Form of the Prologue to the Canterbury Tales," *MP* xlix (1952), 172-81; Arthur W. Hoffman, "Chaucer's Prologue to Pilgrimage: The Two Voices," *ELH* xxi (1954), 1-16; Ralph Baldwin, *The Unity of the Canterbury Tales,* Anglistica v, Copenhagen, 1955.

8. John M. Manly and Edith Rickert, *The Text of the Canterbury Tales,* Chicago, [1940], ii, 476. Tatlock had earlier reached the same conclusion: "The Canterbury Tales in 1400," *PMLA* l (1935), 100-39.

9. *Chaucer and His Poetry,* Cambridge, 1915, pp. 167 f. There is of course no prologue to the Shipman's Tale in Manly or Robinson.

10. W. P. Ker, in Henry Craik, *English Prose,* i, 1907, pp. 40-41. The case for Melibeus as a serious piece was presented by Tatlock, *Development and Chronology,* pp. 189 ff. More recently Professor Lawrence came to its defense in *Essays and Studies in Honor of Carleton Brown,* pp. 100-110.

11. G. G. Coulton, *Chaucer and His England,* London, 1927⁴, p. 157. Cf. also Mather, *Chaucer's Prologue,* etc., Introduction, and Tatlock's reproof (p. 189) of the same position.

12. George H. Cowling, *Chaucer,* London, [1927], p. 162.

13. Adolphus W. Ward, *Chaucer,* p. 113. The fallacy is obvious.

14. Manly has shown (Manly and Rickert, ii, 410-13) that in the first form of the Prologue to the Nun's Priest's Tale the Host himself shut the Monk off. The revised Prologue, as now printed, gives us the additional by-play, not merely of implying that only a man of the Knight's rank would interrupt the well-oiled Monk, but also of revealing a bourgeois weakness of the Knight himself. For not to be overlooked is the critical observation which follows. To the fourth repetition of the definition of tragedy the Knight adds its contrary:

> *As whan a man hath been in povre estaat,*
> *And clymbeth up and wexeth fortunat,*
> *And there abideth in prosperitee.*
> *Swich thyng is gladsom, as it thynketh me.*

This is the common man's attitude: there is tragedy enough in real life, without reading and writing about it.

15. It has been suggested that Chaucer composed the tragedies to comfort John of Gaunt's wife Costanza and that he added the modern instances to bring history down to date. One might rather guess that the tragedies were composed in their own style, *ful plat and eek ful pleyn,* as an exercise after Boccaccio's pattern and that the modern instances were inserted for the sake of contemporary appeal. Certainly, though some of the manuscripts put them there, they did not stand at the end when the Nun's Priest's Prologue was written: cf. l. 2766 and l. 2782.

16. "On the whole it seems clear," says Robinson cautiously, p. 857, "that the *Nun's Priest's Tale* was composed when the scheme of the Canterbury pilgrimage was well under way"; and less cautiously: "It was not merely written with the Nun's Priest in mind, but was adapted with more than

usual care to the character and calling of the teller" (p. 14). This is hard to understand, since the narrator has no character in the General Prologue, but is only one of three innominate priests accompanying the Prioress. The "homiletic material" in the Tale might suggest a priest, but the mock-heroic tone is not what we should expect from a follower of the dignified Prioress. In fact, certain indications point in a different direction, namely, the address to *ye lordes* at ll. 3325 and 3330 (for elsewhere the Pilgrims are addressed by the general term *lordings*) and the phrase *As seith my lord* at the end, whether the Archbishop of Canterbury is indicated, as in the Ellesmere MS, or, as Manly suggests, my Lord Bishop of London, as being the Prioress' immediate superior. It is thus not unlikely that the Tale was originally written for the entertainment of a clerical audience, much as the main part of the Canon's Yeoman's Tale seems to have been read before a group of Canons Religious—and the Canon and his Yeoman invented for its insertion in the *Canterbury Tales*. It would be gratuitous to add that Chaucer here meant to embarrass the Prioress a little.

17. See J. R. Hulbert, "What was Chaucer's Aim in the *Knight's Tale*," *SP* xxvi (1929), 375-85; William Frost, "An Interpretation of Chaucer's Knight's Tale," *RES* xxv (1949), 289-304; H. S. Wilson, "*The Knight's Tale* and the *Teseida* Again," *U. of Toronto Q.* xviii (1949), 131-46; Charles Muscatine, "Form, Texture, and Meaning in Chaucer's Knight's Tale," *PMLA* lxv (1950), 911-29; and Edward B. Ham, "Knight's Tale 38," *ELH* xvii (1950), 252-61, with a review of seventeen critical pronouncements of extraordinary range.

18. Some such revision has in fact been argued for recently, and promptly rebutted; cf. Johnstone Parr, "The Date and Revision for Chaucer's Knight's Tale," *PMLA* lx (1945), 307-24, and Robert A. Pratt, "Was Chaucer's Knight's Tale Extensively Revised after 1390?" *PMLA* lxiii (1948), 726-36.

19. Cf. Albert H. Marckwardt, "Characterization in Chaucer's Knight's Tale," *U. of Michigan Contributions in Philology*, No. 5, April 1947; and Walter H. French, "The Lovers in the *Knight's Tale*," *JEGP* xlviii (1949) 320-28. On "Arcite's Intellect," see Curry's learned article in *JEGP* xxix (1930), 83-99.

20. Cf. Stuart Robertson, "Elements of Realism in the Knight's Tale," *JEGP* xiv (1915), 226-55; the author's claims however are somewhat exaggerated.

21. Cf. Canon Looten, *Chaucer, ses modèles, ses sources, sa religion*, Lille, [1931], p. 56: "Mais il est plus facile de discerner dans la rédaction du *Knightes Tale* telle que nous la possédons, des traces d'inexpérience qu'on peut attribuer à la jeunesse du poète encore inhabile à manier son outil."

22. Langlois, 1365-68; Michel, 1373-76. "Direct copying," says Fansler, *Chaucer and the Roman de la Rose*, New York, 1914, pp. 131 ff. Cf. also Brusendorff, *The Chaucer Tradition*, London, 1925, p. 397.

23. See, for a different view, George Kane, *Middle English Literature*, London, [1951], pp. 62-63.

24. Tatlock, *Development and Chronology,* pp. 175 ff., recognized "a certain crudity in the plot" (p. 177) and "the remote and fragile character of the subject." He ventured to claim that "In vividness and realism of detail (except as regards Constance herself) the poem compares not unfavorably with any of the non-humorous tales." "And finally, the *Man of Law's Tale* shows an ease and mastery and an artistic aloofness in Chaucer's attitude to his material which is far different from his earlier manner. The style of the poem is remarkably unified and harmonious. . . ."—The merits of the Tale were emphasized by Bernard I. Duffey, "The Intention and Art of 'The Man of Law's Tale,'" *ELH* xiv (1947), 181-93. To this I entered a brief objection in *MLN* lxiv (1949), 12-14. More recently Edward A. Block has come to its defense with "Originality, Controlling Purpose, and Craftsmanship in Chaucer's *Man of Law's Tale,*" *PMLA* lxviii (1953), 572-616, hoping "to show that the *Man of Law's Tale* is a work of superb craftsmanship which embodies throughout various controlling purposes and reflects greater originality, imaginative power, and conscious artistry than has hitherto been recognized."

25. See A. C. Edwards, "Knaresborough Castle and 'the kynges modres court,'" *PQ* xix (1940), 306-9.

26. "Chaucer's Man of Law's Tale and Constance of Castile," *JEGP* xlvii (1948), 343-51.

27. Cf. James Sledd, "Dorigen's Complaint," *SP* xlv (1947), 36-45.

28. Kane, *Middle English Literature,* pp. 84-87.

29. For another point of view, attributing to Chaucer a display of imaginative symbolism, see Charles A. Owen, Jr., "The Central Passages in Five of the *Canterbury Tales:* A Study in Irony and Symbol," *JEGP* lii (1953), 294-311; 295-97. The rocks, Professor Owen holds, are a guarantee of Dorigen's conjugal fidelity, a sign that she and Aurelius are unwilling "to accept the real world," and somehow a symbol of that peculiar "firmness" of Arveragus.

Note on Chaucer's Clerk

1. *The Universities of Europe in the Middle Ages,* Oxford, 1895, II, Part ii, pp. 452 ff.

2. Charles E. Mallett, *A History of the University of Oxford,* vol. i, *The Mediaeval University,* New York, 1924, p. 187 and n.3.

3. The only reference I have found to red binding is in C. H. Haskins, *The Rise of the Universities,* New York, 1923, p. 86. It seems that some Paris students, "when it is time to leave Paris, in order to make some show of learning . . . get together huge volumes of calfskin, with wide margins and fine red bindings." But Chaucer's Clerk was of a different sort. There remains the possibility that black and red refer to the ink of the manuscript; if so, 'clad' is a bold metaphor and one would expect *and* instead of *or.*

4. W. W. Lawrence, in *Speculum* xxvii (1952), 236.

5. *Chaucer and His Poetry,* Cambridge, 1915, p. 199.

Note on the History of the Clerk's Tale

1. Germaine Dempster, "A Period in the Development of the *Canterbury Tales* Marriage Group and the Blocks B² and C," *PMLA* LXVIII (1953), 1142-59; 1143-47. Mrs. Dempster posits a version "before the tale and its frame pieces took standard form," ending with E 1169 or "much more probably" with E 1162. The Host stanza could hardly have been written after the Envoy. In fact, "were it not for the accidental preservation of the Host Stanza, we would not even suspect that revision took place."

2. On "internal revision" cf. Manly and Rickert, II, 500 f. and Severs, *Speculum* XXI (1946), 295-302. One particular line offers some difficulty: *this auctour* (l. 1141) would not be clear without some immediate reference to Petrarch. Several manuscripts have *the auctor,* but this would be only a partial help. It is possible of course that the first version did not include Petrarch's moral. If so, l. 1142 was rewritten to introduce it and the *But o word* stanza, containing some repetition of ll. 1139 ff., was added to make the conclusion less abrupt.

3. But "it does not occur in the three MSS which end there," i.e., at 1169 (Manly and Rickert, II, 265; "two MSS," II, 500). These are Bo¹ (1450-80; "contributes to the evidence for pre-CT versions," I, 60) and its companion Ph² (1450-70); and Hk (1440-50) of complex affiliations but "representing a line almost independent, coming off near the top of the large composite group" (I, 287).

4. One such is the word *soveraynetee* (l. 114), which is not in Petrarch, though the idea is. Kittredge (*MP* IX [1912], 435, n. 1) noted this and quoted Petrarch, but commented: "Chaucer may or may not have understood this Latin, but he certainly did not think he was translating it." Another is the repeated emphasis on *gentilesse* and particularly the view that nobility *comth al of God* rather than by heredity: which corresponds exactly with part of the hag's 'sermon' in the Wife's Tale, but is also in Petrarch. These and other similar connectives would be noticed by Chaucer, as they are by us, and would weigh heavily with him when the Clerk's Tale became part of the Marriage Group.

5. Cf. J. Burke Severs, "Did Chaucer Rearrange the Clerk's Envoy?" *MLN* LXIX (1954), 472-78.

6. Manly and Rickert, III, 473; II, 263. The *d* MSS are dated from 1430 onwards, except Ry², which is dated 1420-50. Only one of the five MSS of *a* is dated before 1430, viz. Dd (1400-20), which after l. 686 of ClT is with its group (I, 102). On the relation of *a* to the *b* group, see I, 132.

7. The Manly and Rickert edition is silent on the presence or absence of this title. It is present in those manuscripts printed by the Chaucer Society, except Ph⁴ (HM 140), which ends at l. 1162 and continues with the Envoy without title, and Longleat 257 (Lt¹), which ends at l. 1169 and has the Envoy without title.

CHAPTER IV

THE *TROILUS* EPILOGUE

1. J. S. P. Tatlock, "The Epilog of Chaucer's Troilus," *MP* xviii (1920-21), 625-59. Cf. also James L. Shanley, "The Troilus and Christian Love," *ELH* vi (1939), 271-81.

2. Walter Clyde Curry, "Destiny in Chaucer's Troilus," *PMLA* xlv (1930), 129-68.

3. This is foreseen and forecast repeatedly throughout the poem. It comes first in i, 197-200 and again in i, 330-33; it reappears in iii, 813 ff., when the outcome is anticipated apropos of the trumped-up story of Horaste, with a quotation from Boethius; and again in iv, 581; and emphatically in iv, 834-35. In these and many other places Chaucer reminds the reader that love is bitter-sweet.

4. D. W. Robertson, Jr., "Chaucerian Tragedy," *ELH* xix (1952), 1-37.

5. Cf. John W. Clark, "Dante and the Epilogue and Troilus," *JEGP* l (1951), 1-10, with a list of discussions from 1915 to 1939. As to which sphere Troilus reaches, cf. Jackson I. Cope, *MLN* lxvii (1952), 245-46 and Forrest S. Scott, *MLR* li (1956), 2-5. The evidence is all inconclusive: the moon or the Fixed Stars? Chaucer sometimes reckoned *a summo ad imum* and sometimes the other way about; and in any case one would expect to find Arcita in the sphere of Mars, his special deity, and Troilus in that of Venus, his special deity.

CHAPTER V

OBSERVATIONS ON THE ART OF CHAUCER

1. Ernest H. Wilkins, "Cantus Troili," *ELH* xvi (1949), 167-73.

2. Paull F. Baum, "Chaucer's Nautical Metaphors," *South Atlantic Quarterly* xlix (1950), 67-73.

3. Samuel Moore, "General Aspects of Literary Patronage in the Middle Ages," *The Library,* ser. 3, iv (1913), 369-92; 391. Cf. Bertrand H. Bronson, "Chaucer's Art in Relation to his Audience," in *Five Studies in Literature,* Berkeley, Cal., 1940.

4. Cf. Ruth Crosby, "Oral Delivery in the Middle Ages," *Speculum* xi (1936), 88-110; and "Chaucer and the Custom of Oral Delivery," *ibid.* xiii (1938), 413-32. Miss Crosby has proved, and to spare, that Chaucer in adopting the methods of oral narrative has used over and over again the tags and colloquialisms of the romances. How far or just where this is a literary device remains an open question.

5. Cf. Margaret Galway, "The Troilus Frontispiece," *MLR* xliv (1949), 161-77.

6. "Thow, redere," in the *Troilus* v, 270 is another mark which sets off Book v as different from the other Books.

7. "Chaucer and the Great Italian Writers of the Trecento," *The Monthly Criterion* vi (1927), 18-39, 131-57, 238-42; 38, 33, 36.   On the Ugolino story cf. Theodore Spencer, "The Story of Ugolino in Dante and Chaucer," *Speculum* ix (1934), 295-301.

8. Cf. Skeat, Oxford *Chaucer*, v, 25; Fansler, *Chaucer and the Roman de la Rose*, New York, 1914, pp. 162-65; Brusendorff, *The Chaucer Tradition*, Oxford, 1925, pp. 402-404.

9. Just below the Pardoner says (C 407 f.):

> *For certes many a predicacioun*
> *Comth ofte tyme of yvel entencioun;*

which comes from an earlier couplet in the *Roman* (Langlois 5113 f.).

INDEX

The Library of Congress has catalogued
this book as follows:

Baum, Paull Franklin, 1886–
      Chaucer, a critical appreciation.   Durham, N. C., Duke
University Press, 1958.
      229 p.   23 cm.

      1. Chaucer, Geoffrey, d. 1400.

PR1924.B3   821.17   58–12587 ‡

Library of Congress